DRYDEN

English Literature

―――――

Editor
JOHN LAWLOR
Professor of English Language and Literature
in the University of Keele

DRYDEN

William Myers

Lecturer in English Literature
University of Leicester

HUTCHINSON UNIVERSITY LIBRARY
LONDON

B1

HUTCHINSON & CO (*Publishers*) LTD
3 Fitzroy Square, London W1

London Melbourne Sydney Auckland
Wellington Johannesburg Cape Town
and agencies throughout the world

First published 1973

© William Myers 1973

*This book has been set in Fournier type, printed in Great Britain
on smooth wove paper by Anchor Press, and
bound by Wm. Brendon, both of Tiptree, Essex*

ISBN 0 09 116450 8 (cased)
0 09 116451 6 (paper)

FOR KATEY

The Christian Princess in her Tent confers
With fifty of your learn'd Philosophers.

CONTENTS

INTRODUCTION

Dryden was the last English poet to be interested in history, and possibly only Shakespeare before him united the gifts of a true historian with those of a major poet. It was to Dryden's disadvantage, however, that he was as ready as Shakespeare to apply the vocabulary of private experience to public affairs, even though his assumptions about the relation of meaning to reality and of grammar to reason were those of the Royal Society, not those of a Jacobean dramatist. Logically he could only illustrate and entertain with metaphors and analogies; he could not think seriously with them. As a result he seems decidedly unconvincing when he links notions of kingship, for instance, with those of fatherhood and filial obedience. His father/king figures are mere ideograms compared with Prospero at one extreme or Sir Thomas Bertram at the other, without interest either psychologically or politically. Dryden was also trapped inside neoclassical notions of responsibility which severely limited his freedom to use what words and portray what characters he chose. The result has been that as a commentator on man and society he has seemed superficial. Until recently, critical attention focussed on his manner rather than his matter, as if the obvious limitations of the conventions, linguistic and poetic, within which he worked, were identical with limitations of intellect and sensibility in Dryden himself. It is a major purpose of this brief survey of his work to demonstrate how completely and impressively he in fact learned to deploy a limited and perhaps debased poetic idiom in an examination of the human problems created by the pressures of history.

Dryden's development falls into three phases. In the first, up to about 1678, he accepted a relatively orthodox monarchist theory of politics and concentrated on developing a theory of poetry. Critically he began more or less as a Hobbist, strongly emphasising the pre-eminence of the Fancy over the Judgement in both heroic drama and comedy. Committed first to humour comedy and then to a comedy based on gentlemanly repartee and the general character of men and manners, he consistently argued for delight rather than instruction as the chief end of comic writing. However, this emphasis shifted in the mid-seventies. Judgement became increasingly important in his analysis of the poetic faculties; he came to attach more importance to correctness, and to reject the extravagances both of heroic drama and 'his long-lov'd Mistris, Rhyme', at least on the stage. This change largely preceded the political crisis of the late seventies which consti-tutes the second phase of his development. During this time he was compelled to confront the manifest inadequacy of royalist theory in the context of real power politics, and to examine more rigorously than he had previously done the workings of that divine Providence by which Charles II had been restored in 1660. In the excitement of the Exclusionist crisis, his vision remained restricted to problems of political and theological principle, and the packs and sets of great ones clustered excitedly round the court. With the accession of James II and his own conversion to Catholicism, however, the new unorthodoxy of his theological views and the political weakness of his co-religionists forced him to examine the real basis of political power, and the relation of principle to vested interest, and of vested interest to class. He was at last able to grasp exactly what made history secular; why, that is, events were rarely related to virtue in a Christian rather than a Machiavellian sense. He had then the task of integrating his faith in divine love and human goodness with a steady, thoroughly modern awareness of history's infinite capacity to violate every conceivable kind of value.

To amplify this picture of Dryden and simultaneously to take into ac-count all his poetry, plays and criticism has inevitably, in a work as brief as this, required a barely justifiable amount of unsubstantiated assertion, summary judgement, and a ruthless compression not only of my own ideas but those of the many critics and scholars on whom I have heavily depended. In the interests of simplicity I have confined acknowledgement of this indebtedness to the notes, and have not always done even as much. Many facts, opinions and insights in this book which might seem to be mine belong in fact to others. I must therefore acknowledge the pervasive influence of L. A. Beaurline, H. Erskine-Hill, William Frost, T. W. Harrison, Phillip Harth, Arthur Hoffman, Earl Miner, Alan Roper, Charles Ward and many others. Throughout I quote from Kinsley's edition of *The Poems*. Other quotations are from the Scott–Saintsbury and the California editions of *The Works*, Ker's edition of the *Essays*, Boulton's of *Of Dramatick Poesie*, and the *Four Comedies* and *Four Tragedies* of Beaurline and Bowers. In each case I have used what I judge to be the best generally available text in spite of the occasional anomalies which have resulted. Finally I would like to thank Herbert Orton and Peter Seddon for talking to me so patiently about seventeenth-century English history.

I

THE RESTORATION:

POEMS 1659–1667

Nearly every major work of Dryden's involves the juxtaposing of largely traditional poetic and political conventions. Neoclassical habits and assumptions are brought into frequently ironic relationships with the social perspectives of the lesser landed gentry from which Dryden came. In his first major poem, the *Heroique Stanza's* (1659) on the death of Oliver Cromwell, for instance, he puts this stock of neo-classical panegyric at the service of his Cromwellian convictions. Like most members of his class in the late fifties, he approved of the pattern of government established in 1655: rule by a single person with Parliament was sufficiently traditional to please him. But the constitution was new, and Richard Cromwell's ability to control the army and the Commons untested. It is not surprising, therefore, that the *Heroique Stanza's* should be a little subdued. The attitude to Oliver is 'one of sober admiration'.[1] Nevertheless the poem is remarkably representative of Dryden's talent, mainly because of the relationship it seeks to establish between historical realities and conventional neoclassical idealisations.

Compared with Dryden's surviving juvenilia (the verses to Hoddeson [1650], to Honor Dryden [1653?], and the once fashionably admired elegy to Lord Hastings [1649]), the *Heroique Stanza's*, written when Dryden was twenty-nine, are technically impressive. There are, admittedly, obscurities:

> From this high-spring our forraign-Conquests flow
> Which yet more glorious triumphs do portend,

[1] Superior figures refer to end-of-chapter notes.

Since their Commencement to his Armes they owe,
If Springs as high as Fountaines may ascend.   (109–12)[2]

But even here stanza and syntax energetically combine: conjunctions, prepositions, and relatives control the beginning of each line, verbs and nouns give it weight at the end. The first stanza is similarly controlled:

And now 'tis time; for their Officious haste,
Who would before have born him to the sky,
Like *eager Romans* ere all Rites were past
Did let too soon the *sacred Eagle* fly.   (1–4)

In this case judicious use of alliteration and assonance gives variety and strength to the simple structure which the syntax and metre shape and support. The syntactic plunge *in medias res* is assured as well as dramatic. This feeling for the formal relationships between metre, sentence structure and sound patterning is characteristic of all Dryden's verse. So is the verse paragraph, a prototype of which is evident in the first four quatrains of the poem, skilfully locked together as they are by carefully placed conjunctions. And if the formality of the quatrain makes for more sluggishness than one finds in the later couplet paragraphs, it does act as a control on the poem's baroque conceits:

His *Grandeur* he deriv'd from Heav'n alone,
For he was great e're Fortune made him so;
And Warr's like mists that rise against the Sunne
Made him but greater seem, not greater grow.   (21–4)

In quatrains analogies have to be swiftly concluded.

A first reading of the *Heroique Stanza's*, however, does not give an impression of successful restraint. There is the reference to the ludicrous miracle of '*Bolognia's* Walls' (63–4), and a number of passages that could easily be read as insulting to Cromwell. The allusion to the whale (137–40) must have disturbed readers of Hobbes' *Leviathan*, while the comparison of Cromwell to Tarpæia (135–6) is especially awkward since even her allies, the Sabines, felt compelled to crush her to death for her treason. The most obvious defence of such anomalous references is that they are indeed intended to reflect adversely on Cromwell, and that the *Heroique Stanza's* anticipate

Dryden's mature work in characteristically modifying the effects of panegyric by intruding the art of irony on the art of praise.

The title given to Cromwell in the poem—that of prince—suggests a basis for this irony. Cromwell is a Machiavelli. 'To become a Prince of a private man', Machiavelli had written, 'presupposes either virtue or fortune.'[3] The tensions of the *Heroique Stanza's* derive from the ambiguity in both words. 'Fortune' can mean either 'providence' or 'luck', 'Vertue' either 'goodness' or, as Cowley put in in his anti-Cromwellian satire *Visions and Prophecies*, the exercise of *any* of the 'powers and inclinations which God has infused' into men, 'desire of rule' being one of these.[4] Cowley was by no means alone in associating Oliver with *The Prince*. Marvell's *Horatian Ode* touches on the idea; an anonymous satire, *The Unparalleld Monarch* (1656) does the same, while in the pro-Cromwellian *Killing Noe Murder* (1657) Machiavelli is cited in the Protector's defence.[5] In the context of this strong tradition, parts of the *Herioque Stanza's* must have struck contemporaries as being dense with double meanings.

> Such was our Prince; yet own'd a soul above
> The highest Acts it could produce to show:
> Thus poor *Mechanique Arts* in publique moove
> Whilst the deep Secrets beyond practice goe.   (125–8)

Formally the allusion is to the secret arts of government which only princely minds were capable of mastering; but the reference to Cromwell's political guile is hardly disguised: 'practice' alliterating with 'publique', 'produce' and 'Prince' sounds a strongly Machiavellian note.

But if the tensions in the poem are centred in an unspoken unease about the qualities required to conquer 'new Principalities . . . by ones own armes and valour' they spread out from the person of Cromwell to the whole nation, and in particular to the situation created by his death. As a result the final effect of the poem's irony is to reinforce our sense of Cromwell's greatness. The closing stanzas, for instance, rather oddly suggest that the civil peace which follows the Protector's death may well be short-lived ('Halcyon days' are fleeting). The problems of the succession, however, are paradoxically evidence of Cromwell's greatness, since they point to the incapacities of those who survive him. The last stanza neatly balances the contradictions of usurpation: the more peacefully Cromwell's ashes rest, the greater the evidence that usurpation can succeed, and so the greater the temptation to others to follow his 'great example'. The sense of unease arising from such hints creates a far subtler impression of Cromwell's stature than mere praise could. There is certainly no need for the caution with which critics of the poem have tried to avoid cultivating 'another crop of ambiguities'.[6] Dryden has explicitly repudiated mere adulation:

> Yet 'tis our duty and our interest too
> Such monuments as we can build to raise;
> Lest all the World prevent what we should do
> And claime a *Title* in him by their praise.   (13–16)

The plain-speaking in 'interest', the circumspection of 'Such monuments as we *can* build' and the affrontery of 'claime a *Title*', all point to Dryden's concern to establish intelligent, ironic, and moderating alternatives to the surface of the poem. Cromwell's, however, was a greatness that could survive references to Tarpæia's treason or Bolognia's luck. Superficially the praise may be generalised, with Cromwell emerging as the flat Idea of a Prince. But the ironies are particular, tying a universal if vacuous symbolism to specific tensions in the England of 1658. Dryden presents an appreciation of his prince according to this double perspective because he knows that Cromwell's greatness arises out of historical realities and points to heroic idealism, that it confirms and surmounts the local ambiguities and the grandiose generalities to which the poem so learnedly and guilefully alludes.

There is, however, a constraint in the *Heroique Stanza's* which even if it is quite proper in an elegy, acts finally to limit the appeal of the poem. Quatrains restrict Dryden's range. Turning to the two Royalist poems he wrote after Charles II's return in 1660, one feels immediately the heroic couplet's larger technical scope.

In *To His Sacred Maiesty* (1662), for instance, Dryden discovers his gift for processional effects. The first thirty-five lines develop against a background of strict metrical regularity. The appearance of the king, however, signals a break:

> Soft western winds waft ore the gaudy spring
> And opend Scenes of flow'rs and blossoms bring
> To grace this happy day, while you appear
> Not King of us alone but of the year.   (29–32)

It is as if Charles were proceeding alone behind paired ranks of couplet-courtiers. The opening of *Astræa Redux* (1660) also shows Dryden's ability to strengthen his regular couplets with small irregularities:

> Now with a general Peace the World was blest,
> While Ours, a World divided from the rest,
> A dreadful Quiet felt, and worser farre
> Then Armes, a sullen Intervall of Warre.   (1–4)

In the third line 'felt' has a pivotal function of almost political force, and the unexpected pause after 'Armes' makes the last line satisfyingly ominous. The poem has imperfections; rhyme occasionally conquers sense; but generally metre and image are emancipated without control being lost.

There is a new freedom, too, in the more open ironies of both poems. Dryden, having raised his heroes high, 'liked suddenly to disclose that an atmosphere rarefied is also difficult to survive in'.[7] Charles' irregular living provided opportunities for this. The reference to his proclamation against 'debauched and prophane persons' in *Astræa Redux*, for instance, was surely playfully intended:

> Of those your Edicts some reclaim from sins,
> But most your Life and Blest Example wins.   (316–17)

In view of his well-publicised philanderings abroad, the suggestion that in exile he 'Could tast no sweets of youths desired Age' (53) was also, presumably, ironically meant.

Such ironies, however, are minor matters. The Restoration made it possible for Dryden to assert more positively than had previously been advisable those political convictions and prejudices which he clung to so stubbornly for the rest of his life. In his presentation of Charles as suffering hero in *Astræa Redux*, for instance, he recommends for the first time that wise passiveness in public affairs which was to be a key idea in all his political thinking. He therefore brushes aside the impetuous Booth to celebrate the stolid mercenary Monck, the chief instrument of Charles' restoration and rather like Grillon in *The Duke of Guise* (a play begun at this time), a typically 'honest' soldier. If Monck's sense of honour could look suspiciously like stupidity, it was just such stupidity, or simplicity, which made him,

in Dryden's eyes, the perfect instrument of Providence. Monck believed
in dogged obedience to the authority that commissioned him; it was,
he said, his 'great principle';[8] yet by remaining true to the letter of his
commission from Parliament, he secured, almost by inaction, the
return of the secluded members whose votes restored the King. This
Dryden liked. With Sir Robert Filmer, he believed in obeying usurping
governments, since they had 'a possession by the permissive will of
God',[9] and the working of God in history was one of his deepest
beliefs.

His other was the divinity of kings. He readily identifies Charles
with both David and Christ, even if with predictable frequency and
little discrimination. Particularly difficult to accept is the elaborate
parallelism in *Astræa Redux* between Charles as the bridgegroom of
England and Christ as the bridegroom of the Church, especially in
view of the adroit but rather soiled urbanity with which the poem hints
at Charles' messy personal life. But it is just this emphasis which leads
to an understanding of the nature and complexity of Dryden's political
thinking even at this relatively early stage. It is also crucial to an
understanding of his art. *Astræa Redux* in fact anticipates *Absalom
and Achitophel* (1681) by carefully conceding the unworthiness of
kings in order to give especial emphasis to the sacramental inviol-
ability of their kingship. The argument is one which Dryden doubtless
became more familiar with later, since it was frequently used in
Catholic apologetics. Put crudely, it is that the more visible the
human corruptions of a divine institution, the more directly its
triumphs and virtues can be attributed to God. Dryden was to exploit
such paradoxes with increasingly subtle satirical finesse in his later
works; but even at this stage of his career he had skill enough to ensure
that strong, positive convictions would emerge from the careful,
mockingly sustained ambiguities of his poems to the King. Just as
Cromwell's standing as a princely man is finally enhanced by the
context of ambiguity in which the *Heroique Stanza's* place him, so the
divine right of kings and the activity of God in history are the more
positively asserted in the Royalist poems of the sixties precisely by
means of the aesthetically and humanly inadequate settings in which
they are placed.

Divine right was a moral, not a legal, concept. When in 1660, for
instance, Charles II promised the English people 'resettlement of our
just rights and theirs',[10] he was not suggesting that the rights of either
could be embodied in a code or constitution. No theory could account

for, nor written constitution document, the rights enjoyed by the king
and his people. Thus in *Astræa Redux* Charles' authority, especially
in respect of the prerogatives of mercy and equity, cannot be reduced
to precise formulations:

> Your Pow'r to Justice doth submit your Cause,
> Your Goodness only is above the Laws;
> Whose rigid letter while pronounc'd by you
> Is softer made. (266–9)

The poem carefully identifies the written laws of the realm with
divine justice, which takes precedence over divine power. But just as
the Law of Moses is replaced by the Christian dispensation of Grace,
so the prerogative of mercy is above the written laws of the realm. In
insisting that law is superior to force, Dryden opposes Hobbes. In
insisting that 'equity', 'mercy', and 'prerogative' must take precedence
over written law, he takes up a position which Locke was later to
resist. He does so because he wishes to protect social relationships
from the tyranny of power-based or law-based absolutism. The king
fixes and embodies the ideal relationship between power, law, and
prerogative, and so organically guarantees that the 'perfect union' to
which Charles had called his people in 1660 will be truly flexible and
humane.

It is easy to label such ideas conservative; but then all articulate
political discussion in the seventeenth century was between different
kinds of conservatism, at least once Cromwell had given effect to
Ireton's principle that political rights could only be granted to men
with 'a permanent fixed interest in this kingdom'; that is, to 'the
persons in whom all the land lies, and those in corporations in whom all
trading lies'.[11] On the other hand, at this stage of his career, Dryden's
royalist principles were marked by the progressive optimism of
mercantilism. Colbert, after all, was about to make expanding commerce an integral part of Louis XIV's grandiose absolutism, for which
'most practical men of affairs felt a sneaking sympathy'.[12] It was easy,
therefore, for Dryden to regard England's submission to Charles II as
progressive as well as providential. Hence the emphasis on sea power
and trade in *Astræa Redux*, the sea imagery being as relevant to the
poem's ideas as to its rich decoration.

Ironic and lavishly irresponsible as these poems may appear, therefore, both may properly be enjoyed for the expansive seriousness with

which they celebrate the restoration of Right to the kingdom of
England. They remain, however, superficial beside the *Heroique
Stanza's*. It is almost impossible to find anything of lasting relevance
in their politics, yet suspiciously easy to assert that Dryden did.
Another poem, written at this time, illustrates the point. *To my
Honoured Friend, S*^r *Robert Howard* (1660) has been variously inter-
preted. It is alleged to be about 'the moral nature of poetry',[13] or about
literature and society,[14] or 'the interconnectedness of all activities in
the land'.[15] In fact it meets none of these claims, or rather not seriously
so. It is a light-hearted exercise in friendly banter. Behind a surface of
compliment it suggests that Howard was rather a dull poet. The
surface is graceful, however, especially the account of Howard's
'natural' talent, and the fantastic speculations about whether art is a
product of chance, like Lucretius' universe, or whether there is a
'providence of wit'. Sir Robert, however, has no need of art: he has
enough brute strength to do without acquired skill, and so, by pure
chance, 'Like some brave Captain' (Monck presumably!) restores
moral knowledge to the throne of Poesy. This delightfully witty
section identifies frivolous verse with Puritan government, and
concludes '"A sober Prince's Government is best"' (54) which suggests
an odd view of the respective sobriety of Protector and King. Dryden
then hints that Howard's Virgil has been over-translated, and that his
commentary on Statius is unscholarly. He notes *whom* Howard has
praised (Charles and Monck), not *how*, and offers this as an explanation
of the volume's supposed success. The poem is ironic but unmalicious,
yet it has been consistently over-interpreted. This does not so much
reflect on *To . . . S*^r *Robert Howard*, however, as on the other poems
of this period which use similar analogies for more grandiose purposes. The controlling irony in the modest epistle points to a lack of
control in the more ambitious panegyrics.

  This does not explain, however, why the critics have tended to
misread the former. The reasons for this become clearer in the light of
two other poems written about this time, *To My Lord Chancellor* (1662)
and *To The Lady Castlemain* (1674). In some respects the former is a
brilliant exercise in the use of decorative baroque conceits. Even Dr
Johnson was prepared to acknowledge the skill with which Dryden
handles the comparison of Clarendon to the earth and Charles to the
sky.[16] Significantly, however, it was *To The Lady Castlemain* which
A. W. Verral picked out as 'Dryden's first masterpiece, the first . . .
without technical flaw'.[17] Certainly its fluency has an almost sexual

grace. It is also happily free of intellectual ambition. It does, however, contain these lines:

> You, like the Stars, not by reflexion bright,
> Are born to your own Heav'n, and your own Light:
> Like them are good, but from a Nobler Cause,
> From your own Knowledg, not from Natures Laws
> Your pow'r you never use, but for Defence,
> To guard your own, or others Innocence.   (25–30)

This could easily have been addressed to Clarendon, while the following lines, describing the Muses as 'antient ladies' desperately hoping that Clarendon will give them some attention, could have been written to Lady Castlemain:

> For still they look on you with such kind eyes
> As those that see the Churches Soveraign rise
> From their own Order chose, in whose high State
> They think themselves the second choice of Fate.   (13–16)

The Muses dissolve in the marvellous joke of involving the earnestly Anglican Clarendon in a papal election, but the joke would have been no less telling if applied to Charles' mistress and her rivals. Dryden's analogies and allusions, in other words, are so smoothly interchangeable that decisions as to their seriousness can be extremely difficult. If they carry large meanings in *Astræa Redux*, why not in *To . . . Sᵣ Robert Howard*?

It is sometimes hard to believe that Dryden is really saying anything at all in these early works. What, for instance, are we to make of the lines immediately following those quoted from *To My Lord Chancellor*? The amusing ecclesiastical conceit introduces a suggestion that 'Wit and Religion' went into exile with the King. A potentially solemn reference to the gods forsaking their Trojan shrines, however, is followed by the more frivolous idea that the 'Druyds' were restored in 1660. The paragraph then concludes with the suggestion that Charles is to England as Christ is to his mystical body, the Church. It is hard to see anything intelligent in this protean flow of metaphor. It has been suggested in explanation that 'the cavalier spirit' required 'an emphatic mingling' of classical and Christian imagery;[18] but this hardly justifies the changes of mood and prefabrication of analogy which one finds in *To My Lord Chancellor*, a style clearly more suited to the aesthetic libertine than the Christian humanist. It might seem more reasonable simply to conclude that Dryden was uncertain about the relationship of contemporary life to 'the biblical or classical pasts'.[19] But the difficulty this view has to meet is *To my Honour'd Friend, Dr Charleton* (1663), a poem brilliantly confident about the relationship between Restoration England and the ancient world.

Its excellence is an effect of the ease with which it moves through a mass of conventional reference and allusion. Charleton was prominent in the Royal Society and had tried to prove that Stonehenge was a Danish coronation site. Denmark having recently changed from an elective to a hereditary monarchy, Dryden was able to weave round Charleton's theory a complex of royalist, scientific, commercial, patriotic and religious sentiment. The poem's climax is an imaginary account of Charles returning to Stonehenge (where he had taken refuge after his defeat at the Battle of Worcester), to 'be chose again to rule the Land' (52). It is of course understood that such an election would be like the once-and-for-all affair recently held in Denmark and implied in the proclamation of 1660 which was carefully cast in the form of a contract binding the English people to the Stuart monarchy for ever.[20] The brilliant fusion in this poem of ancient notions of right and the dashing new commercialism of the sixties disposes of the thesis that for Dryden this was a time of ideological uncertainty. There is, however, not a single reference in the whole poem to the country's real situation. It is a rich conflux of ideas only, and this accounts for its success. Like *To The Lady Castlemain* it is a purely mental construct, unembarrassed by the 'real' politics which haunt *To My Lord Chancellor* and which make Dryden's conceits and his principles seem equally superficial. The strength of all the poems of this period is their confidence—indeed their over-confidence—on matters of principle. But easy, serious, or flamboyant as they may be, they remain basically irresponsible, deficient in any exact appreciation of the times about which they were written. Dryden's writing in the sixties, in fact, was not historical, not realistic enough.

This must seriously prejudice *Annus Mirabilis* (1667), his most ambitious early work and deliberately characterised as 'An Historical Poem'. The Anglo-Dutch war which it describes was badly conducted. With the Plague (1665) and the Fire of London (1666), it weakened the Government's standing. Seditious pamphlets suggested divine disapproval of the Court as a cause. Dryden's poem is a reply,[21] unlikely to sway public opinion, but at least a trumpet blast from the other side. His own account of it, however, is not encouraging. He admits that it is neither long enough nor unified enough to be a true epic, but argues that it is none the less heroic, a quality which he conceives to be less a matter of structure, and so of Judgement, as of Wit. Specifically he claims to be imitating Virgil, whose chief gift, he argues, was elocution, 'the Art of clothing and adorning [a] thought . . . in apt, significant and sounding words'.[22] This emphasis on rhetoric at the expense of narrative is hardly proper in a historian, even a poetic one. Equally ominous are his assertions that the function of imagery is to excite wonder, and his definition of Wit as 'lively and apt description' which re-creates an absent object 'as perfectly and more delightfully than nature'. Combined with the propagandising purpose of the poem, such attitudes suggest that his verse could detach itself altogether from history in a tissue of self-indulgent metaphor.

There is general agreement that this is what happened, that the quatrain proved unsuitable for narrative, that the narrative decayed into panegyric, and that the vaunted amplifications were too 'literary' and deficient in 'socal or sociological' import to be truly Virgilian.[23] The poem has been praised for the virtuosity with which the quatrains are organised, for its large tone and strength of statement, its masterly disposition of images, especially of the four elements (earth is effectively associated with the Dutch) and its Marlovian indulgence in the exotic. But by and large it is a 'great . . . bad poem';[24] nor, looking at the first thirty-six quatrains, is it easy to dissent from this judgement. It opens on a rough, low note. The Dutch are 'Crouching' and 'cruel', fit objects of punning jokes and French duplicity. Admittedly with the introduction of Charles meditating on foreign policy, like the cosmic alchemist God is to become later in the poem, a heroic note is struck, but only briefly. In a stanza which Johnson thought like the work of 'some wag', the summoning of the fleet becomes a baroque frivolity— as indeed does the 'porcelain' Battle of Bergen which follows. But just as the whole poem is about to disintegrate in a tinkle of irony, a darkly serious theme appears—the vanity of all 'proud designs'—in stanzas which Johnson rightly found 'one of the fairest flowers of English poetry'.[25]

These inconsistencies of tone cannot, however, be dismissed as effects of Dryden's insensitivity. They are too gross to be other than a deliberate exercise in aesthetic madness. There is moreover a key to the poem's method in Dryden's assertion in the Preface that Virgil is his master in the poem. Virgil's distinctive achievement, the Preface maintains, is that 'the Soul of the Poet . . . inform[s] and move[s] through all his Pictures'.[26] In effect, Virgil's personality, manifest in the tone and style of his verse, has a major co-ordinating function in structuring the *Æneid*. We have only to concede that Dryden's is a very different personality to see how *Annus Mirabilis* can be Virgilian without being like anything Virgil wrote. And if it is Virgilian in this way, we must look not to its narrative line but to the exposure and development of Dryden's own moods and attitudes if we are to discover a structural coherence in its apparent inconsistencies.

The treatment of Monck (now Duke of Albemarle) in the Four Days Battle illustrates the process. The Battle of Bergen is followed by some awkward sketching in of the diplomatic background. We are then fairly quickly introduced to the two preliminary heroes, Prince Rupert and Albemarle, moving to their posts in verse of some splendour: 'war, severely, like it self, appears' (208), and the poem becomes heroic at last. There are tough monosyllabic lines—'Both furl their sails, and strip them for the fight' (221); and the low-slung strength of the British ships is effectively emphasised. Yet when the fight begins this mood of heroic sternness is suddenly and neatly undermined in a stanza which purports to be a noble echo of Virgil but in fact cleverly alludes to an incident in which Albemarle's breeches were blown off in battle, and he had to fight on naked from the waist down. A little later, however, we see Albemarle restored to full poetic dignity, keeping watch through the night like another Henry V, anxiously surveyed by the ghosts of English kings. This condition of moral suspense or emotional confusion is carried over into the opening stages of the next day's fighting, which begins almost in bizarre fashion with a brutally light-hearted description of a drowning:

> The wild waves master'd him, and suck'd him in,
> And smiling Eddies dimpled on the Main. (375–6)

In the succeeding stanzas, however, the similes are given true Virgilian dignity. More importantly, the dangers and horrors of war are honestly and toughly reported, and this finally confirms Albemarle's moral dignity. In a daring allusion to his earlier embarrassment—'His naked valour is his onely guard' (410)—the cynical streak with which so much of the poem has been laced, is tellingly checked, and Dryden frankly, and possibly even humbly, makes Monck's soldierly if naive decencies the moral centre of this section of the poem.

The whole work operates in similar fashion. In an unrelenting programme of tonal deflation Dryden consistently denies us easy and so specious access to heroic triumph. Apparently he does so as a frequently amused and always urbane sceptic, but in reality his intentions are complex and intensely moral. Thus the Four Days Battle peters out, the ship-building and Royal Society passages are clogged up with ludicrously decorative pseudo-scientific speculation, and the July victory over the Dutch is flat, its only issue being an unheroic firing of the Dutch coast. Structurally this preserves the climactic dignity of the Fire, but its cumulative effect is also to suggest Dryden's grave distrust of 'large designs', even his own. When finally the Fire sweeps like a 'mighty Squadron' on to London, and Charles emerges as the poem's climactic figure, he must first cease to struggle as a royal hero, and instead pray humbly as a royal priest, before the divine alchemist (in a calculatedly deflating and much misunderstood stanza)[27] snuffs out the fire. There is a considerable aesthetic toughness in this part of the poem, which matches an equally unyielding moral and theological toughness, notably in stanzas 273–6. The poem's meaning and intentions, however, are implicit in the remarkably modest note on which the final apostrophe to London concludes. The poet's mood, sophisticated, earnest, sceptical, believing, above all modest and discriminating, controls the poem to the end.

So compressed an account of its tonal strategy misses the arrogant grace of its tactics. (Their range, incidentally, is indicated by the intelligent and respectful 'Verses to her Highness the Dutchess' which were printed with it and are part of the poem.) What is clear, however, is that Dryden meant what he said about the poet informing and moving through his poems. This he does not just to express his own personality, nor merely to indulge a love of either elaborate design or intellectual toughness, but most of all to illustrate a complicated, personal moral vision. The stanzas which Johnson praised are the centre of the poem:

> Such are the proud designs of human kind,
> And so we suffer Shipwrack every where!
> Alas, what Port can such a Pilot find,
> Who in the night of Fate must blindly steer!
>
> The undistinguish'd seeds of good and ill
> Heav'n, in his bosom, from our knowledge hides;
> And draws them in contempt of human skill,
> Which oft, for friends, mistaken foes provides. (137–44)

The conduct of affairs of state is a high mystery reserved for kings; the conduct of history is reserved to God. The fact, however, that monarchy thus becomes a metaphor of divinity reduces the impressiveness of kings and of the poems written about them. The doctrine of divine right, after all, assumes a hierarchy of values which from certain points of view must turn all human greatness into a mere masquerade. Thus, though it has rightly been said that 'the new ironic and sceptical intelligence' of the Restoration was generally destructive of belief in monarchy as 'the earthly realisation of a transcendent and cosmic order',[28] in Dryden's case at least, irony is consciously in the service of that order, and of the virtues of humility, obedience and restraint which it implies.

Annus Mirabilis is a great and serious poem. This does not mean, however, that it is any more 'realistic' historically than the other poems of the period. It is wiser, but still oblivious of the secular, autonomous, and pragmatic nature of politics, and of the fact that personal qualities, whether they are heroic like Albemarle's or urbane like the poet's, are of little relevance in public affairs. This is why it is so easy not to take the poem seriously, and why, from certain points of view, it is a less intelligent achievement than the *Heroique Stanza's*. There at least Dryden confronted pragmatism in public life:

> Our former Cheifs like sticklers of the Warre
> First sought t'inflame the Parties, then to poise;
> The quarrell lov'd, but did the cause abhorre,
> And did not strike to hurt but make a noise.
>
> Warre our consumption was their gainfull trade,
> We inward bled whilst they prolong'd our pain:
> He fought to end our fighting, and assaid
> To stanch the blood by breathing of the vein.   (41–8)

There is nothing so deeply 'realistic' as this in *Annus Mirabilis*. The hesitancy of the Presbyterian leaders after 1644, and Cromwell's decisiveness, are psychological equivalents of the balance of impersonal military and political forces in the kingdom. The balance of metrical and syntactical pressures in the first quatrain precisely imitate both, particularly the delicately placed 'then to poise', and the emphasis given to 'sticklers', 'strike', 'hurt' and 'noise'. Notoriously the next stanza was supposed to refer to Charles I's execution. In the light of the tonal complexity implied by the Machiavellian references in the poem, there is no reason why, among other matters, it should not.

What the *Heroique Stanza's* lack, however, is the freedom, technical and ideological, of the post-Restoration poems. As a result, they are not only deficient in the poetic exhibitionism of *Annus Mirabilis*, but more importantly in the humanising diffidence for which that ebullience provides a curiously appropriate setting. Dryden was only to realise the full potential of his talent when the fullness and honesty with which history is reported in the *Heroique Stanza's* was integrated in his work with the discriminating, if idiosyncratic, moral sensibility of *Annus Mirabilis*. Taken together, however, both poems clearly look forward to the end of the century and *The Secular Masque*.

1. A. W. Verral, *Lectures on Dryden* (1914), p. 95.

2. Quotations from the poems are from *The Poems of John Dryden*, Ed. James Kinsley (1958); hereafter Kinsley.

3. *N. Machiavelli's Prince*. Translated ... by E. D. 1640, in *The Tudor Translations*, Ed. W. E. Henley, XXIX (1905), p. 518.

4. Quoted in Felix Raab, *The English Face of Machiavelli: A Changing Interpretation, 1500–1700* (1964), pp. 133–4.

5. ibid., pp. 134–41.

6. Paul Ramsey, *The Art of John Dryden* (1969), p. 60.

7. Arthur W. Hoffman, *John Dryden's Imagery* (1962), p. 11.

8. Quoted in Godfrey Davies, *The Restoration of Charles II, 1658–60* (San Marino and London, 1955), p. 110.

9. Quoted in Alan Roper, *Dryden's Poetic Kingdoms* (1965), p. 61.

10. Quoted in Davies, op. cit., p. 340.

11. Quoted in Christopher Hill, *The Century of Revolution, 1603–1711* (Sphere Books ed., 1969), p. 120.

12. J. H. Plumb, *The Growth of Political Stability in England, 1675–1725* (Peregrine Books ed., 1969), p. 24.

13. Charles E. Ward, *The Life of John Dryden* (1961), p. 22.

14. Earl Wasserman, 'Dryden: *Epistle to Charleton*', in *Dryden, A Collection of Critical Essays*, Ed. Bernard N. Schilling (1963), p. 72.

15. Roper, op. cit., p. 34.

16. See *Lives of the English Poets*, Ed. George Birkbeck Hill (1905), p. 428; hereafter *Lives*.

17. *Lectures on Dryden*, p. 34.

18. Hoffman, op. cit., p. 18.

19. Earl Miner, *Dryden's Poetry* (1967), 6.

20. See Bernard N. Schilling, *Dryden and the Conservative Myth* (1961), p. 239.

21. See Edward N. Hooker, 'The Purposes of Dryden's *Annus Mirabilis*', *Huntingdon Library Quarterly*, X pp. 49–67.

22. 'An account of the ensuing Poem', Kinsley, I, pp. 46–7.

23. Roper, op. cit., p. 79.

24. Ramsey, op. cit., p. 60.

25. *Lives*, p. 431.

26. Kinsley I, p. 47.

27. See Anne T. Barbeau, *The Intellectual Design of John Dryden's Heroic Plays* (1970), pp. 202–3.

28. John Heath Stubbs, 'Dryden and the Heroic Ideal', *Dryden's Mind and Art*, Ed. Bruce King (1969), p. 4.

2

ADMIRATION AND TRUTH:
DRAMA AND CRITICISM 1660–1679

In their fashion, Dryden's curious, stylised heroic plays reflect the political life of their period with some accuracy, though in suspiciously easy ways. In 1681, for instance, it was alleged that scenes from *The Duke of Guise*, in fact written twenty years earlier, referred to the Exclusion crisis then raging. Even more than the early poems Dryden's drama was 'platonised', everything historically or psychologically local being excluded. *Tyrannick Love* (1669) gives us 'patterns of piety',[1] *The Conquest of Granada* (1670) 'patterns of exact virtues'.[2] The plot of *The Indian Queen* (1664), written in collaboration with Howard, is typical. Montezuma, a foreigner in Peruvian service, captures and befriends a Mexican prince, but changes sides when refused the Peruvian princess in marriage. Later he captures her and her father, but the Mexican queen (a usurper) and her general imprison all three. The queen, however, falls in love with Montezuma, and the general with the princess, whom the prince, Montezuma's friend, also loves. The prince defies his mother and rescues the prisoners but, wounded in a love-duel with Montezuma, cannot prevent their recapture. He therefore honourably kills himself. A rising on Montezuma's behalf (suddenly revealed as lawful king of Mexico) resolves the situation. The general is killed, and the queen, devoted to Montezuma still, kills herself. These pre-Columbian Amerindians are quite indistinguishable from the Romans of *Tyrannick Love* and the Moors of *The Conquest of Granada* in their pursuit of love, honour and empire. Characterisation is a matter of type, and, like morality, is based on social roles. Obedience is owned to kings, loyalty to friends, fidelity to a beloved. The form is thoroughly unclassical in spite of Saint-

Everemonde's claim that joining the love-themes of mediaeval romance, and the epic effect of *admiratio*, to pity and terror, the traditional effects of tragedy, was essentially Horatian.[3] Scott more accurately said of heroic conventions that they present 'splendid imagery, eloquent expression, sound morality, everything but the language of human passion and human character'.[4]

Was Dryden aware of these deficiencies? There is certainly evidence of ironic intention in his plays of this type, the irony being primarily directed at the political and psychological theories of Hobbes. Dryden's distrust of Hobbes, moreover, seems bound up with a recognition of the absurdity of the heroic posture. Admittedly it is his villainous characters who make the distinctively Hobbist assumption that the two universal and determining impulses are Fear and 'a perpetual and restlesse desire of Power after power',[5] and that the supreme good is 'Empire'. Such characters are impressive enough in their fullness of life and will, but their impulses have unforeseen results which reveal the ironically controlling hand of an un-Hobbist Providence. (In the Dedication to *The Rival Ladies* [1664] Dryden compares God's control over men to the dramatist's over his characters.)[6] It is not just the villains who fall into this trap however. The true heroes, either in lawful pursuit of *gloire* or as defenders of the Right, are caught in it as well. Besides, it is always the fall of events, never human purposes, which secures the triumph of justice. The effect of so much misguided activity, however motivated, has obvious comic potential, and there is evidence, as Cibber noted, 'that the Poet intended to make his spectators laugh while they admired' such characters.[7] It has been argued, therefore, that 'the heroic plays are a form of satire',[8] a claim supported by the 'clever comic imagery'[9] in parts of *The Indian Emperour* (1665). Apparently Dryden entered a poker-faced conspiracy about his plays with a sophisticated section of his audience. In 1681 he claimed of his purple passages that when he wrote them he 'knew they were bad enough to please',[10] and one may reasonably assume that he shared this consciousness with others.

The difficulty is that once heard this ironic note echoes through everything. Thus in *Tyrannick Love* there are numerous parallels between St Catharine's speeches and the writings of John Tillotson.[11] But if St Catharine is the serious figure this implies, how are we supposed to distinguish the following breathless description of her impact on the Roman intellectual world from speeches that are meant to be funny?

> I hope my business may my haste excuse;
> For, Sir, I bring you most surprizing news.
> The Christian Princess in her Tent confers
> With fifty of your learn'd Philosophers;
> Whom with such Eloquence she does perswade,
> That they are Captives to her reasons, made.   (II,i,127–32)[12]

Once irony is accepted as an element in these plays, it is difficult to take any of them seriously. But even if Dryden did indeed choose deliberately, 'to approach the precipice of absurdity and hover over the abyss of unideal vacancy',[13] a belief in the seriousness of heroic literature was none the less central to his whole sense of the dignity of poetry generally.

Everything he wrote at this time about the nature and functioning of poetry in fact points to his taking the heroic play, as a *genre*, very seriously indeed. Accepting Hobbes' division of the poetic faculties into Fancy and Judgement, he envisaged only a minor role for the Judgement. Admittedly in his first critical essay Fancy stands for Inspiration and Judgement for art;[14] but by 1667 the Imagination is supreme and includes Invention, Fancy, and Elocution; that is, the discovering, shaping, and expressing of poetic ideas;[15] and by 1671 even the 'disposing of actions and passions into their proper places' is placed in the 'field of fancy', the latter being 'the principall quality requir'd' in a poet.[16] Throughout this period, moreover, Dryden consistently defended the heroic play on the grounds that it was the form which gave greatest scope to this supreme poetic faculty. Being limited only by 'the extremest bounds of what is possible', it offered the ambitious poet his greatest challenge. Accordingly, in 'Of Heroic Plays' (1672), he criticises Davenant for 'the scanting of his images and design', and so failing to comply 'with the greatness and majesty of an heroic poem'.[17]

This belief in the importance of both Fancy and the heroic mode is an essential element in Dryden's side of the protracted argument he had with Howard in the sixties over the use of rhyme on the stage. Superficially Dryden's main argument is that rhyme is useful in restraining an over-luxuriant Fancy, but this is hardly more convincing than his claim that it aids (presumably the actor's) memory. Rhyme is really important because it enriches and elevates a play, the function of heroic drama being precisely to present images of 'Nature wrought up to an higher pitch . . . above the level of common converse, as high as the imagination of the Poet can carry them, with proportion to verisimility'.[18] Far from restraining the heroic flight, therefore, rhyme, like the use of battle scenes and elaborate stage machinery, serves to 'raise the imagination of the audience',[19] producing a theatrical equivalent of epic *admiratio*. In view of the effort Dryden put into maintaining this position, and the importance especially of rhyme to his poetic practice as well as his poetic theory, it is almost impossible to imagine him writing his heroic plays with an eye primarily to their satiric effect.

The comic element in the plays is none the less palpable. It must therefore somehow relate to a serious attempt by Dryden to produce *admiratio* in his audience. Exactly what effect he was seeking is suggested by his assertion that the poet should 'endeavour an absolute dominion over the minds of the spectators'.[20] With this aim in view, it is easier to see the contribution irony could make to theatrical *admiratio*, especially if Dryden had a sceptical, cool-headed audience to start with. The more he encourages such attitudes, the greater his final triumph in subduing them. The strategy is a cruder version of that in *Annus Mirabilis*, where the reader is allowed to find Albemarle amusing, only to be effectively chastened as the old soldier's courage emerges as truly heroic when the fighting is really desperate. In the heroic plays, however, it is not so much solid virtue that subdues the audience's aroused and flattered sense of detached superiority, as a *tour de force* of splendid design, explosive acting, and sumptuous images. The wonder we are invited to feel is undiscriminating, the heroic qualities which are its basis being wholly without moral or intellectual content. In the 1660s, however, Dryden had little respect for the 'nature' he claimed to imitate: 'a bare representation of what is true, or exceeding probable'[21]—the moderating disciplines of realism in other words—did not interest him.

It is still possible, however, to enjoy the heroic plays, if only as extraordinary displays of poetic gymnastics. Apart from *Amboyna* (1673), a crude piece of political propaganda, written in haste at the start of the Third Dutch War, they represent the whole of Dryden's contribution to serious drama in the ten-year period following the staging of *The Indian Queen*. In *The Indian Emperour* the virtues of the *genre* become apparent. Given the conventions of love, honour, abstract morality and decorum in which the play is working it is deftly organised. Act One, scene two establishes some tense erotic and political relationships with verve and economy, while the Second, Third, and Fourth Acts work out the events implicit in the First. The play's ideas form richly organised, frequently ironic relationships with these events. Thus when Cydaria askes Cortez 'What is this Honour which does Love controul?' his reply is succinctly anti-Hobbist:

> A raging fit of Vertue in the Soul,
> A painful burden which great minds must bear,
> Obtain'd with danger, and possest with fear.   (II,ii,38–41)[22]

but he quickly abandons honour for love, like any Hobbist puppet. Promptly, however, his rival provokes a battle, and thereby ironically secures by mechanical impulse the ends of a Providence which sanctions Cortez's original view of virtue. Initially it is Montezuma who is impeccably Erastian on church–state relations, condemning Catholic asceticism as commercially minded, and even submitting to the fall of Mexico if Providence decrees it. Finally, however, he is prepared to resort to human sacrifice on grounds of expediency, and like a true Hobbist identifies kingship with power. Cortez, on the other hand, has assumed Montezuma's original attitude of submission: 'We toss and turn about our Feaverish will,' he declares, 'When all our ease must come by lying still' (IV,i,111–12), thus firmly stating Dryden's most consistently held position about man's duty in the face of divine and human authority.

Tyrannick Love is a disappointment. The First Act is ludicrously compressed and the love entanglements are mechanical. Neither Maximin's rantings, nor St Catharine's vulgar martyrdom can counteract the comedy of lines like Berenice's cry to Porphyrius before their execution:

> If I dye first, I will ——
> Stop short of Heav'n, and wait you in a Cloud;
> For fear we lose each other in the crowd.   (V,i,485–7)

On the other hand, there is some impressive interplay between imagery and idea. Mind, State, and Cosmos are validly fused in images of storm and harbour. The storm represents passion, politics, and history itself, above which a Lucretian god, stoical and indifferent, is contrasted with the Christian God, compassionate, reasonable and mysterious, each pointing to different kinds of royalty on earth, and different orders of morality among men. Naturally Dryden counsels patience and submission:

> Th' unknown, untalk'd of man is only blest.
> He, as in some safe Cliff his cell does keep,
> From thence he views the Labours of the deep.   (III,i,47–9)

Even in Dryden's weakest productions ideas organised in images have a structural as well as a didactic function. If *Tyrannick Love* fails, it is because it relies on wild rhetoric to subdue the audience, not on that 'brilliancy of event'[23] which Scott found in Dryden's next heroic play, *The Conquest of Granada*.

It is certainly an extraordinary performance, exhibiting, in Johnson's words, 'a kind of illustrious depravity and majestick madness'[24] through ten fantastic acts. It is very elaborately organised. A stylised antithesis between the passive, obedient and virtuous Ozmyn and the noble impulsive Almanzor is balanced against a second, between the lazy, lawful tyrant Boabdelin and the impulsive, power-hungry Lyndaraxa, all four ending up as supporting figures in a pageant celebrating the established legitimacy of Ferdinand and Isabella.[25] But it is action, not pageantry, which complicates the structure. With abundant material and uninhibited violence of language and image, Dryden vitalises his ideas in the person of Almanzor, whose mind is both an irrational pre-social force of nature, and yet also, paradoxically, the means by which a rational, divinely sanctioned social order is established in Granada. His famous assertion of personal freedom—

> I am as free as nature first made man,
> Ere the base laws of servitude began,
> When wild in woods the noble savage ran.   (I*C.of G.*,I,i, p. 43)[26]

magnificently contradicts Hobbes' views about the state of nature. The equally vital but predatory Lyndaraxa, however, is a pure Hobbist, and (especially in her handling of her lovers in the Fourth Act of the First Part) a very amusing one. Nor is it the villains only who invite laughter. The play may finally indulge Almanzor's dreams of heroic personal fulfilment, but at least he is introduced in a bizarre comic light. The description of the bull-fight in the first scene, like the description of the exposed Albemarle in *Annus Mirabilis*, combines sonorous Virgilian echoes with superbly stylised comedy:

> The undaunted youth
> Then drew; and from his saddle bending low,
> Just where the neck did from the shoulders grow,

> With his full force discharged a deadly blow.
> Not heads of poppies (when they reap the grain)
> Fall with more ease before the labouring swain
> Than fell this head:
> It fell so quick it did even death prevent,
> And made imperfect bellowings as it went.
>
> (IC.of G.,I,i, pp. 38–9)

Even Ferdinand and Isabella, embodiments of political legitimacy, are caught up in Dryden's ironic recognition that there are limitations to the ideal. Isabella's naive declarations about love and honour contrast effectively with Ferdinand's laconic ruthlessness in sentencing the innocent Ozmyn to death. It would be wrong, however, to put too much stress on this side of the play. Strongly and noisily staged, its copious flow of violent action and image might even today gain absolute, if temporary, dominion over the minds of an audience.

It remains, however, the minor work of a gifted poet, its development being more a matter of tempo than meaning. It was highly successful, but this did not persuade Dryden for long that his achievement was really comparable with true epic. Doubts about both the heroic mode and his own analysis of the poetic faculties set in soon afterwards, probably when he began seriously to think of writing an epic poem. He announced his intention to do so in the Dedication of *Aureng-Zebe* (1676), declaring also that he was weary of being condemned to rhyme like 'the Sisyphus of the stage'.[27] The Prologue to the same play condemns rhyme as psychologically false ('Passion's too fierce to be in Fetters bound'), and suggests that, especially in comparison with Shakespeare, his own work is unrealistic. The rejection of rhyme in drama, in other words, like the earlier defence of it, is intimately bound up with a whole complex of thinking on the art of poetry.

Dryden's change of view in the seventies on these matters has generally been attributed to his growing attachment to non-classical, distinctively English literary traditions, in which Shakespearean naturalness is the most important element. In view of his expressed enthusiasm for Rapin and Le Bossu at this time, however, there are strong indications that, in the fundamental reappraisal of his ideas about the nature and function of poetry which took place in the seventies, he became more rather than less attached to neoclassical standards, and that this took place in conjunction with, and not in spite of, an intensifying admiration for Shakespeare.

Entirely consistent, certainly, with an increasing rather than a decreasing respect for neoclassicism is Dryden's growing conservatism on the question of rhetoric. In the *Apology for Heroic Poetry and Poetic License* (1677) he continues to insist (naturally enough in view of his epic ambitions) that heroic poetry is 'the greatest work of human nature'.[28] What is noticeable about this latest defence of the bold rhetoric of the heroic style, however, is its appeal to the authority of nature and the emphasis on the judiciousness needed for the proper use of hyperbole. *The Grounds of Criticism in Tragedy* (1679) significantly associates disapproval of extravagant writing with contempt for ranting actors and the audience who applaud them. In the Dedication to *The Spanish Friar* (1681), Dryden again insists that 'nothing is truly sublime that is not just and proper'.[29] *Admiratio* is no longer accepted as a legitimate theatrical effect, nor, in tragedy, is irregular plotting. In general he seems more willing to submit to the rules, accepting in particular Rymer's dictum that 'No simple alteration of mind ought to produce or hinder an action in tragedy', and thereby radically reducing the importance of debate in his plays.[30] His new attachment to classical norms is not, however, prescriptive, but a complex and humane commitment, in literature and in life, to proportion, judiciousness, and honesty.

This ideal is subtly suggested in the ambiguities of the lines *To Mr. Lee, on his 'Alexander'* (1677), a poem in which irony is beautifully tempered by a middle-aged poet's affection for a young, ambitious, faithful friend. The tension between critical standards and personal loyalties is crucial. In the *Apologie* Dryden had had to dissociate himself from Lee's excessive praise of *The State of Innocence* (1674). His *Alexander*, moreover, was the kind of play Dryden was beginning to dislike. The poem, therefore, though genuine and generous in its praise, quietly affirms the need for wise proportion in life and art. This commitment to proportion is evident in Dryden's growing respect for Judgement, and for the concepts associated with it, 'propriety' and 'thought'. They are the key to the relationship between his classicism and his love for Shakespeare, and they apply equally to poetry and friendship.

The contrary view, however, that the change in the seventies was away from and not towards neoclassicism does gain some support from the 'Heads of an Answer' which Dryden jotted down in his copy of Rymer's *Tragedies of the Last Age* (1677), a work firm in its adherence to neoclassical principles. But it is significant that the 'Heads' do not in fact answer Rymer. They outline possible lines of attack, but with a certain tentativeness. Read carefully, they suggest an unwillingness to jettison either the earlier English drama or the principles of correctness which Rymer defended.[31] They also firmly establish Dryden's acceptance of Rapin's views on the importance of thoughts and words in poetry, as against the fable, its disposition and manners. It is their thoughts, Dryden notes, that make Homer, Virgil, and Shakespeare great, a view he was to repeat in *The Grounds for Criticism in Tragedy*: 'dressed in the most vulgar [i.e. plainest] words', he argues, 'we should find the beauties of [Shakespeare's] thoughts remaining'.[32] On his own admission, it is true, the *Grounds* omit any serious discussion of 'the principal subject of it, which is the words and thoughts that are suitable to tragedy'.[33] Instead we are offered a logically impeccable statement of neoclassical theory. Design, very properly, is dealt with first, and then, at some length, manners or decorum. This, after all, is precisely the area where Dryden's own practice as a dramatist was changing and where Shakespeare most obviously accords with neoclassical principles. But even if he was curiously reluctant to discuss his true centre of interest, the words and the thoughts appropriate to tragedy, he insisted later, ''tis my ambition to be read . . . the propriety of thoughts and words . . . are the hidden beauties of a play',[34] and thereafter constantly asserted that this was the true definition of poetic wit. Not naturalism, then, but thought, or rather wit (understood as 'a propriety of thoughts and words')[35] is at the heart of his delight in Shakespeare, and what he now felt was the poet's chief task, the use of his Judgement.

Ideas, in a language rightly characterised by Scott as 'nervous, pure and elegant',[36] are certainly Dryden's chief contributions to his adaptations of Milton, Sophocles, and Shakespeare in the seventies. Admittedly he tried hard to give *Troilus and Cressida* (1679) a classical *liaison des scènes*—he conceded in the Preface that *dispositio* was a Shakespearean weakness—but if he changes his originals otherwise it is not to increase their naturalism but to highlight ideas. For the first time in his work ideas are given clear pride of place over theatrical and rhetorical effect. Purity of thought replaces high heroics as the goal of his writing, and with it a concern for integrity—aesthetic and intellectual—becomes prominent. His adaptations, indeed, are best read almost as practical exercises in honest thinking; if they are not to be dismissed, that is, merely as presumptuous deformations of their originals.

The State of Innocence, written in a month in 1674, is more a masque than an opera. It is an adaptation of *Paradise Lost*, and Dryden makes it perfectly clear that he had no thoughts of rivalling his original, 'one of the greatest, most noble, and most sublime poems'.[37] Why then did he write it? Principally to place problems he had dealt with super-ficially in the heroic plays—the reliability of human reason, and the relationship of free will to physical pleasure and divine Providence—in the supremely simple context of the Garden of Eden. The simplicity of Dryden's Eden, of course, is baroque in character:

> The soil luxuriant, and the fruit divine,
> Where golden apples on green branches shine,
> And purple grapes dissolve into immortal wine.   (II,i, p. 135)[38]

Moreover a baroque 'dissolving' of ideas and images into each other is a potentially confusing characteristic of the piece. In Act Three, scene one, for instance, Lucifer recalls how God once 'bounteously bestow'd unenvied good' on him. He then overhears Adam's description of the joy in Heaven when he and Eve first made love; Eve describes her ecstatic loss of identity; and Lucifer cries out,

> O death to hear! and a worst hell on earth!
> What mad profusion on this clod-born birth!
> Abyss of joys, as if Heaven meant to show
> What, in base matters, such a hand could do.

The hand is God's, and the 'blasphemy' obvious. But then the whole piece equates beatitude and grace with erotic intoxication:

> Seraph and cherub, careless of their charge,
> And wanton, in full ease now live at large;
> Unguarded leave the passes of the sky
> And all dissolved in hallelujah's lie.   (I,i, p. 129)

Creation is full of the ecstatic bounty of God, the supreme natural manifestation of which is sex. But can reason and will function in such a context? Can man be sovereign over himself in such an abyss of joy? Lucifer the Hobbist says not, that will responds automatically to stimulus; even Adam, unfallen and innocent, has his doubts. But his first speech is not, as has been said, 'over-positive and slickly concise'.[39]

Rather it penetrates the divine mystery of his origins with majestic ease. Neither is Eve's inability to escape intellectually from exclusive awareness of herself, nor her later fear of surrendering 'much loved sovereignty' to Adam, evidence of prelapsarian corruption. Her egoism is innocent; she naturally and properly cherishes her identity. Man's reason, virtue, and selfhood, at any rate in Eden—that is in the purely natural context of an unfallen world—are finite but sufficient in a way Hobbes could never have conceded. It is the sovereignty of God, the invincibility of his foreknown and preordained purposes, which creates the problem. Dryden's solution is his usual one: man is free, not to resist God's purposes, but in choosing to make them his own: 'Obey', Raphael tells Adam, 'and, in that choice, Thou shalt be blest' (IV,i, p. 155). In *The State of Innocence* Dryden makes this favourite idea of his the intellectual centre of a copious baroque design, in which the social, psychological, and religious condition of man is given boldly generalised, yet precise, expression.

Oedipus (1679) is mainly Lee's work. The First and Third Acts, however, are Dryden's, and though he formally defended them he was quickly dissatisfied with the additions to Sophocles' plot. The play opens well, however. Some excellent blank verse discreetly controls images of the disorder brought on Thebes by the plague, and makes for effective presentation of the problem of free will. Alcander finds comfort in the thought that

> There's a chain of causes
> Linked to effects; invincible necessity,
> That whate'er is, could not but so have been . . .
>
> (I,i, pp. 138–9)[40]

Alcander, however, is of Creon's party. Tiresias comes nearer to stating the true position when he argues that 'Whatever is, is in its causes just; Since all things are by fate', and fate is decreed by 'the vast abyss of heavenly justice' (III,i, pp. 184–5). Ignorance of the divine will is thus, as *The State of Innocence* had also asserted, an essential condition of human obedience. *Oedipus* is important, however, in bringing into prominence a new honesty in Dryden's attitude to God's responsibility for history. According to *The Grounds* the moral of the play is that 'no man is to be accounted happy before his death'.[41] This means apparently that there is no security for man even in true principles. The 'just causes' by which the divine will is executed issue in unwitting patricide and incest. Dryden is no longer prepared, in other words, to reinforce his commitment to the view that God is reasonable and just if inscrutable, and that man is free yet subject to the divine will, by offering simplistically comfortable views about Providence. On the contrary, he insists that faith in God's reasonableness and justice must honestly confront utterly unreasonable and unjust events. This has the important effect of giving 'poetic justice', and so decorum, a distinctive role in Dryden's later plays. They are observed only to be challenged; and the challenge which they most often have to meet is the overwhelming indecorum of unwitting incest, which even a studiously correct subjection of character to status cannot blandly cope with. Thus the intensification of Dryden's commitment to neoclassical norms, and his new emphasis on the importance of Judgement rather than Fancy, are associated with a new ruthlessness about the optimistic assumptions built into the conventions he was using.

Compared with Shakespeare's play, *Troilus and Cressida* is unsubtle, but it does show Dryden once again relentlessly testing his ideas. In adapting *Troilus* he was trying to create a Restoration equivalent of his original, consciously different[42] in the way that his Virgilian *Annus Mirabilis* is emphatically Drydenian. Having Cressida only pretend to love Diomede, therefore, cruelly intensifies the specific problem Dryden was interested in. It makes Troilus' impulsiveness the decisive factor in the war—it is he who persuades Hector to fight, just as Hector persuades him to surrender Cressida. The fact that his noble fury is misplaced makes for a disturbing dichotomy between public and personal good. The war providentially secures the restoration of a 'peaceful order', but at the expense of Troilus' heroic spontaneity. The final laconic dialogue on this problem is especially effective. Ulysses' speech is obviously directed against the whigs (the Exclusion crisis was at its height), but its sharp tory moral, 'Let subjects learn obedience to their kings' (V,ii, p. 390),[43] is based firmly on the recognition that Agamemnon's victory rests on brutality and policy, on the triumph of Achilles and his bullies over Hector and Troilus. This sort of truth Dryden was now willing to face, as a Christian and a monarchist; and his new honesty about principles and practice connects interestingly with his new concern to give the sober assessments of the Judgement priority over the enthusiasms of the Fancy.

Aureng-Zebe (1675), his last heroic play, indicates why Dryden now found the mode unsatisfactory. Parts of it were obviously intended, as the actor Booth suggested, to elicit 'a laugh of approbation . . . from the understanding few',[44] but the play is also both a virtuoso performance in perpetually surprising design, and the scrupulously 'correct' piece described in the Epilogue. It is a virtuoso performance in thought and diction also. Words and their meanings, as well as people, are launched into its exhausting confusion of event. Sexual words in particular are crucial to its extravagant comedy and barely concealed anxiety, precisely because sexual rhetoric combines the two most vitalising yet menacing of human capacities, eroticism and the Fancy. It is the Fancy above all, the essential impulse of the heroic mode as Dryden used to view it—which is the source of the play's most disturbing confusions. The reason for this is that the desires which it arouses may not always be matched by performance. Impotence, political and physical, thus becomes a major theme of the play. In a marvellous confrontation between the ageing Emperour and his young, dissatisfied wife, Nourmahal, the semantic black comedy of her nagging and his senility threaten to devastate their entire kingdom. 'Your fury hardens me', the poor man announces at last, and threatens her with 'a Husband's and a Monarch's pow'r' (II,i,327–30)[45] as a substitute for lost manhood. Later, however, talking to Morat, his chosen successor, he declares his preference for power of a more basic kind:

> . . . Youth, the perishing good, runs on too fast:
> And unenjoy'd will spend it self to waste;
> Few know the use of life before 'tis past.
> Had I once more thy vigour to command
> I would not let it die upon my hand. . . .

'Me-thinks all pleasure is in greatness found' (III,159–63;166), Morat, bent on Empire, replies, unintentionally confirming his father's conviction that Hobbes' *summum bonum* does not automatically associate with 'greatness' of a more tangibly pleasurable kind. Not that potency is any answer. As a 'Universal Monarch' (II,34); that is, a sort of Louis XIV of the emotions, it can be dangerous in its own way: 'wishes, Madam, are extravagant', Arimant tells Indamora (and he could equally be talking about the fancies of the heroic poet or those of inflamed youth); 'They are not bounded with things possible' (II,52–3). Fancy and sexuality combined can produce jealousy, and at least one scene in the play on this theme has justly been said to have 'more style and grace than most . . . Restoration comedy'.[46]

Dryden nevertheless thought of *Aureng-Zebe* as a tragedy, and it is certainly a deeply serious work. What is at issue, in fact, is the meaningfulness of language and the coherence of the world. The play allows the inert abstractions of neoclassicism to acquire anarchic accretions of meaning until finally both language and life are deprived of ontological security. The tensions between the safety of fixed meanings and the terror of incalculable realities become extraordinarily acute. Even the play's heroic embodiment of balanced reason and desire, Aureng-Zebe himself, is nearly engulfed in the confusion. His famous meditation. 'When I consider life' (IV,33–44), lucid as it is, is surrounded by enough semantic anarchy to give words like 'joys', 'cuts off', and 'first sprightly running' a certain tension. And later when his step-mother confesses that she loves him because he incarnates his father's youth, his reply, 'In me a horrour of my self you raise' (IV,153), could suggest horrified sexual arousal. Usurpation and incest in society, and the victory of Fancy over Reason in the mind take all coherence from reality and art. Thus after seizing power Morat thinks that he can wipe out 'Murder and Usurpation', both as facts and concepts, simply by saying so. Even people's names are insecure. Lovers 'become' their rivals: Arimant disguises himself as Aureng-Zebe, Nourmahal identifies with Indamora, Aureng-Zebe is a reincarnation of his father. This interchangeableness is closely related to the neoclassical identification of personality with role—king, father, lover, rival, mistress, mother. It is also interestingly similar to techniques of sexual fantasy developed later by de Sade. The decorous simplifications of neoclassical characterisation, in short, become a source of moral confusion in the play, making it possible, for instance, for two women, Nourmahal and Indamora, to become deadly rivals and intoxicated partners in a single act of grand theatrical eroticism.

> I love a Foe, who dares my stroke prevent, (Nourmahal declares)
> Who gives me the full Scene of my content,
> Shows me the flying Soul's convulsive strife,
> And all the anguish of departing life.   (V,312–15)

The language of *Aureng-Zebe* records the chaos which results when Fancy is thus triumphant over Judgement, but it creates such a vivid impression of intellectual and moral anarchy in doing so that the possibility of reason itself being Fancy's creature, hauntingly remains.

Clearly Dryden had to move away from a mode which accorded

mere names and titles such mastery over reality. *All for Love* (1678) enacts his withdrawal. The play's virtues are clarity, logic, and proportion. The blank verse is supple and modest, its regular iambics being discreetly varied by feminine line-endings impossible in couplets. F. R. Leavis points out that the verse lacks 'complexity, confusion . . . ambiguity';[47] but after *Aureng-Zebe* that is its strength. Apart from Antony's adjectival first soliloquy, it is the verbs which give force as well as simplicity to the verse, as in Antony's description of his extravagant emotions:

> But I have *lov'd* with such transcendent passion,
> I *soar'd*, at first, quite out of Reason's view,
> And now am *lost* above it.   (II,20–2—italics mine)[48]

The interchangeable, untrustworthy abstractions of *Aureng-Zebe* are replaced by strong, monosyllabic acts. This speech, however, also shows the continuity of thought between both plays. Antony is at the end of his 'golden Dream of Love and Friendship' (V,245) in which reason and reality have played less and less part. Act Three opens on a note of pure heroic fantasy: Cleopatra is Venus, or Love, Antony Mars, or Honour; but Antony can only fight imaginary giants and indulge in wild fantasies of inexhaustible potency in Cleopatra's arms:

> . . . perpetual Spring
> Is in thy armes; thy ripen'd fruit but falls,
> And blossoms rise to fill its empty place;
> And I grow rich by giving.   (III,25–8)

The dream is not facilely dismissed however. Antony's chosen eroticism compares well, for instance, with the 'rational' Dollabella's automatic self-control:

> But yet the loss was private that I made;
> 'Twas but my self I lost: I lost no Legions.
> I had no World to lose, no peoples love.   (III,166–201)

Dollabella is ruefully self-mocking about a 'premature ejaculation' which, as well as pointing up Antony's political guilt, registers his own psychological and political insignificance. Then there is the eunuch

Alexas, who bears his 'Reason undisturb'd' (II,87), and embodies unanswerable arguments for choosing the interior freedom of eroticism and Fancy rather than World of Caesar.

Not that Caesar's victory is at all trivial. Antony knows well enough that

> ... the World
> Shou'd have a Lord, and know whom to obey ... (V,280–1)

that for the world's sake the heroic dream, Fancy itself, must in all senses of the word die. In conceding this, however, the lovers simultaneously assert the eternal validity of love precisely at the moment of its total extinction. 'Thou best of Thieves;' Cleopatra tells the serpent before it kills her,

> ... who, with an easie key
> Dost open life, and unperceiv'd by us,
> Ev'n steal us from ourselves: discharging so
> Death's dreadful office, better than himself,
> Touching our limbs so gently into slumber,
> That Death stands by, deceiv'd by his own Image
> And thinks himself but Sleep.   (V,474–80)

The harmony and complexity of this speech beautifully involve the mind of the poet with the experience of his character. Cleopatra's words are appropriate to Dryden's thought. In softening her death, the phallic serpent does not sentimentalise the play's insights into mortality. The images of Death-as-Love and Death-as-Sleep acknowledge their own deceitfulness; desire-charged Fancy as a fact enriching man from within, and mortality imposed on him as a Fate from without, in the end ironically combine to annihilate his pitiful search for a secure personal identity and a world which unites meaning with joy.

Caesar does not appear in *All for Love*. There is also a notable neutrality in the references to him. He has no traditional role in the play, neither King nor Usurper, Lover nor Eunuch, Friend nor Rival. The World is certainly lost but there is no indication—and this is important in a convention which requires the triumph of justice—that it is well won. He moves to victory with a fatal inexorability which the neatness of the play's construction emphasises. That Providence should secure the victory of so cold a figure—and we know from elsewhere that Dryden did in fact regard Octavius Caesar as a usurper[49]—is highly significant. It suggests that in the darkening political atmosphere of the late seventies he was regaining that sense of the secular nature of politics which twenty years earlier he had so subtly detected in the career of Cromwell. In an ending which almost definitively outlines the balance of tensions in all of his subsequent work, the curtain falls on the play's only convincing representatives of human values, dead but for ever (at least in art) enthroned, while an enigmatic, traditionless, inhuman authority advances to take possession of the world.

1. *Tyrannick Love*, Preface, *The Works of John Dryden*, Ed. H. T. Swedenberg, Jr, *et al.* (1956), X, p. 109; hereafter California.

2. 'Of Heroic Plays', *Essays of John Dryden*, Ed. W. P. Ker (1900), I, p. 149; hereafter Ker.

3. See Moody E. Prior, *The Language of Tragedy* (1947), p. 155.

4. *The Works of John Dryden*, Ed. Walter Scott and George Saintsbury (1882), I, p. 59; hereafter Scott–Saintsbury.

5. Thomas Hobbes, *Leviathan*, Ed. Michael Oakeshott (1957), I, xi, p. 64.

6. See California X, p. 97.

7. Quoted in Bruce King, *Dryden's Major Plays* (1966), p. 28.

8. ibid., p. 2.

9. ibid., p. 28.

10. 'Dedication of *The Spanish Friar*', Ker I, p. 246.

11. See Bruce King, *Dryden's Major Plays*, pp. 50–4.

12. Quoted from California X.

13. *Lives*, p. 342.

14. *The Rival Ladies*, Preface, California VIII, p. 95.

15. 'An account of the ensuing Poem', Kinsley I, pp. 46–7.

16. *An Evening's Love*, Preface, California X, p. 212.

17. Ker I, p. 151.

18. *Of Dramatick Poesie*, Ed. James T. Boulton (1964), p. 108.

19. 'Of Heroic Plays', Ker I, p. 154.

20. ibid. I, p. 155.

21. ibid. I, p. 153.

22. Quoted from California IX.

23. Scott–Saintsbury IV, p. 5.

24. *Lives*, p. 342.

25. See Anne T. Barbeau, *The Intellectual Design of John Dryden's Heroic Plays* (1970), pp. 105–26.

26. Quoted from Scott–Saintsbury IV.

27. *Aureng-Zebe*, Dedication, Scott–Saintsbury V, p. 195. It should be noted that the play, and therefore the Dedication, were *published* in 1676. All Dryden's plays are *dated* according to *first performance*, 1675 in the case of *Aureng-Zebe*.

28. Ker I, p. 181.

29. ibid., p. 246.

30. See General Introduction, John Dryden, *Four Tragedies*, Ed. L. A. Beaurline and Fredson Bowers (1967), p. 18; hereafter *Four Tragedies*.

31. See Robert D. Hume, *Dryden's Criticism* (1970), pp. 108–23.

32. Ker I, p. 227.

33. *Troilus and Cressida*, Dedication, Scott–Saintsbury VI, p. 253.

34. Dedication of the *Spanish Friar*, Ker I, p. 248.

35. 'The Author's Apology for Heroic Poetry', Ker I, p. 190.

36. Scott–Saintsbury VI, p. 127.

37. 'The Author's Apology for Heroic Poetry', Ker I, p. 179.

38. Quoted from Scott–Saintsbury V.

39. King, op. cit., p. 102.

40. Quoted from Scott–Saintsbury VI.

41. Ker I, p. 213.

42. See *Four Tragedies*, p. 190.

43. Quoted from Scott–Saintsbury VI.

44. ibid. V, p. 184.

45. Quoted from *Four Tragedies*.

46. King, op. cit., p. 117.

47. '*Antony and Cleopatra* and *All for Love*', *Scrutiny* V, p. 9.

48. Quoted from *Four Tragedies*.

49. See *Discourse concerning . . . Satire*, Kinsley II, p. 651.

3

FANCY AND DELIGHT:

COMEDY AND CRITICISM 1663–1672

Dryden always claimed that he felt unhappy with comedy, though he was consistently loyal to tragi-comedy, at least until he gave up the stage altogether. His first attempts at both kinds are less confident than the early heroic plays, and give strength to Scott's suggestion that Restoration 'indelicacy . . . sate awkwardly upon his natural modesty'.[1] The awkwardness of Dryden's first play, *The Wild Gallant* (1663), however, is more social than sexual. Bibber the tailor 'who keeps company with his betters' is a pathetic figure, cruelly gulled by those betters with the false promise of 'a Waiter's place at Custom house' (IV,i,233). Mature Restoration comedy was careful not to base comic effect on class differences as considerable as this. Dryden himself was to complain that farce 'requires . . . much of conversation with the vulgar; and much of ill nature in the observation of their follies':[2] comedy should properly entertain 'those who can judge of men and manners, by the lively representation of their [own] folly or corruption'[3]—but here too *The Wild Gallant* fails. The hero, Loveby, receives money apparently from the Devil but really from his mistress. He may be playing along with the deception—Setstone's account of their meeting (II,i,220–32) suggests that the joke is on him—but if Loveby is not credulous like the other characters (Lord Nonsuch is persuaded that he and his whole household are pregnant by the Devil) his wit and vitality cease to have any relation with the play's governing idea, credulity; and if he is deceived, he becomes inexplicably foolish. Either way his wildness is without function, and both the action and the dirty jokes mere contrivance.

The Rival Ladies (1664) is even more awkward. Instead of separating

its tragic and comic elements in different plots, it promiscuously
co-mingles effects of pity and salacious laughter in a single action.
The result is tonal confusion and Fletcherian pastiche. Its indulgent
display of male fantasy and female sentimentality has a certain brutal
appeal, but a high-flown mixture of rhyme and blank verse is hardly
compatible with a hero whose two boy-servants (he calls them 'pretty
youth' and 'sweet heart') are really girls who readily unbutton to fight
for his attention, although they know he loves another. The First
Act involves an ambush by robbers, the Fifth an escape from pirates.
It is difficult, therefore, to apply the Preface's account of the perfect
comic plot to the play itself. (Perhaps significantly Dryden links its
difficulties with Orrery's gout.) Both early comedies, in fact, betray a
taste for irresponsible plotting, which, joined to the extravagance of
his characters' fantasies, suggests that Dryden was more interested in
weaving elaborate designs of ideas, images, and events than inventing
a plot. It is Design, rather than action properly so called, which has
to be unravelled in the final scene.

His next comedy, however, *Secret Love* (1667), is the first altogether
satisfactory play he wrote, though he himself thought it 'much inferior
to my *Indian Emperour*'.[4] It has a lucidity and order which would be
inexplicable but for *Of Dramatick Poesie* (1668), his first major critical
essay, and effectively 'the preface to *Secret Love*'.[5] It is essential to
consider the essay before examining the play. It purports to be a
debate between four gentlemen, Crites, Eugenius, Lisideius, and
Neander, about the literary merits of the Ancients and the Moderns,
and the French and the English, though very few classical or French
works are actually discussed. Dryden simply uses the debate-form to
soften the formality of what is in effect a treatise on comedy. (The
last rather unsatisfactory section on rhyme in serious plays is admitted
to be an addition.) He begins, therefore, with a broad definition of
the nature and scope of literature. This is disguised as the definition of
a play, and the slightly cantankerous Crites objects because it fails
to distinguish the drama from other literary forms. However, Dryden
uses Crites' own defence of the Ancients to remedy precisely this
defect, since his account of the unities introduces the distinctively
'dramatic' factors in dramatic poesy. Crites is notably conservative on
the question of underplots. It is then Eugenius' function in his defence
of the Moderns to liberalise Crites' first principles. He argues, for
instance, that any structural model, whether in three, four or five
acts, will serve as a standard, and qualifies his approval of the classical

ideals of unity and continuity (*liaison des scènes*) by urging a tolerant attitude to correctness. Lisideius, as spokesman for the French, concentrates on putting a conservative position on plotting, so that Neander in reply can outline the four important modifications to the classical theory of comedy which the whole essay was written to justify. Liveliness is to have pride of place over correctness; delight, not, instruction is to be regarded as the chief end of comedy; tragi-comedy is to be an acceptable *genre*; and comic effect is to be based on 'the ridiculous extravagance of conversation, wherein one man differs from all others';[6] that is, on 'humour' as against the two forms of Greek comedy based on either grotesque ridicule or 'the general Characters of Men and Manners'.[7] The most important argument to emerge from the discussion is the defence of double-plotted plays: 'the under-plot', Neander argues, '. . . is only different, not contrary to the great design.'[8] This concept of a great design to which the action is subordinate, and which therefore admits a second, is central to the whole of Dryden's subsequent development as a dramatist, just as it was implicit in his first two comedies.[9]

Certainly the decision to separate the tragic and comic plots in *Secret Love*, and yet to fuse them in a larger dramatic patterning in which liveliness and duty (i.e. Fancy and decorum) are in graceful tension, accounts for the play's success. It is also an early instance of Dryden deliberately flouting the aesthetic and moral order implied by the rules. The final preservation of decorum in the Fifth Act completes a design created out of the earlier tensions. As we have seen, Dryden was a firm believer in the Fancy at this stage of his career. When he places 'Dramatick laws' under the control of the Judgement, therefore, as he does in the Preface (1668),[10] on the grounds that they give a play 'symmetry of parts' only, the value he attaches respectively to 'air and spirit' (products of the Fancy) and to correctness becomes apparent. The fact that this 'air and spirit' twice puts decorum at risk does not, however, mean that Dryden has jettisoned good order in the interest merely of frivolous delight. He acknowledges two breaches of convention: Philocles joins in the uprising against the Queen when he learns of her secret love for a commoner (in fact himself), and Celadon and Florimel treat 'too lightly of their marriage'[11] in the Queen's presence. Both incidents, however, make an important contribution to the play's *thematic* preoccupation with indecorum. Indecorum points up important tensions between freedom and law in life and in art. Love idealised and love concupiscent in turn disturb

aesthetic and social good order in *Secret Love*. Both fanciful idealisation
and wild gallantry, therefore, operate within a larger framework of
meaning. Indelicacy is part of the design.

The opening dialogue between Celadon and the masked Florimell,
for instance, is really about freedom, not desire. The audience can at
once enter into the humours of the characters and yet observe with
detachment the scene's artifice. They must know who Florimell is:
her disguise becomes, therefore, defiantly artificial, exactly like the
dialogue. The air and spirit of the almost indecorous lovers touches
the form and blends with it. The change from blank verse to couplets
is similarly integrated with the play's design. It coincides with the
appearance of Candiope, also secretly in love with Philocles, in Act
Three. At the same time the pattern of comic plot preceding tragic
plot in each Act is reversed. The theatrical obviousness of these
devices is appropriate in keeping the audience conscious of design as
something distinct from plot, and so of the subtle issues involved in
the play's correctness. Correctness, and the price it exacts, are the
source of all the tensions. The Queen's potentially comic and therefore
indecorous jealousy of Candiope, for instance, delicately points up the
human loss implicit in her dignity. Similarly, when Philocles discovers
her feelings, and as a result nearly falls out of love with Candiope, he
learns that the price of true love is apparently political obscurity, and
his regret at the loss of a crown ('Lost, lost, forever lost, and now 'tis
gone 'Tis beautiful'—V,i,432–3) exactly matches Celadon's feelings
when he and Florimell finally agree on the terms for marriage:

Flor. La ye now, is not such a marriage as good as wenching, *Celadon*?
Cel. That is very good, but not so good, *Florimell*.   (V,ii,560–2)

Dreams have to be modified, happiness compromised, but the
perfection with which the play resolves its own tensions of Design
sustains a dreamlike grace.

Secret Love is a 'humour' play, though it does not read like one.
Dryden's definition of humour, however, does not exclude an excessive
obsession with extra-marital pleasures in a young man of Celadon's
class.[12] But because he is a gentleman in manner as well as status, his
behaviour is never bizarre enough to differentiate him 'from all
others' as the definition in *Of Dramatick Poesie* would seem to require.
Dryden's pleasure in urbane manners would thus seem to be in
conflict with his theoretical preference for humour comedy. There were,

however, no such difficulties in his next play, *Sir Martin Mar-all*
(1667), which he wrote with the Duke of Newcastle. His collaboration
with Newcastle on this play, and with Davenant on *The Tempest*
(1667), proved important, helping to explain his notable attempt in the
Preface to *An Evening's Love* (1668) to break loose from Jonson's
influence and his own initial commitment to humour comedy. It also
throws light on the controversy with Shadwell on Jonson, and the
whole of Dryden's later development as a writer of comedy and
tragi-comedy.

Sir Martin Mar-all was written in haste (the timing of the two plots
is allegedly inconsistent), and is strongly marked by Newcastle's
coarse feeling for Jonsonian comedy. Dryden almost certainly
disapproved of the play, and the fact that Newcastle had taken his
plot from Quinault and Molière probably strengthened his dislike of
French comedy. We may assume that Newcastle was also responsible
for the decision to make Sir Martin a ridiculous fool, instead of an
impetuous boy as in his French originals, and so for the inadequate
relationship between Sir Martin and his clever servant Warner. The
basic joke of the piece is that Sir Martin invariably ruins Warner's
arrangements for furthering his affair with the heroine, Millisent. It is
a poor joke because Warner never tells his master what he intends to
do. Thus Sir Martin is treated as a fool when he stops Millisent's
wedding without consulting Warner; the fact, however, that Warner
had arranged for Sir Martin to be the groom without consulting him,
is surely a point against the man, not the master. Sir Martin's obvious
silliness makes Warner's failure to take account of it a folly in itself.
Dryden seems to have intervened decisively on Newcastle's design in
the Fifth Act to correct this basic flaw in the play. The point that it is
'fair Play . . . , to tell a man before hand what he must do' (V,i,143–4),[13]
is explicitly made for the first time, and in the subsequent action the
characteristically bizarre nature of the events is more striking than any
idiosyncratic oddity in the people. There is a particularly satisfying bit
of theatrical cheek when a gentlemanly pedigree is produced for
Warner (now married to Millisent) in the play's closing seconds.
Certainly the fertile 'irresponsibility' of the Fifth Act contrasts notably
with the clumsiness of the other four, and points away from, not
towards, the so-called 'Jonsonian' comedy of Newcastle and Shadwell.

Dryden preferred more stylised comedy. Hence the attraction of
revising *The Tempest*. Admittedly, beside Shakespeare's play, Dryden's
seems repellent. Its virtues become more apparent, however, when it is

placed beside *Sir Martin Mar-all*. Dryden is more at home in a fantastic world, detached from reality as in a dream or masquerade, than in
Sir Martin's lifeless London. He relishes spectacular theatrical effects
and fanciful writing. But what distinguishes *The Tempest* not only
from *Sir Martin Mar-all* but also from *Secret Love*, is its concern
with ideas, its witty treatment of 'heroic' themes, free will, appetite,
political authority, and the prerogative of mercy. It is characteristically
in the Fourth and Fifth Acts, at 'the heighth, and full growth of the
Play . . . which embroils the actors in new difficulties';[14] at the point
that is when Dryden has to depart decisively from Shakespeare in
order to involve his additional characters, Dorinda and Hippolito, in
the action, that ideas become important, and the play Dryden's own.
Since the function of the traditional Fourth Act is to destroy the
expectations of characters and audience built up earlier in the play, it is
especially suited to Dryden's obsessive interest in man's freedom in a
universe under the control of an absolute and omnipotent God: 'on
what strange grounds we build our hopes and fears', Prospero says
at the end of the Third Act; 'man's life is all a mist, and in the dark,
our fortunes meet us'.

> If Fate be not, then what can we foresee
> Or how can we avoid it, if it be?   (III,ii,154–8)[15]

All the important questions about human relationships, political and
sexual, centre on this problem of reason, foreknowledge, and freedom.
As early as Act Four, scene one, Ferdinand pronounces a theoretical
solution to the problem: 'do but think we chuse it', he says of the
prison Prospero has put him in, 'and 'tis what we would chuse'; but
this is easily said, since at this point 'love and silence' wait upon his
wishes (IV,i,37–9). His civilised passivity is disturbed, however, when
the 'natural' man, Hippolito, who until the play began had never seen a
woman, naively announces that he wants Miranda too: 'she was Mine
first', Ferdinand tells him: 'you have no right to her'. Hippolito,
however, replies:

> I have not yet consider'd what is right, but, Sir,
> I know my inclinations are to love all Women:
> And I have been taught that to dissemble what I
> Think is base. In honour then of truth, I must
> Declare that I do love, and I will see your Woman . . .
>
>   (IV,i,286–92)

The difference between them is parodied in the grotesque political debate between 'Duke' Trinculo and 'Duke' Stephano, whose ludicrous civil war anticipates the duel between the two young men in which the likeable Hippolito is killed. Prospero's designs are in ruins. Impotent and tyrannical, he disturbingly asserts his perfectly legitimate 'divine' right 'To execute Heav'n's Laws' and sentences Ferdinand to death. It is paradoxically a sign of Dryden's determination, even at this early stage, to eschew easy solutions to his problems, that he saves the situation (in the interests of Delight) by a deliberately arbitrary restoration of Hippolito to life. He thus carefully forbids an extrapolation of his happy ending to the human situation in general. The original play's most famous lines—Miranda's 'brave new world' speech—are here divided between Dorinda and Hippolito; and the irony is far more bitter, if less full and subtle, than it is in the Shakespeare.

An Evening's Love provides further evidence of Dryden's uneasiness with farce and with the humour he had defended in *Of Dramatick Poesie*. He came to regard the play as 'an ill Comedy',[16] and as the undoubtedly unsatisfactory main plot is closely linked to Thomas Corneille's *Le Feint Astrologue*, it helps further to account for his dislike of the French comic tradition. Admittedly Molière influences the sub-plot, but the adaptation is freer. The difference between the two parts, indeed, reflects that between *Sir Martin Mar-all* and *The Tempest*. The spirit of the former is evident in the encounter in Act Three between Bellamy, the mock astrologer, and Aurelia, the girl he is wooing. Her affectation of *precieuse* terms is feeble and her credulity dull, while her father is extravagant and stupid. But the play is always technically professional. The *liaison des scènes*, especially, has fluency and shape. By the end of the First Act, for instance, at least five possible pairings have been promised in a deft descent down the social scale. The dreamlike, urbane licence of the piece (two impoverished Englishmen are loose in a Spanish city during a carnival) allows for the manners of gentlemen to mingle freely with the fancies of a poet. Lent, however, begins next day, and the play's impiety (the women are wooed in church and bedded in the last Act, their father consenting, without benefit of clergy) is part of that elaborate consciousness of seriousness which is always implicit in the wilful irresponsibility of a masquerade.

Allusions to falconry, money, potency, and wit, all acting as metaphors for each other, point up the tensions between fantasy and reality. Even the Prologue fuses wit and potency, Dryden's resourceful elaborations of an obscene analogy becoming an outrageously sustained piece of exhibitionism. But wit can also mean plain lying—as Dryden repeatedly emphasises in all his comedies: 'Range, quest, and spring a lie immediately', Bellamy tells his servant Maskall (II,i,267). Wildblood, however, treats Maskall's talent as so much small change, and sees himself as the bird of prey: 'I love to stoop to my prey,' he says 'and to have it in my power to Sowse at when I please' (IV,i,119–20). Women, in his view, are sporting birds too, since they 'work up one another by ... high flying, as the *Heron* and *Jerfalcon*' (IV,i,148–9). The great issue between him and Jacinta, however, is more down to earth, and concerns impotence and poverty masquerading as potency and wealth. Wildblood is always promising Jacinta money, and always losing it to other women, who are all in fact Jacinta in disguise. Her persistence in bleeding him of folly, however, almost makes him lose his self-respect. His dissipation of resources and the lies he tells himself and others are both light-hearted and dangerous. In a beautifully human exchange at the end of the Fourth Act, they almost apologise to each other. The effect is to expose and with great delicacy to place urgency of desire, fear of failure and the other complicated motives which lead men and women to put on masks before making love.[17]

An Evening's Love, however, is a rougher play than this suggests. The comedy is frequently farcical and humorous in ways Dryden was soon to despise, at least for a time: but this does not make it less authentically his. A streak of literary coarseness in fact is vital to his comic art. It is evident in the frankness with which he calls the wit of his wild gallants lying, in the bell-ringing episode that Scott disliked,[18] and in the incidents which echo it, Beatrix and Jacinta repeating the words 'Money, money' to the penniless Wildblood, and Alonzo wilfully refusing to hear the truth ('I'll stop my ears, I'll stop my ears!') in the final scene. It is evident above all when Jacinta calls Alonzo 'that malicious old father of mine' and Wildblood threatens to 'scrape his weeson, that the bristles may not hinder me when I come to cut it' (V,i,399–410). This violence is integral to the characteristically ludicrous last Act; and though finally the tensions between crudity and grace are resolved in the latter's favour, when Alonzo relents and Jacinta and Wildblood sing a duet that 'epitomises their charming self-consciousness in a parody of the pastoral singing bout',[19] the possibility of serious grossness remains, to unsettle the play's conclusion.

These tensions in *An Evening's Love*, following on *Sir Martin Mar-all* and *The Tempest*, apparently made it obvious to Dryden that his theory of comedy had broken down. In his Preface (1671) to *An Evening's Love*, he returned to the subject, admitting in the first paragraph that to do so he was interrupting the critical programme he had set himself. He claims also to have little taste for comedy, and not to 'value a reputation gain'd from' it,[20] but this is mere tactics. He may wish to appear detached and disinterested, but in fact his commitment to comedy is strong. His whole case is that it is of the essence of comedy that it should be handled with both care and ease. Hence the attack on farce and the cruder forms of humour comedy, both of which lack intellectual precision and grace of manner. As a dramatist and critic, he obviously felt the need to adopt such a manner himself in talking about comedy. Thus Fancy is still for him the supreme poetic faculty, but farce is condemned because it 'works . . . on the fancy only'.[21] Dryden is careful, in fact, not to seem over-enthusiastic about the things he values most, especially as he is breaking with orthodox opinion on the question of Jonson. As late as 1668, in 'A Defence of *An Essay of Dramatick Poesie*', he had represented Jonson as the norm of English classicism. Now he presents him, not as the writer of model comedies, but as a special case, 'the only man of all Ages and Nations'[22] to write good humour comedy. Jonson is master of all that Judgement can do. 'To make men appear pleasantly ridiculous in the Stage was . . . his talent: and in this he needed not the acumen of wit, but that of judgement.'[23] He is therefore not a standard for the present age. Farce, or the comedy of Fancy alone, is thus casually juxtaposed with that of Judgement alone. Similar contrasts between humorous characters and witty characters, vulgar conversation and gentlemanly repartee, entertainment and instruction, are introduced later in the same easy way. Each contrasting pair modifies and amplifies the others. They are not lined up like sheep and goats on the right and left hand. Dryden's neoclassicism is not a severe avenue, but a park landscaped with careful asymmetry, through which he moves with a proprietary, almost arrogant, air. This too, however, is calculated. His ideal comedy is about, and for, 'those who can judge of men and manners' with all the '*Urbana, venusta, salsa, faceta* and the rest which *Quintillian* reckons up as the ornaments of wit.'[24] He has in particular to demonstrate that wit has all the variety and copiousness of humour, and that 'repartie' above all 'as it is the very soul of conversation, so it is the greatest grace of Comedy'. He is concerned, in short, to show that the chief poetic faculty, the Fancy, can be fully stretched in the comedy of manners, but it is essential to his sense of how this can be done in a

civilised society that his commitment to comedy should include the
virtue of detachment. Hence the casual way with which a defence
against Shadwell's charges of plagiarism—Dryden quotes the King in
the process—leads to the climax of the essay, a magnificently eloquent
celebration of 'the work of a Poet, and . . . the Graces of a Poem'.[25]

Just as *Of Dramatick Poesie* was above all a defence of *Secret Love*,
so the Preface to *An Evening's Love*, the most brilliant of Dryden's
early critical essays, is in effect an introduction to the finest of his
early plays, *Marriage à-la-Mode* (1672). And if the essay contains his
most convincing defence of Fancy as the supreme poetic faculty, the
play offers us his most gratifying exhibition of what Fancy can
achieve. It is supremely a vehicle for delight, not instruction, for life,
spirit and grace. This does not mean, however, that is is merely a
brilliant confection of baroque design and elegant repartee. It touches
on dangerous issues, if only for the excitement of the encounter.
Polydamas is an unlawful king; even the heroes of the comic action
feel the unease this creates; and when they fight for the usurper, an
audience of royalist rakes must have felt the same tension. Dryden's
favourite themes, sovereignty, free will, Providence, and tyranny
reappear, and as usual the very abstractness to which neoclassicism
reduces 'love', 'authority', 'fate', and 'God' is exploited to ironic
effect. In an exchange between Polydamas and his supposed long-lost
son Leonidas, for instance, about whether the young man should marry
his pastoral sweetheart Palmyra or a princess of the King's choosing,
the Prince quite properly defends his personal liberty against parental
and regal tyranny; but his pat neoclassical terminology catches him in
contradictions which are cleverly representative, not only of his own
personal position, but of mankind's relations with God. First he
attributes love to Fate:

> . . . Sir, ask the Stars,
> Which have impos'd love on us, like a Fate,
> Why minds are bent to one, and fly another.   (II,i,334–46)[26]

yet ten lines later he denies even God's power to force his will:

> I owe you all things Sir, but something too
> I owe my self . . .
> You are a King, Sir; but you are no God;
> Or if you were, you could not force my will.   (II,i,343–4;347–8)

His naivety, courage and youth make the irony gentle, even amusing, but the issues remain serious.

A key tension in the play is that between the purity embodied in Leonidas' pastoral love for Palmyra, together with the literary innocence of the pastoral convention, and the sophistications of Restoration life and letters. Thus the play's two songs are equally bawdy, yet deliberately associated, not with the comic sub-plot, but with the idealistic characters of the main plot: the first is a 'song the Princess *Amalthea* bad' Doralice learn (I,i,2–3), while the second, the notorious song about declining potency, 'Whilst *Alexis* lay prest', is actually performed in the serious part of the play. More important is the contrast between Leonidas and Palmyra's pastoral childhood and the corruptions of the court, evident both in its high politics and its erotic intrigues. The comic action is among the most graceful and indelicate of Dryden's performances, and the contrast between its visible grace and almost invisible obscenity is intricately interwoven with the other contrasts in the piece. Thus in Act Three Doralice introduces the 'pastoral' theme by mentioning a friend of hers who heard one of Dryden's own songs ('After the pangs of a desperate Lover' from *An Evening's Love*) being sung by three tailors in the country long after it had ceased to be fashionable at court. This adroit alienation device invites a sophisticated response from the audience which Melantha then reinforces with a witty, mocking account of her own experiences of rural manners. But the whole discussion is only a preface to Palmyra's lovely and supremely simple account of her idyll with Leonidas. This leads, however, into an intensely idealistic but also violently (if unconsciously) erotic fantasy about their 'dying' together. There is no equivalent to this in Dryden's sources.[27]

In the next scene, however, there is a real sexual encounter between Palamede and Doralice, and instead of the potentially exalted 'death' pun, they play together, with just as much enthusiasm and far greater knowledge, on plainer words like 'cock' and 'lay'. They are interrupted by Melantha (Palamede's betrothed) and Rhodophil (Doralice's husband) and a mock reconciliation follows in which everyone understands, yet no one mentions, the others' infidelities. Lurking behind this collective self-deception is another, voiced by Palamede at the end of the scene, about the limitations which impotence imposes on the libertine ethic. If the comic characters have a Hobbist view of imagination and desire, as has been suggested,[28] Dryden is obviously mocking Hobbes' melodramatic psychology by reminding us again how mental anarchy must submit willy-nilly to physiological law.

The Fourth and Fifth Acts, using Dryden's favourite device of a masquerade, develop this theme of wilful self-deception through a series of palpably feigned sicknesses and disguises comically or deliberately not seen through. Increasing references to impotence blend with Polydamas' growing sense of political powerlessness:

> So blind we are, our wishes are so vain,
> That what we most desire, proves most our pain.   (IV,ii,82-3)

This theme is decisively concluded in Doralice's sad comment at the end of her affair with Palamede:

Many a man and woman, that have lov'd as desperately as we, and yet when they came to possession, have sigh'd, and cri'd to themselves, Is this all? . . . 'Tis better as 'tis; we have drawn off as much of our Love as would run clear; after possessing, the rest is but jealousies, and disquiets, and quarrelling, and piecing.   (V,i,281-4;289-92)

The play's fluent development reveals Dryden's broad sense of the vanity of all longing, whether it is idealistic, power-hungry, or merely fashionable.

This real seriousness, however, is not incompatible with his belief that 'the first end of Comedie is delight, and instruction only the second'.[28] The play's palpable fictions in pastoral–heroic verse and fanciful prose create an atmosphere of literary irresponsibility which finally triumphs. Of course the play exposes weaknesses which it is the business of heroic and pastoral conventions normally to conceal; but it does so with a brilliance of design which is itself invulnerable. An art which presents Restoration England in a fantasy Sicily is the art of masquerade. The more cunningly it exposes human weaknesses, the more it celebrates its own imperviousness to them.

But Dryden was soon to grow impatient with the imperviousness of art to the dangers of life, and of audiences to the necessity for instruction. *The Assignation* (1672) was acted within five months of his completing *Marriage à-la-Mode*, and is radically different in spirit from its predecessor, almost as if Dryden were hungry again for the coarseness in *An Evening's Love*. But there is more than roughness in the farce of *The Assignation*. It was, significantly, a failure; possibly, Dryden felt, because of a fault 'in the play itself, or in the lameness of the action, or in the number of its enemies'.[30] But he went on to defend himself against the charge of atheism, and it may be that the play proved offensive to the Restoration's vulnerable dependence on platitudinous orthodoxies. Not that it is explicitly unorthodox; but it does concede to anarchy, indecorum, and atheism, the right to be considered. It is a theatrical equivalent of the sceptical, open-minded conversations of the poets so enviably described in the Dedication (1673). Neither the play nor those conversations, of course, committed anything so crass as 'blasphemy and atheism'. (Such simplistic unorthodoxy was the crude fantasy of dogmatic defenders of the orthodox who, like Shadwell, failed to see that to modify one's thinking on neoclassical doctrines or Christian dogmas was not to undervalue Jonson or to disbelieve in God.) But it is an uncomfortable play, and if, as has been suggested, it attempts 'to retrace the plot and moral structure'[31] of *Marriage à-la-Mode*, it does so for very different ends.

Though reservations have been expressed about its organisation, it is very competently plotted, the two actions interweaving cleverly in the Fourth Act. The real problem is one of decorum. It is essential to recognise that the repeated breaches of decorum are calculated, the discomfort they create part of the design. Thus there have been objections to the Duke's meeting with Violetta and Laura, when the latter is dressed in clothes belonging to the woman the Duke is in love with, Lucretia.[32] The Duke responds to Laura's protestations that she is not Lucretia with a blank refusal even to look her in the face. Benito, a servant, and dogged believer in his own wit, then arrives and the following exchange takes place between him and the Duke:

Duke. I say they are not they.
Ben. I am sure they are Laura and Violetta.   (V,ii, p. 458)[33]

This is obviously devoid of point; that is the point. The Duke's behaviour makes no contribution to the plot; Benito's rudeness to a reigning sovereign is a gross indecorum. Everything in the incident is deliberately disordered. The principles of sound plotting which Dryden himself had outlined in the Preface to *The Rival Ladies*, the comfortable notion that human actions are adequately motivated, and the whole structure of social and political propriety which comedy was specifically supposed not to challenge are all challenged. If the bare facts of the plot are considered—a duke fighting with his son for a nun's love, another man sexually initiating a boy, an abbess arranging her novice's elopement, gentlemen dressing up as servants, servants aping gentlemen—the fact that the play is actually about indecorum becomes evident.

There is certainly less compartmentalising of the heroic and comic worlds. Frederick, the Duke's son, hovers uneasily between them, first a rake who declares for 'the divine bottle, and the bounteous glass' (II,i, p. 391), but later an earnest lover who cannot be disrespectful to his father even though his mistress demands it:

Luc. But for such ancient fops, as, with reverence, your father is, what reason can they have to be in love?
Fred. Nay, your old fop's unpardonable, that's certain. But—
Luc. But what? Come, laugh at him.
Fred. But I consider he is my father, I can't laugh at him.   (IV,iv, p. 442)

Frederick stands by the sacred name of Father and the moral order it implies; Lucretia merely thinks of the Duke as a kind of incestuous geriatric. Their quarrel is serious, the restraints on their love being far more disturbing psychologically and morally than the pride and self-preservation usual in comic lovers. In spite of this seriousness, however, the play's dignity is repeatedly undermined. Benito contributes to this; so do the spirited Laura and Violetta; but so do more dignified characters, as in the encounter between the Duke and Lucretia in Act Five, which is written in strong, largely phrased blank verse, but reveals the power of Lucretia's wit, and the fumbling inadequacy of the Duke with an insolence that is wholly destructive of tragic 'concernment'.

The ambivalence created by continual indecorum, and by the blurring of distinctions between the heroic and the comic is especially in evidence in the two characters responsible for the happy ending, the abbess Sophronia and Frederick himself. From the stock figure of the abbess emerges a clever, benign woman. She leaves an impression of shrewd, this-wordly 'providence' without ever quite embodying a frankly areligious position. Frederick's case reverses this. A careless worldling to begin with, he finally rebels against his father. If the Duke's crime is unnatural lust, Frederick's is treason. Even the natural right which his youth has to Lucretia's love is sullied when the rebellious army turns to him because he is young; and he sinks low enough to bribe his father's guards. At the crucial point, however, he kneels to his father and submits. The Duke then loses all princely dignity, and claims Lucretia for himself. Frederick replies,

> Ah no; I never can resign her to you:
> But, sir, I can my life; which, on my knees,
> I tender, as the atoning sacrifice:
> Or if your hand (because you are a father)
> Be loth to take away that life you gave,
> I will redeem your crime, by making it
> My own.   (V,iv, p. 469)

The Duke promptly forgives him and surrenders Lucretia. Frederick's references to 'atoning sacrifice' and redemption are obviously sacrilegious. They make the Duke a symbol of God the Father and they suggest that the Son's death is the Father's sin. But counter-balancing this is the corollary that in freely offering up his life Frederick gives the lie to the deterministic hedonism implicit in seventeenth-century atheism. The rebel Son creates, therefore, a valid and heroic image of the atonement, while his Father in the same image points to something deeply disturbing in any image of authority, whether divine or human.

   The Assignation registers a radical shift in Dryden's relations with the conventions of Restoration drama. He had never adopted a sub-servient attitude to decorum and poetic justice, but now, instead of flirting with indecorum simply for the delight of restoring order with flamboyant expertise, he violates the rules in a systematic and provocative way to stimulate his audience into thought as well as pleasure. How conscious his intentions were at this stage it is impossible to know. What is obvious is that *The Assignation* is closer in spirit to his later plays than to its predecessors. The rivalry and to some extent the personalities of Frederick and the Duke anticipate those Aureng-Zebe and his father. Dryden's developing preoccupation with unnatural passion in conjunction with major violations of decorum, and above all his growing readiness to face the paradoxes of religions belief with total intellectual honesty, even in the context of comedy, also connect *The Assignation* with the later plays. These developments were entirely of a piece with his growing sense that 'Comedy is both excellently instructive, and extremely pleasant',[34] a major shift of emphasis from his earlier defence of 'divertisment and delight'. It explains why he never again attempted a play like *Marriage à-la-Mode*.

1. Scott–Saintsbury I, p. 375.
2. *An Evening's Love*, Preface, California X, p. 202.
3. ibid., p. 203.
4. *Secret Love*, Preface, California IX, p. 116.
5. Frank Harper Moore, *The Nobler Pleasure, Dryden's Comedy in Theory and Practice* (1933), p. 41.
6. *Of Dramatick Poesie*, p. 92.
7. ibid., p. 93.
8. ibid., p. 78.
9. See Anne T. Barbeau, *The Intellectual Design of John Dryden's Heroic Plays* (1970), pp. 150–5.
10. California IX, p. 115.
11. ibid., p. 117.
12. See Moore, op. cit., p. 35.
13. Quoted from California IX.
14. *Of Dramatick Poesie*, p. 52.
15. Quoted from California X.
16. *An Evening's Love*, Dedication, California X, p. 200.
17. See *An Evening's Love*, Introduction, *John Dryden, Four Comedies*, Ed. L. A. Beaurline and Fredson Bowers (1967), p. 180; hereafter *Four Comedies*.
18. Scott–Saintsbury III, p. 237.
19. *Four Comedies*, p. 181.
20. California X, p. 202.
21. ibid., p. 203.
22. ibid., p. 204.
23. ibid., p. 205.
24. ibid., p. 206.
25. ibid., p. 212.
26. Quoted from *Four Comedies*.
27. See *Four Comedies*, p. 278.
28. See Bruce King, *Dryden's Major Plays*, pp. 82–94.
29. *An Evening's Love*, Preface, California X p. 209.
30. *The Assignation*, Dedication, Scott–Saintsbury IV, p. 370.
31. Bruce King, *Dryden's Major Plays* (1966), p. 207.
32. In Moore, op. cit., p. 123.
33. Quoted from Scott–Saintsbury IV.
34. 'The Author's Apology for Heroic Poetry', Ker I, pp. 181–2.

4

JUDGEMENT AND INSTRUCTION:
POEMS, COMEDY AND SATIRE 1673–1679

Of the early poems only the *Heroique Stanza's* showed an open-minded, realistic sense of history, and only in *Annus Mirabilis* was Dryden's curiously arrogant yet humble poetic personality the chief unifying factor in the poem. It was difficult to develop either tendency in the theatre. Restoration drama was too conventional to be either historically particular, or directly expressive of the dramatist's own personality. If a personal vision of any kind is to be found in Dryden's plays, the enclosed artificiality of neoclassicism must serve as its base, and even an ironic approach to such an elaborately stylised convention could not prevent the author from remaining in the shadows.

The problem was even more acute in Dryden's lyric verse. The majority are love lyrics. They are neither realistic psychologically, nor stylistically or tonally individual. Not surprisingly, therefore, there have been complaints about 'their frigid and factitious metrical sprightliness and their convention ridden *courtoiserie*'.[1] To accept this description as true is not to concede it as a fault. Some of the songs, at least in the context of the plays, have a serious function, precisely by being sprightly and trivial.

There are three groups of lyrics: a few choruses, quasi-libretti for operatic ritual scenes, and love songs, written for specific plays yet often separately printed and frequently independent of their dramatic context. In the first group there are only two songs written before 1680; 'Gainst Keepers we petition' from *Limberham* (1679), and a remarkable sea-song 'Who ever saw a noble fight' from *Amboyna*, which startlingly combines the mindless heartiness of a shanty with the mindless brutality of a battle. The second group includes all the songs in *The Indian Queen*, most in *The Indian Emperour*, the temptation scene in *Tyrannick Love*, the rituals in *Oedipus*, and the procession in *The Spanish Friar*. The best parts of the *Tyrannick Love* sequence are virtually love lyrics; otherwise only the savage 'Hear, ye sullen Pow'rs below' from *Oedipus* has much interest.

The love songs are thus the largest group and are noticeably more interesting after the early plays. 'Ah fading joy', 'I feed a flame', and the two feeble lyrics in *Sir Martin Mar-all* merely amplify and decorate their dramatic context. Like the 'Epithalamion' in *Amboyna*— a pretty but very minor erotic poem—they lack the insolent independence of the twelve songs from *An Evening's Love, The Conquest of Granada, Marriage à-la-Mode*, and *The Assignation*. In every respect these poems are what Dryden's critics object to. They are virtually interchangeable, the sex is coy, pastoral, and obscene, the girls blank and young, the youths idyllically named, passionately forward but only moderately intelligent. The imagery, puns, attitudes and metres work within very narrow limits. After 1672, even Dryden seems to have become less enthusiastic about the form, there being only four poems of this type in *Limberham, Troilus and Cressida, The Spanish Friar* and *The Duke of Guise*. Like masks, their wilfully narrow range and calculated emptiness suggest precisely that imperviousness to life which he was later to reject. But a mask, having in itself form but no substance, can protect the wearer's individuality as well as obscuring it; it can conceal concern rather than discard it; and even without a living face behind it, precisely as an emblem of frozen life, it can have a particularly disturbing theatrical effect. As a result, in the context of Dryden's better plays, in the movement of the scene and the liveliness and intellectual force of the dialogue, the songs function almost unpredictably. The meretricious tinkle may resonate —all the more strikingly, indeed, for being so obviously meretricious. Thus 'Beneath a Myrtle shade' may adroitly remind an audience of 'the well-known early pages of Hobbes' *Leviathan*',[2] or it may just as easily come across as a degenerate, convention-ridden version of Donne's 'The Dreame'. That very impression of cheapness, however, could have—in an alert production and cleverly sung—a distinctive if momentary relevance by disrupting the many intimations of solemnity that there are in *The Conquest of Granada*. Dryden's calculations, in effect, may well include the weaknesses as well as the strengths of convention-ridden *courtoiserie*. The difficulty is that this can only be brought out in the style of the performance. The intelligence and expertise with which the actors move in their masks is thus all-important but outside Dryden's control.

This is less the case with the prologues and epilogues. It is true that the tonal personality behind them is never in any full or confessional way Dryden's own. In every case the prologues and epilogues which he wrote for his own or other authors' plays were parts for actors in his Company, but parts built on assumptions about the human personality which consciously avoided the neoclassical stereotyping of character that one finds in the plays themselves. It would be excessive to say that the psychology of the prologues is realistic, but their manners are, and it is by no means excessive to claim that Dryden's maturing as a poet between 1660 and 1680 is most enjoyably in evidence in this minor but rewarding form. Technically the changes are not striking. Dryden mastered the couplet in the early sixties, and experimented little except with the triplet and the careful introduction of rough rhythms and harsh diction. It is true that after about 1675 the verse is more powerfully organised in simpler masses, but this is probably more an effect of his major reassessment of the nature and function of poetry at this time, than with more narrowly based technical experiment. What the prologues and epilogues do amply illustrate is the nature of his engagement with poetry up to the mid-seventies, and the shift to a new degree of seriousness which then occurred.

The early prologues and epilogues show Dryden's uncertainty about their function and relevance. (He was similarly uncertain about the kind of play he ought to be writing.) The form varies, frequently involving more than one actor, and the tone is jocular and defensive, with none of the arrogant intimacy with the audience which he was to achieve later. In the 'Second Prologue' to *Secret Love*, however, a roughness of diction, disdain of manner, and grossness of analogy begin to offset the formal yet confiding note natural in publicly recited heroic couplets. There is a readiness, too, from this point on, to mention serious critical issues and then by sleight of phrase to introduce a brutally worded obscenity or an easy topical allusion which, far from diminishing the seriousness of the critical pronouncement, tellingly suggests that there is an important difference between the poet's claims to wit and the audience's pretensions to emancipation. Outstanding among the early prologues and epilogues, however, are the outrageously good-humoured pieces written for Nell Gwynn in *Tyrannick Love* and *The Conquest of Granada*, both of which underline the theatricality of the form. Notable too, and indicative of Dryden's range, are the celebration of Shakespeare in the Prologue to *The Tempest* and the fertile obscenity of the Prologue to *An Evening's Love*. Both have a resourcefulness of analogy and of syntactic control which Dryden obviously enjoys. This *is* the copiousness, vivacity, and delight which it was the business of the Fancy to infuse into comedy. The misfortunes of the Company (their theatre was burnt down), the successes of their rivals (allegedly achieved by sensationalism and grossness and so linked to Dryden's growing dislike of farce), and above all the moral and intellectual shortcomings of the audience are so regularly the subjects of these poems, that repetition of familiar themes becomes a pleasure and a joke in itself.

Some of the most enjoyable of the prologues and epilogues were written for various appearances of The Duke's Company in Oxford. There are beautifully turned compliments but also occasional deft exercises in irony. It is not necessarily a compliment to liken the University, not to the Praetorian Guard who in practice chose the Roman emperor, but to the acquiescing Senate who technically elected him;[3] nor will young men, however scholarly, feel particularly grateful to be told that their relations with the actresses will be as chaste as Apollo's with the Muses.[4] These poems in particular deserve the epithet 'masculine' so indiscriminately applied to Dryden. The Epilogue 'No poor *Du'ch* Peasant, wing'd with all his Fear' (1684) spoken at Oxford by Charles Hart in 1673, is brisk in its allusions to the pox of novelty with which a troupe of French actors have infected the town, tough in its contempt for the witless spectacles which are a success there, and clever but sensible in the turn towards compliment with which it concludes; but it is important to remember that it is tailored to Hart's personality, not Dryden's.

In the Epilogue 'Though what our Prologue said was sadly true' (1684), written for the opening of the New Theatre in March 1674, a new kind of violence appears. A deliberately emphasised hardness is evident in the repetition of 'So may' at the beginning of a series of sharply satirical couplets, replacing the lofty camaraderie with which Dryden had hitherto addressed the rakes and fops in his audience. Similarly the Epilogue to *The Man of Mode* (1676) fantastically universalises the grotesque figure of Sir Fopling Flutter in a mood of angry despair rather than amusement. Between them is the brilliantly organised *volte-face* of the Prologue to *Aureng-Zebe* in which Dryden denounces rhyme, 'Damns his laborious Trifle of a Play', makes another noble obeisance to Shakespeare, and savages the grossness of contemporary manners and neglect of wit. The sardonic conclusion reduces the heroic ambitions of the theatrical companies to the ignoble pretentiousness of continental wars, and the latter to the tawdry splendours of heroic plays acted before a trifling English audience:

> We and our Neighbours, to speak proudly, are
> Like Monarchs, ruin'd with expensive War.
> While, like wise *English*, unconcern'd, you sit,
> And see us play the Tragedy of Wit. (37–40)

There is a grim recognition in this expertly timed and balanced simile of the connection between social and artistic degeneration. Dryden's shift from Fancy to Judgement, from delightful to instructive comedy, and from heroic to classical tragedy, coincides with a bitter reappraisal of the civilisation he confidently celebrated ten years earlier. This tendency towards isolation from his own world, inextricably a part of his growing sense of the seriousness and reasonableness of poetry, naturally intensifies the irony in his verse, bringing into sharper prominence his own poetic personality. The remaining prologues and epilogues of the decade, up to and including those for *Troilus and Cressida*, are intensely preoccupied with the grossness and folly of the age and the frustrated greatness of literature. The strength of the anger, for instance, in the Prologue to *A True Widow* (1679)—a play by Shadwell, though Dryden barely alludes to the author or the piece—has all Rochester's disgust but a force and direction, formally and morally, of which Rochester was incapable.

Farce represented for Dryden the contamination of literature by the brutal folly which was corrupting society, and the embodiment of the spirit of farce was Shadwell, whom he made the hero of *MacFlecknoe* (1682) some time in the late seventies, though he did not publish the poem until much later, after the appearance of a pirated edition. It is now generally held that Shadwell's achievements deserve respect. Reading his attacks on Dryden's criticism, however, makes one wonder why Dryden held back so long from putting him down. Shadwell's defence of Jonson is self-regarding, jealous, and inept, his flattery of Newcastle gross. He was incapable of precise thought or consistent expression. He defines 'a good comical humour', for instance, as 'such an affectation as misguides men in Knowledge, Art, or Science, or that causes defection in Manners, and Morality, or perverts their minds in the main Actions of their lives'.[5] The plural 'men' and 'their' in this astonishingly broad definition hopelessly confuse the issue of how and on whom a humour operates. It also completely fails to consider the basic distinction made in *Of Dramatick Poesie*, between classical comedy based on 'the general Characters of Men and Manners' and its exact opposite, the Jonsonian mode which builds situations around 'the ridiculous extravagance of conversation wherein one man differs from all others'.[6] In moving away from the latter, Dryden was certainly not approaching Shadwell's position. Yet Shadwell could blunderingly complain of 'men of feminine understandings who like slight plays only that represent a little tattle sort of conversation like their own ... [and who] damn all Mr. Jonson's plays.' In the Preface to *The Humourists* he met Dryden's opinion that Jonson's great gift was Judgement by claiming that Dryden believed that Jonson's 'Writings were correct, though he wanted fire; but I think flat and dull things are as incorrect and show as little Judgement in the Author . . . [as] sprightly and mettled Nonsense',[7] an argument which not only noisily ignores what Dryden said, but batters and blunts his carefully sharpened critical vocabulary in the process. Shadwell's crimes, however, were less in his criticism, which Dryden in spite of being called 'insolent'[8] and 'a Jugler, or a Rope Dancer'[9] treated fairly equably, as in his plays, of which the most relevant to *MacFlecknoe* is *The Virtuoso* (1676).

A comparison between *The Virtuoso* and Dryden's notorious comedy *Limberham* is illuminating. Shadwell's play is about two rakes, each of whom pursues a girl who is really interested in his friend. They arrange for one of their rivals to introduce them into the girls' house, and for another, disguised as a servant, to be regularly kicked, beaten and tossed in a blanket. The girls' aunt makes advances to them both, and they acquiesce. Then to clear the house they arrange for all the older characters to meet their respective lovers at the same time. They dispose of their rivals down a trapdoor (where one, disguised as a woman, is nearly raped by the other) and get briskly on with their wooing. Unfortunately the older members of the family have all made their assignations in the same place and so return home unexpectedly. The rival dressed as a woman is locked up before being carted off to prison as a bawd, but he strips himself naked and escapes. After a Luddite riot by the unemployed, the characters all attend a masquerade in the evening. One rival is married off to a maid, and the aunt manages to 'enjoy' both the heroes in quick succession, but this fails to make her nieces jealous and she decides to desert her now bankrupt husband. The lovers pair off according to the girls' preferences, and their remaining rival is jolted in a trunk.

The play is totally without design, its satire, its allegedly humorous mode of characterisation, its situations, and the quality of laughter it provokes, having no significant relation to each other. The roughness of its farce, unlike the violence in Dryden, is nowhere countered by any concession to the claims of decorum, artistic or social. A typical example of the dialogue is this mindless exchange between one of the girls, Clarinda, and her blanket-tossed lover, Sir Samuel, at the masquerade:

> *Clarinda* . . . A Mask might cover deformity, but not folly. You have the very Meen of a Coxcombe; all the motions of your body declare the weakness of your mind.
> *Sir Samuel* . . . Pish! What, are you upon the high Ropes now. Whipstitch, your nose in my breech. Pish, I'll talk no more with her.   (V,iv, p. 170)

There are exchanges as gross as this in Etherege and Wycherley, and in Dryden, but not involving heroines whose idea of fun is to break an old man's pipe and throw away his hat and stick. Even this would not matter if the play were pure farce, but what plot there is is continually frozen dead in the interests of a satire on the Royal Society (the girl's uncle is the Virtuoso of the title) which is both philistine and undramatic. Shadwell's idea of satire is to chop up paragraphs of sub-burlesque prose and parcel them out at random among his characters. Nothing said, from the exaggerated descriptions of scientific experiments, to the wearisome and derivative account of a young squire's education, has any bearing, practical or thematic, on the love intrigue. Even the opening (a poor imitation of *The Man of Mode*) is philosophically pretentious and intellectually and theatrically tedious. The whole play, formally, morally, and aesthetically, lacks purpose and shape.

Superficially, Dryden's *Limberham, or The Kind Keeper* (1679) is as crude. Scott found it 'disgustingly coarse'[10] and it was banned by royal decree after three performances. Dryden, however, believed 'that this comedy is of the first rank of those which I have written, and that posterity will be of my opinion'.[11] If this has not proved the case, the fault is posterity's. *Limberham* is a brilliant, bewildering and terrifying performance. The events are as gross as those in *The Virtuoso*—there is endless opening and closing of doors and hiding in boxes and closets —but there is far greater fertility of invention and pace to the action, and the lockings and unlockings of boxes inside rooms within rooms, become nightmarishly significant. The characters are in three groups, ravenous lustful women, impotent jealous old men, and the three central characters, 'Father' Aldo, Woodall his son, whom he does not recognise, and Pleasance, a bitter, clever, sharp-tongued virgin, whom Woodall eventually marries.

Pleasance is Dryden's finest psychological study. Her satire is strong—of women-chasing rakes she says, '. . . let but little minx go proud, and the dogs in Covent Garden have her in the wind immediately; all pursue the scent' (IV,i, p. 53)[12]—but there is vulnerability in the violence of her speech. At one point she calls Woodall back to mock him, but her words are painfully revealing about feelings for him which she is suppressing: 'Will you not stay, sir?' she says, 'It may be I have a little business with you' (III,i, p. 54). 'Business', however, has only one meaning in *Limberham*. We have already seen Woodall hiding in a box and holding the lid down by main force, while the cuckold Limberham tells Aldo,

Mrs. Pleasance has sent for this same business here, which she lent to Pug [Limberham's whore]; now Pug has some private businesses within this business, which she would take out first, and the business will not be opened: and this makes all the business. (II,ii, p. 46)

And all of Pleasance's nightmare too.

At the centre of the play is the anarchic and improper relationship between the impotent Aldo and his son, the monstrously potent Woodall. Aldo agrees to pimp for Woodall if he is allowed to fondle the girls first:

Wood. Then I'm acquainted with your business: You would be a kind of deputy-fumbler under me.
Aldo. You have me right. You be the lion to devour the prey; I am your jackall, to provide it for you. (I,i, p. 22)

Once again father and son batten on the same sexual pasture. But Aldo is not only Woodall's father; he assumes the role of universal father to the whores in the city. Possibly this is why the play was banned. Patriarchalism was by no means confined to Filmer's books. It was perfectly natural for courtiers at Charles II's death-bed, for instance, to mourn the King as 'their common father'.[13] Moreover, in Act Four, scene one, Aldo actually assumes a kingly, not just a fatherly, relation with the whores in the play. Dryden was apparently attacking the very heart of the social order which as a tory poet he was committed to defend:

Aldo [*to the assembled whores*]. Lift up your voices, and sing like nightingales, your tory-rory jades. Courage, I say; as long as the merry pence hold out, you shall none of you die in Shoreditch.
                              Enter Woodall
A hey, boys, a hey! here he comes, that will swinge you all! down, you little jades, and worship him. It is the genius of whoring . . . A hey, a hey boys! the town's thy own; burn, ravish, and destroy!
Wood. We will have a night of it, like Alexander, when he burnt Persepolis: *tuez! tuez! tuez! point de quartier.*   (IV,i, p. 77)

Woodall is possibly based on Rochester, now Dryden's enemy. After a scene (which could be acted with disturbing seriousness) in which he promises to take Mrs Saintly to bed, and the 'good old soul' 'weeps for joy' (IV,i, p. 81), Pleasance mocks Woodall in terms which recall Rochester's famous 'mountebank' escapades:[14] 'Oh, I find it now!' she says: 'you are going to set up your bills like a love mountebank, for the speedy cure of distressed widows, old ladies and languishing maids' (IV,i, p. 82). Whether the reference is to Rochester or not the general point is clear. *Limberham* exposes a rottenness at the patriarchal centre of English life in sexual farce which is almost tragically extreme. Of course it is also an enthusiastic piece of erotic theatre. Its chief virtue, however, is embodied in Pleasance, who remains in the midst of its anarchy and lubricity, uncompromisingly honest and intelligent. Her trenchancy is supremely evident in the play's most telling line. When Woodall, the thoughtless, inexhaustible stud, is finally revealed as the fumbling Aldo's son, Pleasance's cry, 'What young father Aldo' (V,i, p. 112), puts Rochesters of every sort neatly in place.

    Limberham completes the movement begun with *The Assignation*, away from the comedy of fancy and delight to that of judgement and instruction. Its debt to Etherege and Wycherley is obvious, and especially to the latter's *The Plain Dealer* (1676)[15] with which it shares an outspoken disgust of contemporary life and a marked disrespect for mere likelihood in matters of plotting. Whereas in Etherege's *The Man of Mode* (1676) the action tests people and values in more or less

realistic circumstances, in *Limberham* and *The Plain Dealer* the plot is
shaped with ironic extravagance. The function of this extravagance is
not to delight, however, as it was in *Marriage à-la-Mode*, but to
increase, almost allegorically, the range of the play's plain dealing. This
shift to instruction and judgement, of course, radically alters Dryden's
attitude to Jonson. In the criticism of the late seventies and later he is
once again normative, the master of manners,[16] the supremely just and
moderate writer to whose memory Dryden has 'indignation enough to
burn a *D'Amboys* annually',[17] and finally the companion of Shakespeare
with whom 'None of the living will presume to have any competition'.[18] This clear revision of view on the norms of comedy and
Jonson's relations to them could easily have been taken as a victory for
Shadwell. But to Dryden, more deeply concerned than ever with the
nature and function of literature, it was intolerable that the author of
The Virtuoso should place himself alongside the author of *The Silent
Woman*. Hence *MacFlecknoe*, one function of which was to prise them
apart.

    The first thing to be said about *MacFlecknoe* (1682) is that for a
piece of burlesque its design is remarkably pure, strong and classical.
The barest statement that Flecknoe's reign as England's worst poet is
over introduces a fifty-line speech in which he chooses Shadwell as his
successor. Thirty lines describe the laureate's coronation site, forty
the procession and crowning, and the poem ends with a second
seventy-line speech by Flecknoe which is abruptly concluded when
the heroes of *The Virtuoso* open a trapdoor beneath him. The
mise-en-scène is comparable with that in *To His Sacred Maiesty* or the
procession to the tournament in *Palamon and Arcite* (1700). The
effectiveness of this design is strengthened by an uncompromising
assurance of manner. The poem's firm purpose and exuberant execution
are, in their fashion, a pure and serious example of baroque art. They
are also, of course, integral to its plain dealing, its total disrespect for
the sort of circumlocution one might expect in mock-heroic verse. In
this it has something of *Limberham*'s tough indifference to its own
excesses, but in suggesting the stupid blindness of small men to
commonsense, and the poet's own casual superiority to the demands of
mere naturalism, the forthright grotesqueness of *MacFlecknoe* has
nothing of *Limberham*'s ferocity. Extravagant analogies and frankness
in phrasing may express simultaneously the dullness of folly and the
liberty of wit, but there is little scorn in the poem and no hatred. Its
sheer bulk creates an impression of tolerant farce:

> No *Persian* Carpets spread th' Imperial way,
> But scatter'd Limbs of mangled Poets lay:
> From dusty shops neglected Authors come,
> Martyrs of Pies, and Reliques of the Bum.
> Much *Heywood, Shirly, Ogelby* there lay,
> But loads of *Sh——* almost choakt the way.   (98–103)

'*Sh——*' in the last line is packed with excremental possibilities.

Good humour, however, is not enough. There is something potentially very awkward for Dryden in his constructing such a huge machine for Shadwell's destruction. In spite of its brilliant conception and energetic execution, *MacFlecknoe* can still be read as an essentially dishonest attempt to annihilate an opponent by ridicule instead of meeting him on the real grounds of contention between them, the nature of comedy and the standing of Jonson, on both of which issues Shadwell has at least some claim to have had the better of the argument. Ridicule is a dangerous weapon in intellectual debate; it publicly assumes a humanly impregnable stance, an evident rightness which makes argument unnecessary. Dryden's technique is thus to expose himself at least as much as his opponent to the judgement of the discerning reader. If the destruction of Shadwell is not to be merely an exercise in unscrupulous crowd-pleasing, Dryden has to make tangibly evident the intellectual and moral qualities which justify him in treating one of the more prominent of his fellow playwrights with such jovial contempt.

Anyone at all familiar with seventeenth-century drama will of course recognise from Flecknoe's second speech that Dryden could have documented his case against Shadwell in copious detail. More important is the fact that the whole poem is consistently penetrated by his personal experience of the sublime in heroic literature and the comic in modern drama. The following lines illustrate how economical he is in combining his different purposes:

> *Sh——* alone my perfect image bears,
> Mature in dullness from his tender years.
> *Sh——* alone, of all my Sons, is he
> Who stands confirm'd in full stupidity.
> The rest to some faint meaning make pretence,
> But *Sh——* never deviates into sense.   (15–20)

There is more than comic directness here. This is one of many allusions in the poem to Cowley's *Davideis*:[19]

> *Abdon* alone his gen'rous purpose knew;
> *Abdon* a bold, a brave, and comely Youth,
> Well-born, well-bred, with Honour fill'd and Truth, . . .
> *Abdon*, whose love to' his Master did exceed
> What *Natures Law*, or *Passions Power* could breed,
> *Abdon* alone did on him now attend
> His humblest *Servant*, and his dearest *Friend.*[20]

The fact that such a style is nearly as ponderous as Shadwell himself does not prevent a parody of it bringing *MacFlecknoe* into a close, complicated relationship with the sublime in literature and in religion, and this is very relevant to the differences between Shadwell's consistently trivial reiteration of critical pieties and Dryden's growing sense of the judiciousness required by classical art.

MacFlecknoe has three 'subjects', literature, monarchy, and religion, each of which is a subtle, extensive, and developing metaphor for the others.[21] David as psalmist, anointed king, and inspired prophet embodies each in an ideal form; Shadwell is his lumbering antitype. The crudity of Restoration life and letters is thus brought ludicrously into contact with the sublime mysteries of politics, religion, and literature, specifically with the unchallengeable dignity of Virgil and Milton, who are also constantly alluded to in the poem, as well as the less convincing heroics of Cowley. The effect, however, is not of highly disparate literary experiences grotesquely juxtaposed, but of an unexpected harmony, a complete and triumphant integration. And it is the poet himself in and through whom this integration takes place. Dryden, delivering himself of the verse and giving it force, effectively demonstrates his personal ability to assimilate and reconcile the sublime and the comic, Milton and Shadwell. He may thus legitimately dismiss the latter with complete indifference to the man's actual, if modest achievements.

But it is not just Shadwell who is dismissed. In the famous description of the Barbican beginning 'Close to the Walls which fair *Augusta* bind', Dryden not only appropriates and transforms one of Cowley's finer passages, he strikingly repudiates his own attempts to rival in the theatre the epic effects of other, better poets on the page. The Barbican is not just the site of Shadwell's coronation, it is a training school for actors,

> Where unfledg'd Actors learn to laugh and cry,
> Where infant Punks their tender Voices try,
> And little *Maximins* the Gods defy.
> Great *Fletcher* never treads in Buskins here,
> Nor greater *Johnson* dares in Socks appear.   (76–80)

The reference to Jonson is crucial. It enables Dryden to admit to his own deficiencies as a writer of comedy as well as of heroic plays without deferring to the pretentious claims of his opponent to be guardian of the Jonsonian tradition. The allusion to *Tyrannick Love* is no mild exercise in self-mockery either—this is one of the hardest passages in the poem, and dangerous too, since Shadwell had been particularly scornful of the huffing heroes in Dryden's plays. But it is precisely Dryden's capacity for self-criticism which points up the profound lack of it in Shadwell's polemic and in his plays.

What the poem sets out to do in fact is to substitute for the pretentious definitions and egotistical sarcasms of literary controversy a compelling if humorous illustration of the relationship between the actual works which constitute the English classical heritage and the lewd, ugly, comic realities of contemporary English life. Dryden's mastery of this great tradition is joined to worldly relish for fact, for the historical present, as witnessed by London dirt, London shops, and London garbage, and the duty they impose on the poet to be honest and tolerant. *MacFlecknoe* obviously does not have or require the sense of history which Dryden briefly revealed in the *Heroique Stanza's*, but Flecknoe's second speech is magnificently specific, at least about the literary past and the standards of realism, reason, and decorum it exacts in the present. The poem is thus a brilliant display of amusing but deeply considered literary worldliness. The poet who possesses it with such Virgilian assurance is not a mere participant in a literary argument. Rather he embodies a comprehensive vision of men and books, so firmly based in tradition and truth to nature that it turns the superficial critic and maker of farces into a huge figure of fun. Dryden's purpose in *MacFlecknoe*, therefore, is not only to destroy Shadwell, but also, emphatically, to establish himself.

1. Edwin Morgan, 'Dryden's Drudging' in *Dryden. A Collection of Critical Essays*, Ed. Bernard N. Schilling (1963), p. 42.

2. Bruce King, *Dryden's Major Plays* (1966), p. 64.

3. See 'Prologue, To the University of Oxon, Spoken by Mr. Hart . . .' (1684).

4. See 'Epilogue To Oxford . . . ' (1684).

5. Dedication, *The Virtuoso*, *The Complete Works of Thomas Shadwell*, Ed. Montague Summers (1927), III, p. 102.

6. *Of Dramatick Poesie*, pp. 92–3.

7. T. Shadwell, *Works* I, p. 187.

8. *The Sullen Lovers*, Preface, *Works* I, p. 11.

9. *The Royal Shepherdess*, Preface, ibid., p. 100.

10. Scott–Saintsbury VI, p. 2.

11. *Limberham*, Dedication, Scott–Saintsbury VI, p. 10.

12. Quoted from Scott–Saintsbury VI.

13. Quoted in Kinsley IV (1960).

14. See Vivian de Sola Pinto, *Rochester, Portrait of a Restoration Poet* (1935), pp. 105–10.

15. See Frank Harper Moore, *The Nobler Pleasure: Dryden's Comedy in Theory and Practice* (1933), p. 146.

16. See 'The Grounds of Criticism in Tragedy', Ker I, p. 219.

17. Dedication of *The Spanish Friar*, Ker I, p. 246.

18. Dedication of *Examen Poeticum*, Kinsley II, p. 791.

19. See A. L. Korn, '*MacFlecknoe* and Cowley's *Davideis*' in *Essential Articles for the study of John Dryden*, Ed. H. T. Swedenberg, Jr (1966), pp. 170–200.

20. *Davideis* IV, *The English Writings of Abraham Cowley*, Ed. A. R. Waller (1905), p. 385.

21. See Earl Miner, *Dryden's Poetry* (1967), p. 95.

5

THE EXCLUSION CRISIS:

POEMS, PLAYS AND SATIRES 1679–1681

In 1680 Dryden translated three of Ovid's Epistles and wrote a Preface on the principles of translation for a volume of all the Epistles which his publisher Tonson was bringing out. The achievement is small compared with his later translations, but pleasant, with a certain significance also in the history of his poetic development. He had long maintained that Ovid 'had a Genius most proper for the Stage . . . a way of writing . . . fit to stir up a pleasing admiration and concernment, . . . and to shew the various movements of a Soul combating betwixt two different Passions'.[1] He imitates this theatricality by softening and regularising his verse. The couplets are smooth, and without the intellectually aggressive paragraphing of the 'masculine' prologues. Instead they develop by emotional association which is meant to be both feminine and Ovidian. The result is a theatrical stream of consciousness; even the well-organised irony of love-stricken and psychologically complex inconsistency is 'dramatic'. The language is neat, and devoid of the glutinous abstractness of heroic love. It suggests, however, though in an entirely acceptable way, a stylised performance by a talented actress. This capacity of Dryden's to vary the manners of his verse is especially significant as he was increasingly to answer his ideological opponents by confronting them, in the manner of *MacFlecknoe*, not merely with 'answers', but also with a judicious, and knowledgeable 'man'.

As poet laureate, he was especially preoccupied with ideology at this time. His sometimes irrelevant use of political allusions also suggests a personal as well as a professional concern with politics. In

Dido to Aeneas, for instance, he translates *quis sua non notis arva tendenda dabit* as

> What People is so void of common sense
> To Vote Succession from a Native Prince?   (17–18)

This is an unobtrusive reference to the Duke of York's British birth, his chief rival for the succession being the Dutch William of Orange. But if Dryden was personally obsessed with politics in the early eighties, he was not alone. From 1678 until Charles II's death, 'the stage', in Scott's words, 'absolutely foamed with politics'.[2] So did the country.

The problem was the Stuart hankering for Catholicism. James had become a Catholic in 1669. In 1670 Charles secretly promised Louis XIV that he would become a Catholic also—at a suitable time—and in 1673 he used his prerogative to grant religious liberty to Catholics and Non-conformists. The Anglican Commons reacted fiercely, passing the Test Act of 1673 which required all civilian and military office-holders to declare their opposition to the Catholic doctrine of Transubstantiation and to be communicants in the Church of England. (This forced the resignation of Treasurer Clifford, to whom Dryden promptly dedicated *Amboyna*.) By 1678 the alliance between squire-archy and Church, which the long years of Charles' first Parliament had firmly cemented, found itself unexpectedly in harmony with the City and the Dissenters. Titus Oates' 'revelations' about a 'Popish Plot' to kill the King united the country in a violent anti-Catholic hysteria. Catholics were hounded to death by a mob of petty perjurers, which the King did nothing to prevent, and a campaign was mounted to exclude James from the throne, which, through three short Parliaments between 1679 and 1681, he guilefully resisted. He even submitted to an Act which forbade Catholics to come into his presence without a signed and sealed licence from the Privy Council, a law which, it has been remarked, 'for sheer offensiveness to the ruling monarch has perhaps never been equalled'.[3] Just as representative of popular feeling was the refusal of the sheriffs of London to accept the King's commutation of the sentence of hanging, disembowelling and quartering, passed on the Catholic Lord Stafford, to one of beheading.[4]

The Exclusionist campaign (especially in the extreme version which favoured the accession of Charles' illegitimate son, the Duke of Monmouth) was manifestly an attack in principle and practice on the

Constitution. Whig control over City offices meant that juries were packed, and the legal system run on party lines. Hereditary succession, the royal prerogative and due process were all equally in danger. When Charles dismissed his last parliament in 1681, he accused the Commons of presuming to suspend Acts of Parliament on their own authority alone, and of passing 'Strange and illegal Votes, declaring divers emminent Persons to be enemies to the King and Kingdom, without any order or Process of Law'.[5] The Commons was trying to be what it had once been in the Interregnum, an absolute assembly in Hobbist fashion, unrestrained by Right or Law. Nor was arbitrary power from the Commons the only kind of tyranny the Court party professed to fear. In *His Majesty's Declaration Defended* (1681), Dryden argued that Monmouth as a usurper could easily become a dictator, since 'Conquerors are not easily to be curbed'.[6]

The two great seventeenth-century political bugbears were arbitrary power and anarchy. In June 1682 a Royalist paper compared Monmouth to '*Oliver*'s *Richard* the Fourth',[7] implying that the whigs wished to re-create the confusion which followed Oliver's death, a time when the whig leader, Lord Shaftesbury, then Sir Antony Ashley-Cooper, had exercised to some effect his fevered political talents. (He and Monck were made privy councillors on the day of Charles' return.) Shaftesbury may have wanted to emulate Cromwell himself and use the Exclusion crisis in a desperate bid for power. Backing Monmouth was very risky. Next in succession after James was his daughter Mary, married to the formidable William of Orange. William also wanted to exclude James (who was both his uncle and father-in-law), but would never have allowed his other uncle's bastard to pop in between the election and his hopes. Shaftesbury's hopes, however, may well have centred precisely on the prospect of anarchy and civil war, brought about by Charles, or James, or William, being ready to resist Monmouth's claim by force, in which case it might again become apparent, as Dryden himself had observed, 'How strangely high endeavours may be blest'.

Lawlessness was rife. Huge 'pope-burnings' were organised to rouse the mob. Monmouth disobeyed the King and returned from exile to massive public adulation. Even Dryden was beaten up in Rose Alley in 1679, possibly on the orders of Shaftesbury,[8] or of Rochester, and certainly because he had offended some powerful personage. One might therefore expect the prologues and epilogues of the period from 1679 to 1681 to be particularly bitter. In fact they are rather more benign. Dryden confronts the Shadwell-like farce of brutal and degenerate times with a good humour akin to that of the earlier prologues and epilogues, but made relevant to the seriousness of the national situation. A carefully assumed personality as much as carefully considered argument meets the whig challenge, and the response is none the less effective for being manifestly staged. Dryden's very capacity to choose one of a thousand poses suggests a subtle combination of personal qualities which his social stance conceals but which make that stance possible. In a publicly distraught age suggestions of a privately maintained wisdom that is impervious to the grossness of the times are particularly effective.

What holds the attention, however, is the public performance. Dryden's prologues and epilogues at this time are astonishingly rich in figures which he and others, including Swift, were to use again to greater effect. *The Prologue at Oxford, 1680* (1684) interestingly anticipates *A Tale of a Tub*, while the graceful but sturdy *Prologue To His Royal Highness Upon . . . his Return from Scotland* (1682) is an excellent statement of tory principle, which emphasises the royal character of mercy, and so looks forward to *The Hind and the Panther* (1687). It is their authoritative and highly individualised tone, however, more than their ideas, which makes these poems memorable. A number, including the prologues to *Caesar Borgia* (1680), *The Loyal General* (1680) and three to Oxford—'The Fam'd *Italian* Muse' (1693), 'Discord, and Plots which have undone our Age' (1684), and 'Tho' Actors cannot much of Learning boast' (1684) —handle political controversy with the same cheerful carelessness that Dryden had shown towards critical debate in earlier prologues and epilogues. The prologue 'Gallants, a bashful Poet bids me say' (1693) and the Epilogue to *Tamerlane the Great* (1681) return to the spirit of the sixties without making any political points at all. In the best prologues and epilogues of this time, however, Dryden takes complex and wide-ranging perspectives on the contemporary scene. The relevance of his conceptions matches the assurance with which he executes them. *The Prologue . . . spoken at Mithridates King of Pontus* (1681), for instance, uncomfortably juxtaposes the diseased sexuality of the fashionable world with the coarse perjuries of whig witnesses. The disgusted poet defines his own integrity in terms of its opposites, yet paradoxically his plain speaking—and this *is* a bitter poem—is wilfully close in spirit to the rutting of lords and the swearing of Oateses.

In contrast is the lovely *Prologue to the Dutchess On Her Return from Scotland* (1682) where James and his second wife had been in diplomatic exile. The young Mary of Modena symbolises literature and new life repossessing a waste land:

> For Her the weeping Heav'ns become serene,
> For Her the Ground is clad in cheerfull green:
> For Her the Nightingales are taught to sing,
> And Nature has for her delay'd the Spring.　(26–9)

The obviousness of the placing of 'For Her' disguises more delicate subtleties. The long e's [i] in the first couplet, the pleasing 'are taught to' instead of 'begin to' in the second, and the appositeness of 'delay'd' after the last, late-arriving 'for her' anticipate the loveliest lines in Pope's *Autumn Eclogue*. But the poem also implicitly recognises the limitations of its mode and the slightness of its subject. This gracious superficiality, however, is itself evidence of the freedom and richness of life which the defeat of faction makes possible. The 'discords' alluded to in the closing couplets include the clash between the overt intentions of the last line—'Who best shall love the Duke, and serve the King'— and the slight double meaning it is capable of bearing. The fact that this does not destroy the poem's crystalline purity is due to the tact and wisdom of the poet's manner.

　　Two poems addressed to the King also call for attention. *The Prologue Spoken to the King and Queen* (1682) at a performance of Banks' *The Unhappy Favourite* fluently announces obvious tory ideals, but is touched by an occasional flatness of analogy ('Must still our Weather and our Wills agree?') which hints at a prosaic toughness not otherwise evident in the poem. This is especially so in the last line—'Still to have such a King, and this King Long'. All noble attitudinising apart, practical politics demanded a long reign for Charles, so that his brother's might be as short and feeble as tories could decently wish for. Remote as the issues in the Exclusion crisis now are, the practical urbanity of such court poetry still has power to please. The supreme example of the courtier's stance being an amusing but effective response to whiggery is *The Epilogue Spoken to the King at . . . Oxford on . . . March the Nineteenth 1681*, during the most dramatic week in the whole Exclusion crisis. Charles had summoned Parliament to meet at Oxford. The whigs arrived with bands of armed retainers. An agitator called College made excited, obscene speeches on the 'Protestant' side (for which he was later hanged, drawn and quartered). On the other side cries of 'Let the King live and the Devil hang the roundheads' greeted the King.[9] When Parliament met on the twenty-first, Charles was to propose restricting the powers of a Catholic successor, but less stringently than he had suggested earlier, and he knew that the offer would be rejected. He would then dissolve Parliament, and, backed by a French subsidy, destroy the whigs at his leisure. He was calculating on their over-reaching themselves so that their defeat would be the more humiliating. When Dryden's prologue was spoken, therefore, the whigs were riding high and the royal party was subdued.

The sense of imminent climax, of the whole nation converging on Oxford, is well caught in the opening analogy. The poem moves off along a false but alluring trail of seriousness, which even on re-reading reverberates with a real desire for political quiet. Then suddenly and coolly the poet whips off one courtier's mask, and ends his poem by revealing another:

> But while your daies on publick thoughts are bent
> Past ills to heal, and future to prevent;
> Some vacant houres allow to your delight,
> Mirth is the pleasing buisness of the Night,
> The Kings Prerogative, the Peoples right.
> Were all your houres to sullen cares confind,
> The Body wou'd be Jaded by the Mind.
> 'Tis Wisdoms part betwixt extreams to Steer:
> Be Gods in Senates, but be Mortals here. (23–31)

This is more than a spirited defiance of the Exclusionists' Dissenting morality and an arrogantly abrupt ending. Not only are the *hubris* of ambition, the narrowness of intrigue, and the legalism of constitutional theory swiftly and unexpectedly placed in a telling comparison with a rich, relaxed, and 'Mortal' existence; even sacred political concepts like 'Prerogative' and 'Right' are required to survive in this unexpectedly human context if they can. Wisdom in politics and life is a subtle blend of involvement and detachment, of principle and pragmatism, which only a polity as simultaneously royal and mortal as Charles II himself can sustain. Once again a prologue anticipates a major poem, in this case *Absalom and Achitophel* (1681), which Dryden was to begin once the Oxford Parliament had been dissolved and Shaftesbury arrested.

He had already made an important contribution to the Exclusionist controversy, however, in his 'Protestant play' *The Spanish Friar* (1681). It was banned at the accession of James II. When his daughter Mary replaced him she promptly ordered it to be performed, and had then to hide behind her fan because of its relevance to her own usurpation. This is not surprising, since in a carefully limited way the situation of Leonora in the play is similar to what her own had been in 1680, just as Bertram and Torrismond embody the different options open at that time to her husband William. He could either have opted for armed intervention in the name of his wife's specious title, or he could have bided his time, trusting that Providence would finally secure him in his own as the 'hidden' lawful heir. The play has thus a precise if deliberately indirect relationship with the specific problem of the succession. It is not like the earlier plays a conflict in political principle only.

This does not mean that it is not also a typical essay in neoclassical stagecraft. The plot is certainly formulaic. Sancho, the lawful king, lies in prison. Leonora has inherited his throne. Bertram, her unscrupulous minister, feels threatened by the military successes of Torrismond, who, though he does not know it, is Sancho's true heir. Torrismond's foster-father, Raymond, joins Alphonzo in a plot against Leonora, who is very unhappy about her ambiguous position, and becomes more so when she falls in love with the noble Torrismond. However, she allows Bertram to murder Sancho; then when he demands to marry her, she uses the opportunity to dismiss him and promote Torrismond.

Torrismond's birth is never a mystery difficult to penetrate, but something of a *coup de théâtre* is achieved in Act Four when he himself discovers his royal origins and cries out

> The usurper of my throne, my house's ruin!
> The murderer of my father—is my wife!   (IV,ii, p. 496)[10]

Every conceivable assumption about the workings of poetic justice in such a situation is shattered. Marriage should be the reward for successfully resolving the conflict between good and evil impulses and contradictory duties. When in the Fourth Act the consummated and lawful marriage of a perfectly typed, nobly mannered hero to a passionate and queenly heroine is revealed as the lawful union of lawful heir and murdering usurper, the resulting fusion of legitimate and illegitimate elements alarmingly disrupts both neoclassical

decorum and monarchist principles. There are no laws left to obey, yet
duty remains for poet and subject alike. Raymond cannot rebel against
Leonora without rising against his lawful prince. Alphonzo's son,
Lorenzo, cannot be loyal to Torrismond, his friend (and, though he
refuses to believe it, his king), without at the same time fighting his
father. The impasse is brilliantly illustrated in a confrontation between
the tory rebel, Raymond, and his foster-son, the lawful heir, Torrismond. When Torrismond makes his parentage public, to protect
Leonora from the rebels, Raymond, who has known it all along, is so
bent on punishing Leonora that he simply denies it, so as to have an
excuse for continuing the fight on behalf of legitimacy. For his battle
cry, however, he is forced to use the whig 'Our liberty for us!' against
Torrismond's royal 'My right for me!'. Torrismond takes the
traditional patriarchalist line on the duty of subjects to obey a usurper.
There is thus no doubt that Dryden's 'Protestant play' is also an
intensely tory one,[11] but at the same time he seems perversely to
emphasise the impotence of tory principles in practice. Thus the
situation in the play is ironically resolved by the rake Lorenzo and the
Machiavellian Bertram, who has astutely hidden Sancho away because
he was uncertain how Leonora would react to the old king's murder.

   The Spanish Friar is a remarkable blend of platonised passion in a
stage world and substantial political anxieties in a real one. Pedro, for
instance (a rebel in Sancho's cause), describes a situation familiar to
Londoners in 1640 and 1660 as well as 1680:

> The doors are all shut up; the wealthier sort,
> With arms across, and hats upon their eyes,
> Walk to and fro before their silent shops;
> While droves of lenders crowd the bankers' doors,
> To call in money.   (IV,i, p. 485)

This particular image was first introduced by the Spanish Friar himself,
Father Dominic, who as Lorenzo's pimp in his affair with Elvira
gleefully describes Elvira's husband, Gomez, as 'keeping sentry at his
door' like 'a citizen, in a cold morning, clapping his sides, and walking
forward and backward a mighty pace before his shop' (IV,i, p. 474).
Coarse comedy of this kind keeps the heroic action close to a far more
historically convincing world than is ever suggested by *Marriage
à-la-Mode*. The spirit of *Limberham*'s harsh instructive comedy
controls *The Spanish Friar*.

In spite of Dryden's determination to gratify his audience's anti-papist passions in the monstrous figure of Dominic, the comic characters are no more patly divisible into the sympathetic and the unsympathetic than the heroic characters are into the virtuous and corrupt. Thus when the 'hero' Lorenzo is caught by Gomez with Elvira, it is Dominic who proves the wit and rescues him, just as it is the contemptible cuckold Gomez whose anti-clerical satire is the most biting. Dominic is less the assimilable monster, a pimping Catholic priest, than the enormous embodiment of Lorenzo's rakish code who indulges at the same time in the cant terms, not of the Papists, but the Dissenters. When he casually proposes killing Gomez, Lorenzo is thankful that his own sin 'comes far short' of Dominic's (IV,i, p. 477). But does it? Superficially Lorenzo is a comic Antony: 'There are hedges in summer, and barns in winter', he tells Elvira, '. . . we will leave honour to madmen, and riches to knaves; and travel till we come to the ridge of the world, and then drop together into the next' (III,ii, p. 455). When Elvira robs Gomez, however, she and Lorenzo do 'kill' her husband, at least symbolically:

Here's that will . . . provide better entertainment for us, than hedges in summer and barns in winter [Elvira says]. Here's the very heart, and soul, and life-blood of Gomez; pawns in abundance, old gold of widows, and new gold of prodigals, and pearls and diamonds of court ladies.   (IV,i, p. 480)

This acute recognition of what constitutes 'life' in a world which sanctions the values of acquisitiveness sharply qualifies the idealism of the main plot, especially as it is Lorenzo who finally rescues the kingdom's lawful heir, Torrismond. 'I have been at hard-head with your butting citizens', he yells; 'I have routed your herd'. Then he turns to his father: 'Now, sir, who proves the traitor? My conscience is true to me; it always whispers right, when I have my regiment to back it' (V,ii, pp. 507–8). He is also notably contemptuous of patriarchalism. In fact he constitutes an unqualified satire on 'the various Court rakes who joined Monmouth's cause and added the new rationalistic Whig political doctrines to their Hobbist and libertine beliefs'.[12] Dryden was later to attack Shadwell for making heroes of just such men,[13] 'broad republicans', he called them elsewhere, '. . . men of atheistic principles . . . Hobbists in their politics and morals'. [14] This only makes Lorenzo's part in saving the kingdom in *The Spanish Friar* even more remarkable.

Aristocratic thuggery, however, does not finally triumph. Dominic, the hedonistic cynic, diagnoses its weakness when with his final blessing he declares, 'May your sisters, wives, and daughters be so naturally lewd, that they may have no occasion for a devil to tempt, or a friar to pimp for them' (V,ii, p. 520). The work involved in pimping and procuring suggests the artificiality of the rakes' code, for naturalness is one of the play's key values. Elvira turns out to be Lorenzo's sister. Mindless appetite thus blunders into natural law which it is compelled to respect, whatever lust may urge. This makes nonsense of Hobbes' identification of pleasure with the good. Some moral principles, at least, are as stubbornly facts of nature as hungry bodies.

Yet, as we have seen, the play also insists on the impotence of principle. Man is thus trapped in absolute contradiction. He can only submit to the will of God, and lie still. Sancho, the old king, 'majestic in his bonds' (III,iii, p. 468), emobodies this most fundamental of Dryden's convictions; yet even this image is grotesquely parodied in Dominic's Falstaffian account of Gomez and Lorenzo fighting:

Well, this noble colonel, like a true gentleman, was for taking the weaker part, you may be sure; whereupon this Gomez flew upon him like a dragon, got him down, the devil being strong in him, and gave him bastinado upon bastinado, and buffet upon buffet, which the poor meek colonel, being prostrate, suffered with a most Christian patience.   (V,ii, p. 516)

The play thus boxes itself in, allowing no escape from the inventiveness with which it treats of human helplessness, nor the troubled aesthetic balance it achieves between Dryden's convictions and the difficulties involved in accepting them.

'What Charles II needed,' however, according to one modern historian, 'was a Burke, a master of emotional rhetoric'.[15] *The Spanish Friar* illustrates Dryden's disqualifications for the role. He is too uncertain about the practical effectiveness of moral idealism, too ready to identify integrity with balanced, ironic truth-telling, to be a great propagandist. Even his Defence of Charles II's *Declaration* following the Oxford Parliament is notable for its 'moderation . . . compared with the addresses'.[16] (The gentlemen of England took fright when they realised that Exclusionism could lead to republicanism and civil war, and hastened to memorialise their loyalty to the King.) Dryden went on to memorialise the whigs' defeat in *Absalom and Achitophel*, yet even in this overtly propagandist poem his approach is a carefully balanced one.

This moderation is not mere caution. As *The Spanish Friar* illustrates, Dryden was deeply aware of the importance, in principle and practice, precisely of the gap between principle and practice in life. The essential task of morality was to adjust to a stubbornly amoral reality. Even when he argues the tory case in abstract terms towards the end of *Absalom and Achitophel*, therefore, he is careful not to predicate an ideal social order:

> If ancient Fabricks nod, and threat to fall,
> To Patch the Flaws, and Buttress up the Wall,
> Thus far 'tis Duty; but here fix the Mark:
> For all beyond it is to touch our Ark.   (801–4)

The untouchable, divinely sanctioned political reality had never been for him primarily a matter of law or principle, but the flawed kingdom of England as it was, the existing complex of rights actually deriving from the past, however imperfect they might be in principle.

In contrast to this were the traditionless and graceless perspectives of the City. The great issue between Dryden and a man like Slingsby Bethel, for instance, can be seen as a disagreement about what it meant to inherit a 'propriety'. Bethel's political and economic writings stress the importance of commerce in a modern state. They even made 'commercial prosperity a function of religious freedom'.[17] Dryden on the other hand saw things in terms of possession, not exchange. In the *Vindication of the Duke of Guise* (1683) he wrote:

The Estate of England is indeed the king's; . . . but it follows not, that the people are his goods and chattels on it; for then he might sell, alienate, or destroy them as he pleased: from all which he has tied himself by the liberties and privileges which he has granted us by laws.[18]

For this reason, Dryden argues, 'the preservation of his right destroys not our propriety, but preserves us in it'. To a man like Bethel, however, property was precisely the right to sell, alienate, and destroy at will, a species, in effect, of arbitrary power: 'Living on the Spoil', Dryden was to call it in *The Medall* (1682).

The fundamental differences between them are further illustrated in Dryden's attitude to the political contract, which he deals with at the beginning of the final phase (759–810) of *Absalom and Achitophel*. Superficially the 'argument from original sin' is hardly impressive.

What it amounts to, however, is the assertion that a society is created by its past and is unalterable because the past is indivisible. If a contract is part of that past it is binding forever. If it specifies that kings are answerable to the people, then so be it; if it does not, then they are not. This is not so much because of the nature of the contract, however, as the nature of the social arrangements of which it is only a part. The mass of existing rights and proprieties in society constitute a single, providentially sanctioned polity to which the citizen owes a far more fundamental obligation than to any real or hypothetical agreement between king and people. This obviously reactionary view has two redeeming features. It involves a romantic but still flexible, organic, and generous idea of power and possession (as against the legalistic ethic of aggressive capitalism) and it is based on a real respect for history, practically not abstractly conceived.

The tensions arising from this careful balancing of the ideal and the real are triumphantly encountered and overcome in the famous opening paragraph of the poem. The commonplace parallel between the courts of King David and King Charles is a strong reminder of the sacredness of politics. The bland celebration of an uninhibitedly pagan golden age, however, casually suggests an insolent indifference in nature itself to any calls to sacredness whatsoever. It is not at all clear at this stage how Dryden is going to adjudicate between the two, but what is evident enough is his capacity to encounter the clash between them enthusiastically. He is manifestly delighted at the prospect of toying with contradiction, blasphemy, and disbelief in the very act of producing a loyally heroic defence of Charles' divine right as a Christian king. This flaunted refusal to isolate Right from reality is thoroughly reassuring. Here is a man intellectually and emotionally qualified to speak reasonably on behalf of the Stuarts. He is not prepared to shout history down. He is not a Burke.

This spirit of moderation is reflected in the apparently antithetical impulses towards epic and comedy in the poem. The ultimate coherence of Dryden's vision, however, is dependent on his being able to reconcile them. It is obvious from the start that he is going to succeed. *Absalom and Achitophel*, in a much simpler and more obvious sense than *MacFlecknoe*, is an heroic poem. In the very act of being so, however, of conforming to Dryden's mature sense of what heroic writing should do, it succeeds effortlessly, and so with propriety, in being funny.

It is, first of all, a brilliant, lively design. Its characters are grouped with the vigour of Rembrandt's so-called *Night Watch*, with the same carefully calculated disposition of the major and minor figures; Zimri and Shimei on the one hand, with Balaam, Caleb, Nadab and Jonas on the other, between and behind them. The composition neatly divides into four roughly equal parts. The first three, the setting of the scene, (1–227), the temptation (228–476), and the Exclusionist campaign (477–754), establish a strongly organised momentum in favour of the whigs, which the last section, itself divided into three (a general statement of principle, an account of the royalist party, and the king's speech), is intended decisively to resist. The grouping of the characters within this firmly conceived plan, the rhetorical organisation of the verse paragraphs, and the masterly transitions from one mood to another, combine to produce the effect of a virtuoso exercise in design which almost insistently invites comparison with the great allegorical canvasses of seventeenth-century historical painting.

In such an undeniably heroic context, the chief figures have room to speak and gesture grandly. Dryden is careful to give both Absalom and Achitophel in particular the greatest possible scope as serious actors in a great action, so that if they cannot be right in principle, they can at least have the opportunity to be impressive in practice. They are carefully and seriously characterised, therefore, as heroic types. Absalom (Monmouth) is youthful ambition, Achitophel (Shaftesbury), the satanic Machiavelli. In making Absalom a serious and not a mock heroic figure (there is none of the copious exaggeration of *MacFlecknoe*) Dryden nevertheless succeeds in creating a subtly amusing effect. Absalom, like all aspiring princes, begins by admitting his ambition; this in its turn convinces him of his personal greatness; personal greatness then justifies the ambition. The reader, of course, is aware of the circularity of the argument. Unlike Torrismond in *The Spanish Friar*, whose similar instincts are lawfully inherited and incorporated into an intellectually consistent, morally passionate respect for existing authority, Absalom reveals himself as too stupid and venal to be a hero. Achitophel, on the other hand, is trapped by the heroic context in a different kind of self-exposure. He is carefully made to follow the precedents set by Milton's Satan and Shakespeare's Angelo.[19] He is, admittedly, a lesser figure than Satan. Milton after all deals with a subject which dignifies even epic literature, whereas Dryden is exposing unheroic man by giving him a truly heroic context in which to fail. But this does not make him an unimpressive figure. On the contrary, the organisation of the verse paragraphs, the rhetoric, and the imagery in the early part of the poem hardly seem Dryden's but functions of Achitophel's personal manipulative energy. He is the very vivid embodiment, in fact, precisely of that atheistical, pragmatic activism in politics which Dryden regarded as the gravest threat to a humane, traditionally based social order.

Achitophel is thus more a study in manners than in ideas. This was inevitable in view of Dryden's firm commitment to neoclassical theories of heroic poetry. '*L'Epopée*', Le Bossu had written, '*est plus pour les mœurs et pour les habitudes que pour les passions*'.[20] At the same time, just such a preoccupation with the habitual workings of the soul, rather than its immediate and passionate reactions to events, was also neatly adapted to Dryden's political concerns as well as his epic ambitions in the poem. He was engaged, after all, in a real political fight, against men as well as principles. *Ad hominem* argument had a practical relevance as well as an appropriateness to heroic theory. Nor was it incompatible with his sense of the nature of epic poetry to illustrate by comic means the inhumanity inherent in whiggery. His later translations of Homer were to have an unmistakable, if not necessarily very happy, comic element. The vices and follies of men (and gods), so long as they were habitual and the overall effect was one of wonder, were well within the tonal range of the heroic poet. The epic, in fact, could sustain a co-ordinated appreciation of the ideal and the real, of principle and practice in amusing as well as magnificent interaction. The brilliant portraits of Zimri (Buckingham) and Corah (Oates) are as appropriate to the poem's heroic character, therefore, as the more obviously splendid portraits of Absalom and Achitophel.

The decision to attack the inadequacies of whiggish manners had its dangers, however. The tories, in this respect, were not above criticism themselves. An aristocratic imperviousness to the pressures of ordinary morality is all very well—its success in the opening paragraphs of the poem is devastating—but it is finally hollow. Nothing illustrates this more clearly than the contrast between David's sexuality and Achitophel's. Initially David's seems outrageously splendid and royally fruitful, as its results in the person of Achitophel apparently illustrate:

> Of all this Numerous Progeny was none
> So Beautifull, so brave as *Absolon*: . . .
> What e'r he did was done with so much ease,
> In him alone, 'twas Natural to please.

His motions all accompanied with grace;
And *Paradise* was open'd in his face.
With secret Joy, indulgent *David* view'd
His Youthfull Image in his Son renew'd:
To all his wishes Nothing he deny'd,
And made the Charming *Annabel* his Bride. (17–18; 27–34)

The movement, from mythical promiscuity in one generation, through paternal affection, to an idealised eroticism in the next, is psychologically deeply satisfying. Not surprisingly Achitophel's sexuality makes a different impression:

Else, why should he, with Wealth and Honour blest,
Refuse his Age the needful hours of Rest?
Punish a Body which he could not please;
Bankrupt of Life, yet Prodigal of Ease?
And all to leave, what with his Toyl he won,
To that unfeather'd, two Leg'd thing, a Son:
Got, while his Soul did hudled Notions try;
And born a shapeless Lump, like Anarchy. (165–72)

The advantage is obviously with David. The second passage does not, of course, imply that Achitophel is sexless or his son deformed. Rather it refers to the human impoverishment involved in his political bequest to future generations. When we consider the third father and son in the poem, however, the Duke of Ormonde (Barzillai) and the Earl of Ossory, David's style of fatherhood begins to look a little tawdry. The graciously idealistic tone surrounding the loyal Barzillai, who 'Mourn'd' and 'Suffer'd with his Prince', and who sees his heroic son die so unexpectedly if triumphantly (817–63), points to an altogether more impressive moral inheritance than Absalom's.

On examination, indeed, the latter turns out to be a distinctly dubious one. In the first place it is significant that a moral inheritance is all David can give Absalom. Besides, even the lines I have quoted blasphemously identify Absalom with Christ, and David with the Father. In addition they rely heavily on blurred words like 'ease' and 'grace'. Achitophel, it is true, wastes his ease instead of enjoying it, so that again superficially the advantage is with David. But if 'ease' suggests royal abundance in contrast to Shaftesbury's intense aridity, qualities which associate naturally with 'grace' and so merge, at any rate semantically, with the idea of divine favour, the link remains a

thin one. It is surely significant that the heroic Duke of York is in no
way associated with the ease which is apparently both the king's and
the poet's favourite stance, but which merges just as naturally with
David's indefensible indulgence of '*Amnon's* murder' as with divine
or kingly grace. Nor does the poem's sophisticated toleration of
Absalom's youthful brutalities resolve the problem. It merely involves
us in the king's guilt. Indeed the more the poem flatters our appetite for
royal 'tory' manners the more bewildering the morass we find ourselves
in.

It would be a mistake, however, to conclude that this was not
intended. There is a Swiftian deliberateness in the way Dryden
deprives us of our moral bearings in the early part of the poem. The
Jews, for instance, are criticised for setting up a golden calf, yet priests
are mocked if their gods are not of beaten gold. The Jebusites are
admitted to have 'the Native right', yet are attacked for following
'Egyptian rites'; and the gross satire on the Real Presence is later
contradicted by the condemnation of Nadab's blasphemous Eucharist.
Finally the 'ease' Dryden has been at pains to celebrate is dealt a
devastating blow in a second reference to David's adulteries. 'My
Father', says Absalom,

> . . . whom with reverence yet I name,
> Charm'd into Ease, is careless of his Fame:
> And, brib'd with petty summs of Forreign Fold
> Is grown in *Bathsheba*'s Embraces old.   (707–10)

An ageing, bribable adulterer is every bit as disgusting as a bankrupt,
toiling politician. With thoroughly un-Burkean coldness, Dryden
shows 'Royal' manners to be as inconsistent and blasphemous as the
temptation speeches of Achitophel. He thereby rejects heroic idealisations of monarchy on the one hand, and, on the other, the sort of
defensive cynicism which so brilliantly but misleadingly opens the
poem, and he does so because his vision is too realistic for the first and
too serious for the second.

When Absalom makes this final attack on his father at the end of the
third section of the poem, he decisively confuses the issues between
them. This is why the emergence of David in his own person to resolve
the contradictions in the poem is structurally and morally of such
importance. There has been general critical agreement that the fourth
section is damagingly weak, and the note of Royalist triumph on

which the poem ends unconvincing. Such readings, however, tend to ignore the possibility that the David who takes the stage as the climactic figure in the tableau is intended to embody not a triumph but a contradiction, that he is neither the maimed debauchee of whig propaganda, nor the impossibly magnificent Prince of Tory adulation, but at one and the same time a dangerous and unprincipled politician like Achitophel, and the image of God on earth. His position is certainly less comfortingly assimilable than that of Agamemnon in *Troilus and Cressida* or of Sancho in *The Spanish Friar*, both of whom are restored to full royal authority by the deviousness of others. In David's case, the sin of policy is wholly his. The entire strategy of the poem is obscured, and its structural balance destroyed, if this is missed, if both the blasphemy and the truth in the phrase 'Godlike *David*' are not felt with sustained, perplexing, and equal force at the very point when the reader expects a simple, triumphant resolution of the poem's dilemmas.

Absalom's declaration, 'Desire of Greatness is a Godlike Sin' (372), therefore, states a central theme of the whole work. Certainly the juxtaposing of divinity and sinfulness is as persistent as the poem's recurring preoccupation with various manifestations of 'ease' and 'grace'. The death of Barzillai's son, for instance, is called 'Providence's crime', The blasphemous comparison of the begetting of Absalom to the Father's begetting of the Word is matched on the whig side by Absalom's messianic ambitions, and by a grotesque conflation of Shimei (Bethel) with Christ:

> When two or three were gather'd to declaim ⎫
> Against the Monarch of *Jerusalem*,   ⎬
> *Shimei* was always in the midst of them.   ⎭
> And, if they Curst the King when he was by,
> Woud rather Curse, than break good Company.   (601–5)

The bleakly funny portrait of the harsh, uneasy City man becomes as a result a far more acute and serious study than it first appears. We are not only invited, in an essentially aristocratic way, to laugh at the preposterous hypocrisy of the man's manners, we are invited also as Christians to evaluate the significance of his kind of blasphemy.

The fundamental question posed by the poem, in fact, is about which sins are truly godlike; and in order to make this question real, Dryden has to make the sins real too. When David enters the action at the end of the poem, therefore, he does so with a speech that is unmistakably wicked. He proposes to defeat his enemies by using the same perjurers against them as they had used against him during the Popish Plot hysteria:

> By their own arts 'tis righteously decreed,
> Those dire Artificers of Death shall bleed.
> Against themselves their Witnesses will Swear,
> Till Viper-like their Mother Plot they tear:
> And suck for Nutriment that bloody gore
> Which was their Principle of Life before.
> Their *Belial* with their *Belʒebub* will fight;
> Thus on my Foes, my Foes shall do me Right.   (1010–17)

(In fact this process had already begun at the trial of the unfortunate College.) Shocking as this is, it reflects none the less for Dryden a profound theological mystery, the unfaltering determination of God in working out his providential purposes by means of evil as well as virtuous instruments. He sees David's policy, in fact, as an authentic revelation of the divine nature. The King's remarks about the whigs in the lines immediately preceding the ones I have quoted make this very clear:

> Law they require, let Law then shew her Face;
> They coud not be content to look on Grace,
> Her hinder parts, but with a daring Eye
> To tempt the terror of her Front, and Dye.   (1006–9)

David's revenge, in effect, reveals more of the nature of God than was revealed even to Moses on Mount Sinai. Dryden is asserting once again that political success is almost inevitably based on unprincipled nastiness, but instead of concluding from this that history and morality are unrelated, and politics irredeemably secular, he insists that even immoral government can witness to an essentially divine order of things provided it is 'royal'; that is, providentially constituted by time, flexible and patient in its mode of possession, but ultimately sovereign in its exercise of power. The lack of principle in kings, far from justifying the rebelliousness of Achitophel, finally strengthens the case for obedience by witnessing to the sovereignty of God.

This may be hard doctrine, but the resulting impression of intellectual daring which it creates certainly gives the poem's conclusion enough weight to counterbalance the witty audacities of the opening. Many of the complaints made about the conclusion are thereby met; but doubts remain. Johnson argued that the ending is arbitrary, all the difficulties being made to disappear miraculously, as if at the trumpet blast of some 'destined knight'.[21] It has been suggested in reply that the dissolution of the Oxford Parliament was just such a trumpet blast,[22] but this will not do. *Absalom and Achitophel*, after all, is an historical poem, and the next ten years proved its history wrong. The problem did not go away. Subsequent events, indeed, made the poem an interesting historical curiosity, not the impressive and still engaging analysis of politics which one finds in Marvell's *Horatian Ode*. Johnson was also right to see the failure in narrative terms, for even if the poem does not attempt to be a narrative, there is a case for saying that it ought none the less to have done so. By treating the Exclusion crisis as a pageant rather than an action, Dryden sidestepped the vital question of where political power, as opposed to political Right, really lay. He could therefore personalise the whig enemy in the character of Achitophel, even though Shaftesbury's support of Monmouth was probably a desperate gamble; and he could ignore the real threat to the succession which lay not in a single man but in a party, the Williamite Whigs. Thus Buckingham and Bethel are in the poem, but not Sidney, Godolphin and Sunderland.[23] More significant is his failure to explore the nature of party and vested interest in the country generally. This most important of issues is lost in the witty but blurred portrait of the moody murmuring Jews, clustered round Jerusalem rather as the whole issue of Catholic treason is buried in the clever, empty phrase 'From hence began the Plot'. It cannot be denied, of course, that Dryden has a strong sense of the real nature of Restoration political in-fighting, and his brilliant attempt to incorporate this into a Christian vision of man and history explains the strength and complexity of the poem's paradoxical conclusion. He fails, however, to see the problem in historically adequate terms. He is still not sufficiently realistic.

1. *Of Dramatick Poesie*, p. 60.
2. Scott–Saintsbury VII, p. i.
3. Christopher Hill, *The Century of Revolution, 1603–1711* (1969), p. 201.
4. See Kinsley IV, pp. 1901–2.

5. Quoted in Godfrey Davies, 'The Conclusion of Dryden's *Absalom and Achitophel*' in *Essential Articles for the study of John Dryden*, Ed. H. T. Swedenberg, Jr (1966), p. 219.

6. Quoted in Charles E. Ward, *The Life of John Dryden* (1961), p. 163.

7. Quoted in Kinsley IV, p. 1912.

8. See Ward, op. cit., p. 144.

9. Quoted in David Ogg, *England in the Reign of Charles II* (2nd ed., paperback, 1967), p. 616.

10. Quoted from Scott–Saintsbury VI.

11. See Bruce King, *Dryden's Major Plays* (1966), pp. 148–60.

12. King, op. cit., p. 157.

13. See Scott–Saintsbury VII, p. 181 (n).

14. 'Dedication of Plutarch's Lives', Scott–Saintsbury XVII, p. 11.

15. J. H. Plumb, *The Growth of Political Stability in England, 1675–1725* (1969), p. 28.

16. Davies, op. cit., p. 218.

17. Bernard N. Schilling, *Dryden and the Conservative Myth*, p. 209.

18. Scott–Saintsbury VII, p. 215.

19. See Martin Price, *To the Palace of Wisdom* (1964), pp. 56–8.

20. Quoted in Kinsley IV, p. 2039.

21. *Lives*, p. 437.

22. Arthur W. Hoffman, *John Dryden's Imagery* (1962), p. 87.

23. However it is worth pointing out that the Earl of Ossory had been one of William's firmest adherents.

6

THE TORY TRIUMPH:

POEMS 1682–1686

Absalom and Achitophel was published on the ninth of November 1681. Two weeks later a whig jury ordered Shaftesbury to be released, and the mob rejoiced. In late February a medal was struck to celebrate the acquittal and within three weeks Dryden replied. *The Medall* (1682) initiates the most partisan period of his writing life. It has been called 'a good round piece of indignant invective',[1] which it is; but then so are the prologues and epilogues of the next few years, the contributions to *The Second Part of Absalom and Achitophel* (1682), *The Duke of Guise* (1682), *The Vindication of the Duke of Guise* (1683), *The History of the League* (1684), and *Albion and Albanius* (1685). Only the Preface to the *Sylvæ* (1685), the *Life of Plutarch* (1683), and *Religio Laici* (1682) are relatively free of the spirit of reprisal. Ideologically Dryden moved Right. Halifax (Jotham) is tolerantly treated in *Absalom and Achitophel*. In the Epilogues to *Constantine the Great* and *The Duke of Guise*, (1683), however, his party, the Trimmers, are damned with unqualified hatred. Dryden evidently approved of the carefully organised excitements of the period following the Exclusion crisis which made it easier for the Court to set about systematically reshaping the power structure in the country at large. Borough charters were called in in an attempt to undermine the independence of future borough representatives in Parliament and to break the whigs' lucrative hold on local government. Charles also set about somewhat vindictively persecuting his enemies in the courts. Triumphant toryism was an unpleasant spectacle, and Dryden, in his modest way, was triumphant with the rest.

Though the whigs' defeat at Oxford was decisive, this was not immediately obvious. There was probably some objective justification for the intensity of *The Medall*, but even if there were not, its hard fervour and characteristically tight, simple structure would readily persuade us that real dangers threatened, calling for a swift response. Between two attacks on Shaftesbury, Dryden directs his powerful invective against the mob, the City, and the Commons. In the final section, Shaftesbury, the country at large, and the poem itself swell magnificently with the same visionary madness. Heaven, as Shaftesbury sees it, turns out to be an opposition fantasy about life at Charles II's court, whereas his allies, the Dissenters, are intoxicated with the promise of an eternal prayer-meeting in a gloomy mad-house. This gives Dryden an opportunity for one of his deft transitions. He becomes a prophet in his turn, and bitterly prognosticates a future that will repeat the history of the previous forty years. Events were to prove him substantially right. *The Medall*, though a smaller achievement, is more firmly centred in the realities of power than *Absalom and Achitophel* was. The Revolution of 1688, which in a sense it predicts, was to preserve political instability in England for another thirty years. Only when the great whig oligarchs had cozened and betrayed their allies in the shires, and established in their own interest a tight central authority such as Stuarts and Cromwellians alike had been aiming at all along, would the anarchy so savagely described in *The Medall* finally subside. The poem is in fact saved from the sort of lame conclusion which spoils *Absalom and Achitophel* by its acuter appreciation of the historical intractability of the problem of social stability in England:

> Thus inborn Broyles the Factions wou'd ingage, ⎤
> Or Wars of Exil'd Heirs, or Foreign Rage,   ⎬
> Till halting Vengeance overtook our Age: ⎭
> And our wild Labours, wearied into Rest,
> Reclin'd us on a rightfull Monarch's Breast.   (318–22)

The indefinite article in the last line implies uncertainty about Stuart fortunes; nor does it seriously offend against the bleakly ironic spirit of this conclusion if the modern reader recalls that in the event an exhausted nation ended up in the bosom not of a James or a Charles, but a Walpole.

Dryden's other major satire in 1682, his contribution to Tate's *The Second Part of Absalom and Achitophel*, illustrates the range of even his angry verse. *The Medall* is intellectually acute and tonally arrogant.

A reference to the dispute about whether reason or will had primacy in the divine nature (an important distinction as *Religio Laici* makes clear) illustrates the point:

> Almighty Crowd, thou shorten'st all dispute;
> Pow'r is thy Essence; Wit thy Attribute!
> Nor Faith nor Reason make thee at a stay,
> Thou leapst o'r all eternal truths, in thy *Pindarique* way!   (91–4)

Playful as this mixture of metrics and theology may be, the fact that the 'divine' crowd would find it incomprehensible gives the intellectual sharpness to the lines an additional arrogance. *The Second Part of Absalom and Achitophel* involves Dryden in altogether rougher, sweatier sport. His contribution (310–509)—an attack on the whig press—culminates in a hundred lines devoted first to Settle (Doeg), a party hack Dryden had helped to savage in the abusive *Notes and Observations on the Empress of Morocco* (1674), and the old enemy Shadwell (Og). Dryden had recently been the object of a particularly nasty press campaign himself, involving his relations with an actress, his friendship with Howard, and the honour of his wife. (The mud sticks still to poor Lady Elizabeth.) Shadwell had played his cumbersome part, also, in *The Medal of John Bayes*. Dryden's reply is both coarse and dignified. He crushes his enemies under a great weight of insult without ever compromising the respect due to his craft and so to himself. He manages to make short, Germanic nouns and adjectives sound gross and so appropriate to his enemies, while the mildest Latin word, the smallest active English verb, or the most light-weight polysyllable becomes naturally and spontaneously expressive of his own energy and spaciousness of mind:

> To make quick way I'll Leap o'er heavy blocks,
> Shun rotten *U_{zz}a* as I wou'd the Pox;
> And hasten *Og* and *Doeg* to rehearse,
> Two fools that Crutch their Feeble sense on Verse;
> Who by my Muse, to all succeeding times,
> Shall live in spight of their own Dogrell Rhimes.   (406–11)

'I'll Leap', 'my Muse', and 'succeeding times' are Dryden's; 'fools', 'Crutch', even 'spight', are Og's and Doeg's. Similarly Doeg can be

compared to a dog with whom a woman has committed buggery, and
Og to

> A Monstrous mass of foul corrupted matter,
> As all the Devils had spew'd to make the batter.   (464–5)

yet Dryden himself remains verbally immaculate.

Between *The Medall* and *The Second Part of Absalom and Achitophel*
he and Lee completed *The Duke of Guise* which had been
started as early as 1660. A scene written at that time appeared to refer
to Monmouth's defiant return from exile in 1679, and as a result the
play was banned in July, though the real reason for the ban was
probably uncertainty at Court about how strong the anti-whig
campaign should be.[2] By September, however, there were tory Sheriffs
in London and the play was licensed and acted in December. It was
immediately attacked, and Dryden produced his *Vindication* in
reply, a work far more interesting than the play, which is intellectually
simplistic, psychologically crude, and metrically dead. As controversy,
the *Vindication* is vigorous and amusing. It also gives a clear account of
Dryden's political principles and his ideas on the relation of politics to
literature. It was his constant practice, he maintains, not to present
living people in his plays, but to develop his design to 'discover the
original and root of the practices and principles'[3] of his political
opponents.

By the end of the year his extreme fervour in the tory cause may have
been beginning to wane. In 1684 he did publish a translation of
Maimbourg's *History of the League*, but only because the King
insisted. However, a month before publication an alleged Protestant
conspiracy, the 'Rye House Plot' was discovered and the fierce old
toryism flared again. In the Dedication of the *History*, he warns the
King that 'pardon's are grown dangerous to your safety, and conse-
quently to the welfare of your loyal subjects'.[4] He remained patholog-
ically sensitive to the dangers of faction.

This is evident in his rather nasty pageant-opera *Albion and Albanius*,
intended originally to celebrate Charles' final triumph over his
enemies, but altered to take account of his sudden death. Staging it
must have been fun: the figure of Proteus changes into a lion, a
crocodile, and a dragon on stage. The concluding tableau makes great
play with Shaftesbury's ugly medical condition; but this is not
surprising in a work in which the satire never rises above the level of

Democracy's orders for the disarming of Augusta: 'Pull down her gates, expose her bare' (I,i, p. 251),[5] the allusion being to the Rump's orders to Monck in February 1660 for the reduction of London. The lyrical passages are pleasing, however, as are those in *King Arthur*, an opera meant to be performed with *Albion and Albanius*, but only staged in 1691 in a castrated version, all political references having been excised, so as 'not to offend the present times'.[6] The absence of ideas in this piece makes it particularly vacuous. The songs are metrically and thematically more robust, however—the 'Harvest Home' chorus is deservedly well known. Otherwise *King Arthur* is only of interest in showing Spenser's influence on Dryden, notably in Arthur's temptation by naked nymphs, and the figure of the false Emmeline. Both pieces also indicate that political victories coarsened Dryden's thinking and that thought was the essence of his art.

King Arthur, Dryden wrote in 1691, 'was the last piece of service'[7] he performed for Charles II. In fact the last thing Dryden did for Charles was to write a long 'Funeral-Pindarique' on his death, the *Threnodia Augustalis* (1685), a title Johnson felt was 'neither authorised nor analogical'.[8] There is no hiding the poem's intellectual sluggishness. Johnson was over-scrupulous in objecting in principle to mixing 'heathen fables' with biblical imagery, but he was right in practice to condemn the description of prayers for the dying King elbowing their way incontinently into the courts of Heaven:

> So great a Throng not Heav'n it self cou'd bar;
> 'Twas almost born by force as in the Giants war.
> The Pray'rs, at least, for his reprive were heard;
> His Death, like *Hezekiah*'s was deferr'd.   (103–6)

Three related factors explain the failure. It was Dryden's first original pindaric ode; it called for the treatment of people rather than 'practices and principles'; and it provided few opportunities for ironic counter-pointing. The simplicities of heroic convention are therefore unmodified. Of James, Dryden writes:

> No Wife, nor Brother, such a Grief cou'd know,
>   Nor any name but friend.   (76–7)

For over a decade he had been cleverly putting the validity of just such distinctions to the test. Only occasionally a line or two resists the torpor. Of the poets financially dependant on royal patronage we read:

> Yet somewhat to their share he threw;
> Fed from his hand, they sung and flew,
> Like Birds of Paradise, that liv'd on Morning dew.
> Oh never let their Lays his Name forget!
> The Pension of a Prince's praise is great.   (378–82)

The blend of sincerity and irony is subtle, affectionate and finally loyal, but insufficient for any sustained complexity.

It is a relief to turn back to 1682 and *Religio Laici*, a poem mercifully free from the pressures of Exclusionist controversy and tory triumphalism. To begin at the Preface, however, is to drop into the middle of all the old disputes, mixed up with some obviously amateur theology. In the seventeenth century this was inevitable. Religion was a political matter, the consideration of which, Halifax wrote in *The Character of a Trimmer*:

is so twisted with that of Government, that it is never to be separated, and tho the Foundations of it are to be Eternal and Unchangeable, yet the Terms and Circumstances of Discipline, are to be suited to the several Climates and Constitutions, so that they may keep men in a willing Acquiescence unto them without discomposing the World by nice disputes.[9]

This is exactly Dryden's view in *Religio Laici*. In the Preface 'Acquiescence' is his co-ordinating theme. He begins by admitting his 'own weakness and want of Learning';[10] he then mentions his more dangerous opinions, but only to 'submit them with all reverence to my Mother Church'. Next he takes up one of the poem's main concerns, deism, and argues carefully towards an idea of intellectual humility: 'Let us be content, at last,' he says, 'to know God, by his own Methods.'[11] Finally he turns to Catholics and Dissenters. He does not attempt to make the former change their beliefs, but he does demand their unconditional submission to English political institutions. He then devotes nearly a third of the essay to an account of the political disruptiveness of Calvinism, ending with a demand for the submission of the Dissenters to the Established Protestant Church of England: 'We shall be glad to think them true Englishmen,' he says, 'when they obey the King, and true Protestants when they conform to the Church discipline'.[12] On the strength of this Preface it may be excessive to argue that publishing *Religio Laici* 'was a political act';[13] but it is clearly legitimate to analyse the relationship between its avowed purpose of securing the political ascendancy of the Established Church and the logic of the poem.

From the attack on deism with which it opens, an interesting 'political' argument certainly emerges. Dryden rejects theory as the sole or overriding criterion in religious disputes, just as in his political writings he rejects a purely rational approach to constitutional problems. The constitution is an historical inheritance, and religion is a divine gift. There are no more grounds for replacing the Church of England with the rationalist 'Church Catholic' of Lord Herbert of Cherbury than for changing the English constitution in accordance with theoretical ideas of goverment. (Lord Herbert's five 'Catholic Principles', with the important exception of the third, on worship, are outlined in the poem's second paragraph (11 42–61).) This does not mean, however, that the Church is institutionally independent of the State. Dryden is too good an Erastian for that. He is also careful to vest all teaching authority in the Bible rather than the Church as such, insisting (as Anglicans had throughout the century) that the important truths of Christianity were so clearly stated in scripture that authoritative ecclesiastical interpretation was unnecessary. The only area of Church authority was thus Halifax's 'Terms and Circumstances of discipline', local and accidental matters, of peripheral importance theologically. The argument develops so casually and fluently that one hardly notices the extent to which a loyal defence of Anglicanism has in effect minimised the Church of England's authority. This very tactic, however, strengthens Anglican claims in another direction. Since the tests of orthodoxy are few, general, and unspecific, there are no grounds in conscience to justify a Protestant's failing to conform.

Religio Laici, then, supports yet carefully limits the Church's power. Discourse (or Reason) and, in its various forms, Inspiration, are subjected to a similar logic. Thus Reason without Revelation is said to lead, not to the abstract and beautiful consensus proposed by the Deists, but to the bewildering confusions of pagan philosophy. To stimulate discourse is to precipitate social disorder. On the other hand, the equally disruptive claims of inspiration have to be kept in check. Catholic doctrines about infallibility, and the Calvinist emphasis on the inspirations of the Spirit are at least as socially disruptive as rational discourse. Scripture, Tradition, and Grace may be necessary as checks on the claims of reason, but they are also a useful check on each other. A balance has to be struck, in effect, between the Church as an institution, the Bible as an inspiration, and reason and Grace as mutually supporting divine gifts. Dryden moves through these theological contrasts with the same skill and grace he showed in handling the carefully arranged critical antitheses of the Preface to *An Evening's Love*.

The sort of balanced view which results is not so much a product of intellectual analysis as of wise emotional synthesis. Thus while Dryden takes an impeccably Thomist, and therefore intellectually precise view of the place of Reason in the economy of salvation—human intelligence can perceive that God exists, but not Who or What He is—the poem nevertheless succeeds in persuading us that his position is not primarily a philosophical one. It is reasonable in a purely wordly sense to set limits on reason—hence the claim in the Preface that Dryden is 'naturally inclin'd to Scepticism in Philosophy'.[14] Actually he was also a sceptic in a more technical sense. A Pyrrhonistic distrust of reason is one of the firmer positions taken in the poem, though this does not mean of course that he did not simultaneously recognise that there were at least some 'rational inducements for accepting Christianity'.[15] He was above all concerned, however, to balance the two positions by means of the logic, common sense, and faith which his layman embodies.

Exactly the same balance is struck in his handling of scripture. Of the Bible he writes,

> It *speaks* it *Self*, and what it does contain,
> In all things *needfull* to be *known*, is *plain*.   (368–9)

He thus manages to make the Word of God sound like a good piece of Royal Society prose, and this in spite of his lengthy treatment of Père Simon's scholarly exposure of all surviving versions of the Old Testament as textually corrupt. He uses the contradiction, however, to enrich the tonal as well as the intellectual balance of his poem. It is a source of urbane satisfaction to him that such an unworldly and exact exercise of Reason as Simon's—'The crabbed Toil of many thoughtfull years' (235)—should produce in the end so conveniently negative a result. Reason discovers human weakness and confusion even in the text of scripture, just as scripture exposes the deficiencies of Reason. It would be unscriptural, therefore, and unreasonable, to imagine that the important truths contained in the Bible were anything other than few and obvious. Disputes on exegetical detail are for minds that 'make *Algebra* a Sport', not for plain Englishmen.

The whole poem seems determined to replace religious certainty with self-respect in just this way. Dryden's programme is to do without infallibility, 'systematically disarming the Deist's trust in the absolute rightness of reason, the Catholic's trust in the Church . . . and the Dissenter's trust in . . . Scripture'.[16] It does not matter, therefore, if he mis-states his opponents' position. He is wrong, for instance, in his account of Catholic teaching on Tradition, and probably knew he was, since the 'judicious and learned Friend' of the Preface,[17] Tillotson, had put the true position in his *Rule of Faith* (1666).[18] More noticeably, he is guilty of 'a tactic of juggling with words'[19] when he glosses 'infallibility' as 'omniscience'. The effect, however, is not one of dishonesty. Dryden grossly caricatures Catholic doctrine because he does not need to state it accurately to dispose of it. In the brilliant couplet,

> More Safe, and much more modest 'tis to say
> *God wou'd not leave Mankind without a way* . . .   (295–6)

he simply exposes reliance on infallibility as humanly unsound and makes further technical discourse unnecessary. Similarly, he dismisses Deism, Catholicism, and Dissent in turn as tainted with the spirit of Commerce: The lines

> Ah! at how cheap a rate the *Rich* might sin!   (90)
> She parcel'd out the Bible by *retail* . . .   (377)

and

> And sav'd himself as cheap as e'er he cou'd . . .   (397)

establish far more impressive common ground between theological truth and social values than a thin array of logical connections and analogical correspondences ever could. Dryden's commitment to a supple, manly, and uninhibited humanism is the fundamental reality to which both his religion and his politics apparently submit. The 'private judgement' in the last but one paragraph of the poem is not that of a tame conformist, but of an adult intelligence. The layman of the title brings to theological discussion a modest but penetrating urbanity. The influence of Horace's *Epistles*, acknowledged in the Preface, is highly appropriate for this reason, and Scott rather misses the point when he says of the passage beginning, 'Shall I speak plain' (316), that the lines seem 'to be a plain admission, that the author was involved in a question from which he saw no very decided mode of extricating himself'.[20] One of the most telling characteristics of the passage is the (rather misleading) impression it gives that this is just the sort of question from which a plain man doesn't need to be extricated. If Dryden submits to the Church without having solved every problem in his own mind, that is not to be taken as evidence of intellectual dishonesty or slavish superstition. He remains a free and civilised man.

This is also, however, potentially the poem's weakness. By placing reason, revelation, and the Church in so intellectually elegant and frankly human a context, Dryden makes his layman of the title grow more and more and his religion less and less. *Religio Laici* may begin with an account of the 'wild Maze' in which the pagan philosophers ended 'their vain Endeavours', but later we are told,

> Then those who follow'd *Reasons* Dictates right;
> Liv'd up, and lifted high their *Natural Light*;
> With *Socrates* may see their Maker's Face,
> While Thousand *Rubrick-Martyrs* want a place.   (208–11)

In thus contending that 'virtuous heathens might be saved', Dryden was clearly flirting with Arminianism,[21] though it must be borne in mind that the originally Catholic doctrine of universal atonement was developed independently in the Church of England and was continually challenged by the Calvinists in the Church who conformed in 1662.[22] The important question, however, is not Dryden's orthodoxy in accepting this particular doctrine, but why he so emphasises it. It is repeated over and over again—in the Preface, in 'The Objection of the Deist', in Dryden's reply to the Deist, and (slightly modified) in the famous passage which Scott found so confused. The poem's consistent programme of minimising both the Church's teaching authority, and the capacity of man to know religious truth, has apparently destroyed altogether the case for a Christian church, substituting the ideals of pagan virtue and civil obedience instead.

In fact, the reverse is the case. Dryden reiterates this apparently quasi-deistical position in order to enforce a profoundly supernaturalist view of Christianity. The most important lines in the poem are these:

> But if there be a *Pow'r* too *Just*, and *strong*
> To wink at *Crimes*, and bear unpunish'd *Wrong*;
> Look humbly upward, see his Will disclose:
> The *Forfeit* first, and then the *Fine* impose:
> A *Mulct thy* Poverty cou'd never pay
> Had not *Eternal Wisedom* found the way:
> And with Cœlestial Wealth supply'd thy Store:
> *His Justice* makes the *Fine, his Mercy* quits the *Score.*
> See God descending in thy Humane Frame;
> Th' *offended,* suff'ring in th' *Offenders* Name:
> All thy Misdeeds to him imputed see,
> And all his Righteousness devolv'd on thee.   (99–110)

The last four lines of this 'Plain and Natural, and yet Majestick'[23] passage form a kerygmatic statement of the doctrine of the Atonement which will bear comparison, for rigour, clarity, and beauty, with the hymns of Thomas Aquinas. Simply as an argument in the debate, the paragraph marshals all the difficulties in Dryden's case and resolves them with ease. It is 'minimalist' exactly as his case against the Dissenters requires. It is doctrinally precise, yet far more open to both 'Calvinist' and 'Catholic' theories of grace than most Anglican formulations. It supports the claims of Christianity against the arguments of the Deist by demonstrating that it was necessary for the God-man Jesus to intervene in history; but it makes all other doctrines, apart from those of the Incarnation and the Atonement, matters of secondary importance, and so confirms the distinctively Anglican claim that Christian doctrine is a plain, simple matter.

But Dryden is not just scoring in a debate. The lines may be intellectually neat, but they are also theologically strong. They minimise man and his faculties and institutions, certainly, but they are not anti-human, and they maximise the mercy and justice of God. Dryden grants man the capacity to know and obey the moral law, to know and act on the truths of natural religion, to know and respond to the Word of God in scripture, but he insists that the knowledge and the response are of secondary importance. The chief fact is not what men believe they know, but what God in his Own Person has done. God is Truth; and 'Truth by its own sinews will prevail' (349). The passage in which this last line occurs is remarkable because it allows even Christians who are ignorant of basic doctrine to be saved. It alleges in fact that there are no 'saving doctrines' in Christianity at all, but a doctrine of salvation instead. Thus,

> . . . many have been sav'd, and many may,
> Who never heard this Question brought in play. (320–1)

the 'Question' being none other than the absolutely central one of the divinity of Christ. (Scott was wrong, therefore, in finding this passage intellectually confused, though for its own excellent reasons it may give that impression.) The specific problem under discussion is the value of Tradition as a source of religious truth. Dryden points out that the two heresiarchs who most notoriously minimised the active presence of God in human affairs, Arius, who questioned Christ's divinity, and Pelagius, who taught that man could be saved by works alone, both relied on Tradition. Truth, on the other hand, has an effectiveness that human sin and error cannot touch. *Religio Laici* has seemed to verge on Pelagianism more than once, but only to demonstrate the insignificance even of orthodoxy when confronted with the fact of God's condescending love.

In thus emphasising divine mercy over human faith, Dryden is not making a religious statement only. Human values are as crucially involved in the question as religious dogmas. The Deist's strongest argument, for instance, strong enough in Dryden's view 'To startle Reason, stagger frail Belief' (185), is that the Christian God's apparent partiality offends against human notions of justice. This would not startle Calvinist belief, of course, since the doctrine of predestination predicates a 'voluntarist' theory of God, which places the divine essence in God's Will, Reason and Justice being merely what he chooses they shall be. Dryden's rejection of this absolutist concept of God almost certainly derives from his consistent opposition to Hobbist concepts of man. Hobbes' state, his 'Leviathan or Mortal God', is said to be divine precisely because of its authoritarian basis. Dryden, on the contrary, holds that a polity is godlike to the degree that its prince respects his own laws, as God respects his own rationality, and exercises also the godlike quality of mercy. God is thus in essence rational love, with mercy, justice, and power as His attributes.

But if Dryden does take this Thomist view of the divine nature simply because Voluntarism offends his sense of human dignity, his vision of God resolves itself into the rationalisation of his desire for a civilised society. His theology must thereby lose a great deal of its integrity. It was one thing for Benjamin Whichcote to assert of the truths of scripture that 'God made Man to them, and wrought his Law upon Men's Hearts; and as it were, interwove it into the Principles of our Reason'.[24] It is another to argue from men's hearts what God's ought to be. Religion is authentic only if it is autonomous and primary; and the only way it can demonstrate its autonomy is by thwarting human desire. Dryden explicitly acknowledges this:

> This *onely* Doctrine does our *Lusts* oppose:
> Unfed by Natures Soil, in which it grows;
> Cross to our Interests, curbing Sense, and Sin;
> Oppress'd without, and undermin'd within,
> It thrives through pain; its own Tormentours tires;
> And with a stubborn patience still aspires.   (158–63)

It is not enough of course just to say this. Nor is it a very impressive sign of religion's autonomy if the only interests it opposes are those of some legendary pagan Babylon. To be really persuasive religion must be 'Cross to' the interests of a man of the world in 1682. The layman's faith must somehow oppose the layman's humanism.

The natural civilised man of the poem is the embodiment of rationality. His are the virtues of unenthusiastic Discourse, of simple, plain prose. The significance of the epigraph in this connection has frequently been noted.[25] It reveals in Dryden something of the distrust of rhetoric which was felt by rationalist theologians and scientists alike in the Restoration period. In the text of the poem, therefore, Dryden blames 'Wit and Eloquence' (373) for distortions in scriptural interpretation. But precisely this stance of worldly wisdom is implicitly undermined when elsewhere Eloquence is identified with the divine Word, the Son of God Himself:

> Then for the *Style*; *Majestick* and *Divine*,
> It speaks no less than God in every Line:
> *Commanding words*; whose *Force* is still the same
> As the first *Fiat* that produc'd our Frame.   (152–5)

There is thus an opposition in the poem between religious and secular values which is registered in its stylistic unevenness. The layman's rationality, plain speaking, and commonsense are inconsistent with the revelation, grace and eloquence of Christianity, and each is represented by divergent and inconsistent stylistic impulses. The struggle for primacy between prose and poetry in the poem is thus an exact record of the religion's struggle for autonomy and Dryden's for integrity.

The obvious strategy for securing the victory of faith and eloquence, and for producing a well-structured poem, would have been to work steadily *towards* a vision of transcendentally autonomous and splendid religious truth, to start, as I have done in analysing the poem, from the commonsense, prosaic assumption that '*Common quiet* is *Mankind's concern*' (450) and, having allowed Discourse to carry the poem as far as it could, to step eloquently and boldly beyond it in a decisive celebration of religious mystery. This would be to end where the poem now begins. Even as it stands, the final paragraph (without the last couplet) could logically and emotionally serve as a perfectly proper introduction to a conclusion made out of the first eleven lines of the poem. But this would have been a specious strategy. Dryden after all is primarily a poet, with a natural, this-worldly appetite for gracious rhetoric. To gratify this appetite, at the expense of rationalistic good sense, in an eloquent proclamation of doctrines which reason was not permitted to dispute, would merely have confirmed the dependence of his religious ideas on his human aspirations.

The poem's tonal strategy, therefore, is exactly the reverse of this. It opens with eleven perfect lines, as noble and beautiful as any religious verse in English. The analogy is, admittedly, derivative—it was used by both Donne and the Cambridge Platonists—but its currency only makes its resonances richer, and its metrical shaping by Dryden brings it to incontestable perfection. It dominates the poem. As the argument develops, however, first at a level of high dignity, then after line 110 in increasingly informal, patronising and ultimately acrimonious ways, the memory of the opening slowly creates a feeling of dissatisfaction at Dryden's failure to be eloquently religious, a feeling which the jibing pettiness of the final couplet rudely confirms. Another way of interpreting these developments, however, is to see them as a careful refusal on Dryden's part to create poetic conditions for an unconditional ideological triumph. He chooses instead to end his poem with its opposing tendencies in tense equilibrium.

The last six lines deserve close attention. They show us the poet dropping his public manner and, almost in an aside, as he turns away from his audience, speaking to and for himself. The result is a private, irrelevant jibe at Sternhold and Shadwell. In dismissing them, however, Dryden simultaneously dismisses 'Discourse' also, and so ironically concedes the justice of the reader's desire for eloquence and mystery. With a kind of arrogant self-effacement he implicitly acknowledges the triviality in religious terms of his own thinking on the subject, and the inappropriateness of a man such as himself giving expression to lofty religious experience. (The derivative nature of the sun and moon image thereby gains additional point.) The worldly, vindictive conclusion is thus in its way an exercise in humility, precisely in its unpolished ruggedness. The style of the poem as a whole, after all, is manifestly the result of a free decision on Dryden's part—the first paragraphs show how different it might have been—but the choice is a just one: morally if not aesthetically it would have been inappropriate for a middle-aged worldly sceptic to have been, in the end, enthusiastic. Yet since both religion and his own delight in noble verse still urgently demand that he should nevertheless be eloquent about his faith, his failure to respond is sacrificial as well as irreligious. Thus in a thoroughly idiosyncratic way, yet one wholly consistent with the poem's style and method, Dryden's religion finally proves its autonomy. It fulfils the essential condition:

> Cross to [his] *Interests*, curbing Sense, and Sin;
> Oppress'd without, and undermin'd within,
> It thrives through pain; its own Tormentour tires;
> And with a stubborn patience still aspires.   (160–3)

There is thus a full and completely honest record in *Religio Laici* of the tensions between worldliness and grace in both the Anglican *via media* and Dryden's own style of life and art. It is this which makes it in every sense a great confessional poem.

1. Howard Erskine-Hill, 'John Dryden: the Poet and Critic', *Dryden to Johnson*, Ed. R. Lonsdale (1971), p. 41.
2. See Charles E. Ward, *The Life of John Dryden* (1961), p. 184.
3. Scott–Saintsbury VII, p. 151.
4. ibid. XVII, p. 83.
5. Quoted from Scott–Saintsbury VII.
6. *King Arthur*, Dedication, Scott–Saintsbury VII, p. 135.
7. ibid., p. 129.
8. *Lives*, p. 438.
9. *The Complete Works of George Savile, First Marquess of Halifax*, Ed. Walter Raleigh (1912), p. 67.
10. Kinsley I, p. 302.
11. ibid., p. 304.
12. ibid., p. 310.

13. Edward N. Hooker, 'Dryden and the Atoms of Epicurus' in H. T. Swedenberg, Jr (Ed.), *Essential Articles for the study of John Dryden* (1966), p. 232.

14. Kinsley I, p. 302.

15. As Harth maintains. See *Contexts of Dryden's Thought* (1968), p. 101. Harth's definition of 'fideism' is so strict that only the most radically antiintellectual enthusiast could claim to be a fideist.

16. Martin Price, *To the Palace of Wisdom* (1964), p. 64.

17. Kinsley I, p. 303.

18. Phillip Harth, *Contexts of Dryden's Thought* (1968), pp. 202–4.

19. ibid., p. 209.

20. Scott–Saintsbury I, p. 260.

21. Thomas H. Fujimura, 'Dryden's *Religio Laici*: An Anglican Poem', *PMLA* LXXVI, p. 216.

22. See Harth, op. cit., pp. 151–6.

23. The Preface, Kinsley I, p. 311.

24. Quoted in Sanford Budick, *Dryden and The Abyss of Light. A Study of 'Religio Laici' and 'The Hind and the Panther'* (1970), p. 119.

25. See Budick, op. cit., p. 161n.

7

A CATHOLIC REIGN:
POEMS 1685–1688

Charles II's death made a long reign by his Catholic brother a disturbing possibility and for all the ease of James II's accession and his quick successes with the Commons and against Monmouth, a sense of uncertainty remained. Early in 1686 Dryden became a Catholic. It was a decision which completed his development as a poet, and it did so, paradoxically, because in political terms it was foolhardy. The King might be a Catholic, but his co-religionists were few, vulnerable, and unpopular. Until James' accession they had not even a bishop. The Test Acts kept them out of public life, and the Penal Laws, though rarely enforced, threatened the private practice of their religion. No one doubted the ultimate accession of William and Mary who publicly supported the Test, for all their approval of toleration in principle; and there were therefore few self-interested converts to Catholicism during James' reign. It is the very unpopularity of Dryden's move, however, which is important. It radically altered his relations with English society.

In the first place it made him, if anything, more remote from the Court. A letter to Etherege while he was working on *The Hind and the Panther* (1687) echoes the general Catholic dissatisfaction with James' conduct of affairs. Dryden would have preferred a king with more of his predecessor's 'noble idleness'.[1] As official propagandist he did engage Edward Stillingfleet in a controversy over papers left by Charles and James' first wife on their conversion to Catholicism. He also undertook, but did not complete, a translation of Varillas' *History of Revolutions in Europe*, and published for the Queen a translation of a biography of St Francis Xavier. But he wrote virtually no poetry for the King. Only the birth of James' son less than three weeks before the famous trial of the seven bishops stirred him to do his duty as laureate. The other works of these three and a half years are both remote from the Court, and marked by the rich detachment of his final creative period, a detachment with which his new social position as a Catholic had much to do.

Following the *Threnodia* Dryden completed two important poems in pindarics, besides an unfinished ode on the marriage of Anastasia Stafford, whose father had been executed in the anti-Catholic hysteria of 1680. The latter is at least evidence of his new willingness to look beyond the Court and the theatre for events on which to build grand ceremonial affirmations. The advantages of this broader social base are especially marked in *To the Pious Memory Of . . . Mrs. Anne Killigrew* (1686) which gains immeasurably from faint but distinct allusions to a family life more human and accessible than the inert brotherhood and friendship of *Threnodia Augustalis*. Of course there is a certain incongruity between a family as ordinary as the Killigrews and the poem's pompous baroque manner which sweeps a luxurious blend of classical and Christian allusion down the fervent metrical current of the pindaric. But the disparity makes space for irony, and so for the poet himself to act as a co-ordinating and judicious presence in the poem.

As a result it is less dependent on the 'success' of its allusions than the *Threnodia* was. The political metaphor in Stanza VI, by which Anne Killigrew the poetess is depicted as conquering the adjacent kingdom of painting, is based on Louis XIV's 'acts of reunion'; in Stanza VII the contrasting portrait of James represents an English ideal of royalty. The two stanzas accordingly treat Anne Killigrew's paintings as exemplifying first the French, then the English styles.[2] Our pleasure in the poem, however, does not depend on our picking up these or more general royalist allusions. Its irony operates independently of minor details. Our sense of Anne Killigrew, for instance, whether as an ordinary, if gifted, girl, or as the Idea of a Young Poetess, makes faintly ludicrous the lines

> One would have thought, she should have been content
> To manage well that Mighty Government . . .   (89–90)

and we do not need to register a reaction to Louis XIV or divine right to feel this. But though there is something remarkably, almost dangerously, frank about the ironic element in the poem, its effects are by no means unsubtle. In such lines as

> Her Pencil drew, what e're her Soul design'd.
> And oft the happy Draught surpass'd the Image in her Mind.
>
> (106–7)

the ambiguity of a professional's feelings towards an amateur may be daringly obvious, but far from reflecting on Anne Killigrew personally, Dryden's judiciousness and honesty in effect prevent her from being reduced to a platonised idea of genius. A line like 'All bow'd beneath her Government' (104), for instance, suggests something of Pope's delighted tolerance of Belinda in *The Rape of the Lock*. These constant reminders of ordinariness in the midst of so much splendour unobtrusively enrich even the poem's more avowedly solemn passages, notably the famous attack in Stanza IV on stage obscenity. The last line of this stanza—'Her Wit was more than Man, her Innocence a Child!' (70)—reminds us yet again of Anne's real standing as an artist. It does not of course weaken the fierce indignation at obscenity in the main body of the Stanza (after the extraordinary force of 'T' increase the steaming ordures of the stage' [65] it could hardly do so); but it does strengthen our sense of the issues involved in moral condemnations of art. Professional standards have of course to be asserted: an adolescent girl's prudishness cannot be allowed unqualified control over what poetry and painting may depict. But neither can art afford to neglect the ordinary susceptibilities of naive, virtuous and gentle people. The main emphasis of the poem is the reverse of this. The mild littleness of common life is drowned in images of stars, spheres, and seraphims. The fact, however, that this is affectionately qualified by ironic recognitions of prosaic domestic reality, emancipates our appreciation of the grandeur from the burdens of florid dogma and impossible psychology. The grace, massiveness and force of the technial achievement are, as a result, much more available and satisfying.

A Song for St Cecilia's Day, 1687 lacks the unity which Dryden's best poems achieve when ironic manipulations of the conventions control and unify the verse. He is personally 'absent' from the poem because it nowhere establishes intelligent relations with an existing world. But it has none of the dogma implicit in *Threnodia Augustalis* either. The result is a technically clever exercise in decorative verse, more satisfying in parts than as a whole. The critics disagree about whether the central stanzas are 'more effective ... on paper than when set',[3] or, on the contrary, are 'neatly suited to ... varied homophonic treatment'.[4] Doubts have also been expressed about the suitability of the opening and closing choruses for choral treatment, but at least they read superbly. The intermediate stanzas are more awkward, though when read aloud the sense of disastrous metrical clashes being successfully tamed can be satisfying at least to the reader. The passages on brass, percussion, wind and strings are in no particular order, but the transition through Stanzas VI and VII to the 'Grand Chorus' is clever, thematically and metrically. As a whole the poem may be weak, but it is technically adroit in its separate parts.

The allusions and conceits in *Britannia Rediviva* (1688), Dryden's poem on the birth of the Prince of Wales, are so dense and abstruse (twenty-seven are explained in footnotes) that he might almost be returning to the idiom of *Upon the Death of Lord Hastings* (1649). There is no sense of simple yet subtly qualified ideas surging down the page in expertly shaped metrical patterns. But though the poem's fertility is hectic, it records real and powerful tensions between immediate triumph and impending disaster. For instance, the lines

> Nor yet conclude all fiery *Trials* past,
> For Heav'n will exercise us to the last;
> Sometimes will check us in our full carreer,
> With doubtful blessings, and with mingled fear ... (267–70)

may refer to the impending trial of the seven bishops; they certainly record the boiling excitement of the times, of which the undiscriminating impetus of the poem—itself in full career—is manifestly a part. *Britannia Rediviva* ends on a tough note with a paragraph deriving from Plutarch's *Life of Aristides*; it emphasises James' love of justice, even though, as one of Dryden's editors has rightly pointed out, mercy was his own 'Darling Attribute'.[5] Very probably he realised that his hopes for the reign had suffered a fatal reverse. The poem is strained, therefore, not because of its principles but because of its frantic optimism. It is completely lacking in the political insight of *The Hind and the Panther* (1687).

Until recently it would have been thought nonsense to claim that *The Hind and the Panther* was 'realistic'. Superficially it is a ludicrous exercise in allegory. In the first part we are introduced to a semi-

mythical Forest, Caledon (or England) and the poem's two protagonists, the Catholic Hind and the Anglican Panther. There are a number
of other beasts, representing various Protestant sects, of whom the
most important are the Fox, representing the Socinians (who denied the
Divinity of Christ) and the Presbyterian Wolf. The beasts are united
in their hostility towards the Hind until the Lyon (James II) enforces
her right to take her turn at the drinking pool. In the second part she
and the Panther discuss their differences on the Eucharist and Church
authority, and in the third part, they spend the night in the Hind's
cottage arguing about the Lyon's efforts to secure the repeal of the
Test Acts, something the Panther bad-temperedly resists. The
conversation begins to get acrimonious, and each tells a threatening
fable to the other. The poem ends, however, with a triumphant
reference to the Declaration of Indulgence, issued when Dryden was
finishing the third part, by which the King by-passed the Anglican
Commons and on the strength of his royal prerogative alone granted
full civic rights to Dissenters and Catholics alike.

The awkwardness of this scheme is increased by Dryden's tendency
to present his beasts facetiously as leisured ladies. Attributing human
personalities to animals may have appealed to his comic sense, but
when he gives exceptional prominence to a line like 'The Lady of the
spotted-muff began' by placing it right at the end of the first part, he
seems hopelessly to confuse the three ill-assorted elements in his
scheme, churches, beasts, and *grandes dames*. When the Hind declares
herself to be the infallible church of Christ the effect of artistic
ineptitude is even grosser:

> The Dame, who saw her fainting foe retir'd,
> With force renew'd to victory aspir'd;
> (And looking upward to her kindred sky,⎫
> As once our Saviour own'd his Deity,⎬
> Pronounc'd his words—*she whom ye seek am I.*⎭
> Nor less amaz'd this voice the *Panther* heard,
> Than were those *Jews* to hear a god declar'd.
> Then thus the matron modestly renew'd.   (II,394–401)

There is no possible defence for this. But since the dynamic of Dryden's
art from the early seventies onwards had been to create tensions by
abusing decorum, failures such as this, instead of providing grounds
for dismissing the poem as symptomatic of 'aesthetic insanity',[6]

point rather to its method of operation. It is consciously inconsistent. Its meanings lie in the risks it takes and the insecurities they create.

It is necessary first, however, to consider the actual issues of principle with which it deals, and the vision of God, man, and society which they assume. The theological discussion centres on the Catholic doctrine of the Real Presence, but this does not make Dryden's general position very different from that of *Religio Laici*. Catholic teaching on the Eucharist, after all, is simply an extension of the doctrine of the Incarnation which the earlier poem had emphasised, and both doctrines underline the insufficiency of human reason in grappling with religious truth. It thus forms as natural a centre to Dryden's revolt against the tyranny of abstract reasoning as it does to his new theology. It is not surprising, therefore, that just as *Religio Laici* opens with an attack on deistical rationalism, so *The Hind and the Panther* begins with an attack on the equally rationalist Socinians. Both poems accept but limit the role of reason: 'Let reason then at Her own quarry fly' (I,104) is how the later poem points to the constitutionally subordinate function of the understanding in a cosmos made richer by the mysteries of God-in-Trinity, God-made-Man, and God substantially present in what is apparently bread and wine, than that open to sense and logic on their own. Theologically important as these doctrines are, therefore, they also confirm man's need to escape from the psychological shallows of rationalism:

> If then our faith we for our guide admit,
> Vain is the farther search of humane wit. . . .
> Why chuse we then like *Bilanders* to creep ⎤
> Along the coast, and land in view to keep,   ⎬
> When safely we may launch into the deep? ⎦
> In the same vessel which our Saviour bore   ⎤
> Himself the Pilot, let us leave the shoar,   ⎬
> And with a better guide a better world explore. ⎦
>
> (I,122–3; 128–33)

This freedom—based on a far greater autonomy than he had hitherto been prepared to grant to religion—is what Dryden now believes the Anglican Church is wholly deficient in.

His real objection to the Church of England is thus that she is humanly as well as theologically inadequate. Her attitude to the doctrine of the Real Presence, the pivot of the discussion in the second part, makes this clear. The ambiguity of her eucharistic witness suggests intellectual dishonesty on a politically sensitive doctrinal question, and makes her ironically a grotesque parody of Transubstantiation itself:[7]

> Your churches substance thus you change at will,
> And yet retain your former figure still.   (II,50–1)

Equivocation on so central an issue has inexorable consequences and implications. In the first place, it weakens the effectiveness of her discipline, so that Anglican church government is the ecclesiastical equivalent of government by the Trimmers:

> Like tricks of state, to stop a raging flood ⎫
> Or mollify a mad-brain'd Senate's mood: ⎬
> Of all expedients never one was good. ⎭   (II,272–4)

More important is the lack of 'innate auctority' which it points to. But this is inevitable in a church 'Who has herself cast off the lawfull sway' (I,455). The Church of England's 'rebellion' against Rome is thus the equivalent in terms of church discipline of the feeble attempts of reason to replace faith as the ground of religious truth. In rejecting her proper constitutional position within the Universal Church, she has enfeebled herself in terms of vision and authority, as any rebellious polity must. Significantly Dryden assimilates the counter-reformation emphasis on tradition in Catholic apologetics into his own 'political' vision. Tradition is now for him the theological equivalent of the 'Ark' of the English constitution: 'An old possession stands, till Elder quitts the claim' (II,237) is how, typically, he puts his case for accepting ancient but not demonstrably biblical teachings. Presiding over both Scripture and Tradition, however, like the king over statute and common law, is that 'innate auctority' which alone of Christian churches the Catholic Church lays claim to. Thus by probing Anglican attitudes to one doctrine only—the Eucharist—Dryden accumulates evidence of a total failure on her part to embody an adequate ideal of human society, a failure which may be summed up as a deficiency in 'royalty'. She lacks the fullness both of authority and Tradition, ecclesiastical equivalents of divine right and a constitution sanctioned by history, in effect the essential elements of that 'English' pattern of government which he had spent a lifetime defending.

There is thus not the slightest alteration in his basic commitment to tory humanism as a consequence of his conversion. His use of the standard Catholic apologetic of emphasising the 'Englishness' of the Catholic Church's system of government,[8] however, suggests an interesting shift in the relationship between his faith in God and his faith in man. Previously the Stuart monarchy had been the supreme confirmation of his anti-Hobbist views. Now he looks first to the Catholic Church for tangible confirmation of his beliefs. The Church of England has no standing in her own right even in *Religio Laici*. In *The Hind and the Panther*, the Catholic Church is her own mistress. Dryden still believes that government by kings is the best way of politically underwriting an adequately noble view of man—the magnificent passage on the Creation (I,251–90) makes that clear—but monarchy is no longer the chief means of sustaining his beliefs. In becoming a Catholic he secured an historically firmer and broader base for his ideas than the Stuart family had been able to provide.

The Hind and the Panther, however, unlike *Religio Laici*, is not primarily about ideas at all, but about specific and pressing political problems. Even the theologically oriented second part is penetrated by allusions to the political situation. In a sense the poem tries 'to "fix" a situation that changed from week to week',[9] but its main preoccupation is with divisions of power within the kingdom as a whole in the long term. As a member of a vulnerable minority, Dryden had little interest in the kind of politics Charles had played at Oxford. He was working for a political alliance, a joining of interests in depth and on a permanent basis, between the Crown, the Catholic community, and the class of landed Anglican proprietors from which he himself came. National politics of this kind, however, are far less susceptible to consistent allegorical treatment than the court politics of *Absalom and Achitophel*. As Dryden notes in the Preface, 'No general Characters of Parties, (call 'em either Sects or Churches) can be so fully and exactly drawn, as to Comprehend all the several Members of 'em'.[10] His method, therefore, is enthusiastically to jettison consistency and to represent the various powers at work in the State in a series of shifting and unstable symbols. The resulting aesthetic incongruities reflect actual tensions in seventeenth-century English life. The Panther and the Hind are haughty *grandes dames* indulging in the icy courtesies of social rivalry; they are also churches. The mixture suggests how disturbingly divine grace and animal savagery challenge the insecure civilities of polite society. The exquisitely sustained tensions at the end of the first part confirm that the poem is primarily about power. The Hind's delicate advance to the pool, in a context of suspended violence, suppressed tensions and uncertain results, is simultaneously dramatic and formal, a set-piece yet tense, a dangerous ritual. The beast fable is especially apt. It combines violence with heraldic formality. The images are simple, the situations naked as a fable requires, yet the scene is full of meaning. The beasts stand for ideas and principles certainly; but because they skulk and snarl, the dominant sense we have of them is that they are sects and parties, carefully eyeing each other either as competitors or as prey.

The world of *The Hind and the Panther* is more minutely specified than that of *Absalom and Achitophel*, paradoxically because it is so elaborately unstable. Its disorder is radical. The panther mates with both a Lyon and a Wolf, while the wolf and the fox merge and separate through the whole course of human history. 'Rebellion' thereby ceases to be a matter of ideas or causes, but a principle of organic disorder in the evolving human condition. The history of the wolf (I,154–250) takes us beyond the world of Caledon to that of biblical Israel. Conscious echoes of *Absalom and Achitophel*, however, blend the two into a composite image. Similarly the Eden of the Creation dissolves into the Lyon's Caledon (I,251–90). England is thus carefully related to, and distinguished from, its archetypes. Finally, however, the fabulous lawns and forests of Caledon are replaced by the recognisably local landscapes of the Fable of the Swallows and the country estate of the Fable of the Doves. The third part (actually half the poem) has thus 'more the Nature of Domestick Conversation'[11] than the first two. And just as a recognisably English world emerges from the fluid geography of the poem as a whole, so the heraldic and heroic Lyon is finally transformed into the Master of the Doves' farm.

This was a clever move. The House of Commons was full of such men, conscientious Anglican gentlemen whom Dryden invites to identify with the King rather than the Panther. A pamphlet of 1660 claimed that England was 'governed by the influence of a sort of people that live plentifully and at ease upon their rents ..., each ... of whom within the bounds of his own estate acts the prince'.[12] Dryden simply reverses the comparison and invites the gentry to recognise the values, interests, and attitudes which they undoubtedly shared with James personally. James was indeed very much the country gentleman in manners and outlook; 'his conception of kingship was founded on the misty squirearchal dream of Clarendon and Pym—not the authoritarianism of Strafford and Laud'.[13]

Superficially all that stood in the way of full rapport between such a king and such a Commons was the apparently trivial issue of toleration for the Catholic minority. Nor was Dryden falsifying the facts in presenting his plain good man as being firmly in favour of religious toleration, and the Anglican opposition to it as being characterised by bad-tempered evasiveness. But the picture of mean-spirited intolerance resisting the noble purposes of a benign prince obscures the fact that the issue between James and the gentry was not in substance a matter of religious or moral principle at all, but a radical conflict of political interest. Neither side grasped how total the conflict was. Hence the angry bewilderment with which they regarded each other's betrayals of precisely those Clarendonian prejudices which they had in common. The conflict of interest was in fact so great, however, that it finally destroyed both parties. The gentry exiled the Stuarts only to be subdued in their turn by the whig oligarchs. Dryden obviously did not see the tensions of the time in these terms exactly, but *The Hind and the Panther* was written in the thick of them and accurately registers their character and complexity.

Dryden insists that the poem 'was neither impos'd on me, nor so much as the Subject given me by any man'.[14] Nevertheless it must be seen in the context of the strenuous campaign by the authorities to secure a repeal of the Test Acts. But the gentry were bound to the Test by more than conscience. Following the Uniformity Act of 1662, the Church at a local level had virtually become their property, and the basis of a profitable monopoly of local power. In addition the policy of calling in borough charters was threatening to destroy their *de facto* control of the boroughs. Thus it was the logic of modern government, which James without knowing it was caught up in, and not just Catholic emancipation, that constituted the real threat to the nation's 'natural rulers' in the countryside. They were faced, in fact, with 'something very like a social revolution',[15] comparable with the efficiency and probity of the administration of Cromwell's major-generals. 'Not since the Norman Conquest had the Crown developed so sustained an attack on the established political power of the aristocracy and the major gentry'.[16] The squires, however, 'were as deeply entrenched in their neighbourhoods as the baronage of Henry III. And they possessed a like intractable nature; both felt that, if the need arose, they had the right to rebel.'[17]

It is Anglicanism, not as a church but as a vested interest, therefore, which is depicted in the Panther and the Doves. Distinct yet related facets of the same political grouping are suggested by the plain good man. With the portrait of the Buzzard (the Scottish Latitudinarian Gilbert Burnet who fled to the Netherlands with Shaftesbury) completing the picture, Dryden can be said to have presented a full and complex study of the struggle for power within the English ruling class at the end of the seventeenth century. (Burnet is the one weakness in the account; not that he is treated all that unfairly, but he is an inadequate representative of the whig nobility who were the real threat to Crown and squirearchy and whose 'churchman' he undoubtedly was). It is the complexity of this subject-matter which justifies the poem's elaborate fluidity, and not mere cleverness or whimsicality in the poet. The Panther does not, for instance, have a rhetorical 'ethos' which 'is clearly calculated to alienate the reader's sympathies',[18] merely to load the dice in the Hind's favour. Dryden is writing in the light of observed fact. The acrimony of the pamphlet war, the vindictiveness of the attacks on the late king and the late Duchess of York, and the covert violence with which the Commons habitually threatened James, are all perfectly registered in the Panther's personality. Her restless self-restraint in the Hind's cottage, and the savage, barely concealed, moral of the Fable of the Swallows, exactly capture the mood of the gentry in James' reign. By conviction bound to the doctrine of passive obedience, they felt the tensions between conscience and vested interest with particular acuteness.

Yet the Panther remains always potentially noble, substantially so indeed beside the Wolf. This is not surprising, since Dryden, after all, was writing about his own people, and must have had personal knowledge of how savagery and civility, principle and interest, messed uncomfortably together in their minds. He also wished, in the end, to win them over to his point of view. In seeking to base the government of England on an alliance between Crown and gentry, he was in fact genuinely thinking of the latter's interests. Accordingly he felt free to express once again his intense hatred of commercialism, which he was right to see as a far graver threat to their power than the king. One of the most impassioned sections of the poem, especially noticeable because it follows an impressive celebration of the universality of the Catholic Church, is the deeply angry description of colonial enterprises beginning 'Here let my sorrow give my satyr place' (II,556–67). It has an important structural and moral relationship with the image of the Church as the ocean immediately preceding it (II,549–55), and the earlier image of the Church as a vessel piloted by Christ (I,128–33). As such it suggests the enormous gulf between the global visions of Catholic landowner and Dissenting merchant.

It would be wrong to conclude from the intensity of Dryden's response to religion and the rise of capitalism, however, that he was unseeing as well as reactionary. In fact he was particularly well placed to be an excellent observer of the times. It was precisely because he combined to a unique degree a purely personal sense of involvement in the events he was describing with an equally pervasive intellectual and moral detachment from them, that *The Hind and the Panther* is possibly the most significant 'historical' poem in the English language.

The reasons for this personal involvement are obvious enough. Dryden was seriously indignant at the insults borne by himself and others in the pamphlet war. As a monarchist and a gentleman he felt keenly the apparently inexplicable inability of the king and the natural rulers of the countryside to work together. Above all, there was the masterful sincerity of his new faith. 'The presence of . . . a confessional or affirmative passage in each part', it has been suggested, '. . . is one of the many devices to keep the poem informed with the strength of personal convictions'.[19] Perhaps 'devices' implies too much calculation. The poem is spontaneously rooted in Dryden's religious faith and his steady willingness to accept the social and moral consequences of his conversion. In particular the opportunity it gave his delighted enemies to heap humiliating obloquy upon him, and the wounding isolation from his social equals if not from his loyal friends, are exactly recorded and integrated with a distinctively Catholic piety in the majestic passage in the third part beginning 'This breathing-time the *Matron* took' (III,277–97).

It is this last and most impassioned ground for involvement, of course, which is the imaginative as well as the moral basis for the poem's detachment. His conversion made Dryden a stranger in his own country, and he did not even have the consolation of approving the King's policies. The hotly satirical portrait, in the Fable of the Swallows, of Father Petre, James' confessor and adviser, suggests his profound distrust of the Court. Moreover, as a poet, Dryden's stake in the country was anyway radically different from that of anyone else of his class. The resulting independence of vision ensures that the intensity of individual passages in *The Hind and the Panther* is balanced by an overall air of almost irresponsible casualness, which its unruffled indulgence of inconsistency and indecorum keeps constantly before us.

The counterpointing of involvement and detachment is especially effective in Dryden's response to the charge brought repeatedly against the Catholic Church, that the Papacy was the Antichrist.[20] It is this charge which explains Dryden's bizarre choice of a hind and a panther for his protagonists. They form a remarkably adroit response to his opponents' repeated representations of Rome as one of the grotesque blatant beasts of biblical prophecy. Dryden was rightly afraid of the fanatical, pope-burning mob-hysteria such gross propaganda fed. His response, however, is supple and elegant. The Hind is a symbol of purity, helplessness and immortality. She is also a skilful debater. She thereby combines the two qualities which most effectively counter the Antichrist charge—innocence and sophistication. She confronts fanaticism with virtue and wit. She uses her canonical commitment to poverty and chastity, not only to stress her political helplessness and harmlessness, and her moral purity, but also, slyly, to imply that her opponent has been corrupted by the worldly advantages of Establishment. Similarly she combines the important monastic virtue of hospitality with an obviously ironic respect for the Panther's loyalty, and an enjoyably disingenuous concern (since she wants 'an unerring guide'—II,663–90) for her safety. The Hind's graceful innuendos however, never compromise her good faith. Her simplicity, poverty and purity continually re-emerge with all the clarity and strength of their first appearance in the unchallenged loveliness of the poem's opening paragraph. The harmlessness of the Hind, politically, psychologically, and spiritually, is thus equally compatible with the urbanity and the faith of the poet. Together they represent a thoroughly civilised and deeply religious response to the humourless, learned sadism of the Antichrist fanatics.

The poem, however, was not primarily directed at pamphleteering controversialists, but at plain good men in the shires. The consequences for them of not supporting the Crown is what Dryden was determined to make clear, and in the context of practical politics he *was* prepared to counter violence with violence. Unfortunately the Declaration of Indulgence made it impossible for him to complete his fiercely 'realistic' design for the third part effectively. Specifically he was forced to give the Fable of the Doves a singularly feeble ending. The whole balance of the second half of the poem is thereby upset, since the third part is built round the two carefully balanced subordinate fables with which the Panther and the Hind in turn obliquely threaten

each other. Once James had openly offered to form an alliance with the
Dissenters, Dryden could hardly continue predicting dire results for
the Anglicans if they did the same, yet both subordinate fables were
obviously meant to have distressingly violent endings.

The Fable of the Swallows is beautifully adapted to this and other
purposes. It emphasises the Panther's malice, but it also represents
moderate Catholic opinion on Father Petre's policies, and it faces the
harsh future Catholics could expect at William's accession with
considerable toughness. It is a dark little tale with a deliberately
savage ending. To balance it a similar conclusion is obviously called
for in the Fable of the Doves. Significantly Dryden's source, Ogilby's
Of the Doves and the Hawks, ends on just such a note:

> Their Bowels rend, and tender bodies plume
> And, more than *Kites*, the *Dovish* Race consume.[21]

Even if the reader is unaware of this source, Dryden cleverly builds up
an atmosphere of suspense, in expectation of a violent ending. Long
satirical passages increase the tension by delaying the denouement. Of
course, he wished to make his opinion on Burnet and the pamphlet
war explicit. But he also wished to associate rationalism and Dissent, in
the minds of the Anglican reader and the Catholic establishment at
Court, with a Damoclean threat of anarchy. In a passage which points
to the sort of horrors that the poem, but for the Declaration, might
have described in greater detail, he outlines the social and religious
prospects facing Anglicanism if ever the Latitudinarians and Dissenters
win power in the Church:

> Nor Sighs, nor Groans, nor gogling Eyes did want;
> For now the *Pigeons* too had learn'd to Cant.
> The House of Pray'r is stock'd with large encrease;
> Nor Door, nor Windows can contain the Press:
> For Birds of ev'ry feather fill th' abode;
> Ev'n Atheists out of envy own a God:
> And reeking from the Stews, Adult'rers come,
> Like *Goths* and *Vandals* to demolish *Rome*.   (III,1207–14)

'*Rome*' means, of course, Catholicism, but also the fabric of civilised
society. The Test in effect provides no defence against 'Dutch'
Latitudinarians and Atheists anarchically seeking their share of the

ecclesiastical pickings. The passage is alive with fear of the cynical whiggery which Dryden had embodied in Lorenzo in *The Spanish Friar* and which was later faithfully reflected in the tightly knit group of self-interested pragmatists who were to exercise total control of government machinery in eighteenth-century England.

What *The Hind and the Panther* records, in fact (behind the empty triumph of a conclusion forced on Dryden by events), is his recognition that the highly principled, deeply meditated sense of human dignity, which he now believed the Catholic Church as well as the English monarchy bore witness to, was facing brutal extinction in English political life. However traditionally based this vision may have been, it was at least grounded in full and sensitive experience of the world. Dryden's loyalty to it in the context of an extraordinarily acute awareness of the indifference of history to values of any kind is especially impressive. No poem in the language struggles so hard to capture the supra-personal, apparently inhuman character of the historical process, and yet to relate it passionately, intelligently, and coolly, to an uncompromising idealism. In *The Hind and the Panther* Dryden finally resolves the tensions between his personal vision and his historical sense. The *Heroique Stanza's* and *Annus Mirabilis* have at last come together.

1. *The Letters of John Dryden*, Ed. Charles E. Ward (1942), p. 27.

2. See Earl Miner, *Dryden's Poetry* (1967), p. 259.

3. John Hollander, 'The Odes to Music' in *Dryden. A Collection of Critical Essays*, Ed. Bernard N. Schilling (1963), p. 154.

4. Ernest Brennecke, Jr, 'Dryden's Odes and Draghi's Music' in *Essential Articles for the study of John Dryden*, Ed. H. T. Swedenberg, Jr (1966), p. 456.

5. California III, pp. 482–3.

6. C. S. Lewis, 'Shelley, Dryden, and Mr. Eliot', *Rehabilitations and Other Essays* (1939), p. 9.

7. See Sanford Budick, *Dryden and The Abyss of Light* (1970), p. 226.

8. See Phillip Harth, *Contexts of Dryden's Thought* (1968), p. 271.

9. Charles E. Ward, *The Life of John Dryden* (1961), p. 224.

10. Kinsley II, p. 467.

11. ibid. II, 469.

12. Quoted in Christopher Hill, *The Century of Revolution, 1603–1711*, (1969) p. 195.

13. J. P. Kenyon, *The Stuarts* (Fontana Library ed., 1966), p. 147.

14. Kinsley II, p. 468.

15. Hill, op. cit., p. 206.

16. J. H. Plumb, *The Growth of Political Stability in England, 1675–1725* (Peregrine Books ed., 1969), p. 70.

17. ibid., p. 34.

18. Harth, op. cit., p. 44.

19. Miner, op. cit., p. 192.

20. See Budick, op. cit., pp. 191–217.

21. John Ogilby, *The Fables of Æsop Paraphras'd in Verse* (Augustan Reprint Society, 1965), p. 52.

8

A PROTESTANT REVOLUTION:
POEMS AND PLAYS AFTER 1688

Dryden's immediate response to the loss of his laureateship following the revolution of 1688 was to return to the theatre. Possibly his greatest play was written within the year. *Don Sebastian* (1689) is also perhaps the only play in English to discover a tragic logic in the Christian religion. It is also closely connected with the events of 1688–9. Its hero is the historical king of Portugal, Sebastian, whose disappearance on a foreign expedition led to the formation of a Portuguese 'political party . . . comparable to the English Jacobites'.[1] But the throne with which the play is most concerned is the Islamic one of Moley-Moluch, himself a usurper threatened with the machinations of a younger brother, Zeydan, and an evil minister Benducar. Sebastian is taken prisoner when he attempts to secure the rights of Almeyda, whom he loves, and who has at least as good a claim to the throne as Moluch. Moluch, inevitably, also falls in love with her. His chief adviser is Dorax, formerly a Christian and Sebastian's friend, but now bitterly estranged from him. Moluch is also served by a prominent 'ecclesiastic', the Mufti, who is chief victim in the subplot which concerns the intrigues of an amorous Portuguese nobleman, Antonio, now the Mufti's slave. A play so obviously formulaic could have made political allusions almost without meaning to, but it is just this element of conventional innocence which heightens the political tension. When Muly-Zeydan and Benducar talk about doubtful titles and younger brothers in the opening scene, for instance, before their identities and situation have been precisely established, there must have been some unease in the first-night audience about what exactly the former laureate was about. Similarly when Sebastian offers to die for his subjects:

> For Subjects such as they are seldom seen,
> Who not forsook me at my greatest need . . .   (I,i,400–1)

there was no doubt a careful silence throughout the theatre.

Like everything else in the play this aspect of it reaches an apparent climax in a brilliant Fourth Act, when the tragic and comic actions are fused in fantastic night scenes which are successively tense and thick with intrigue and then as ebullient and fanciful as the carnival scenes in the earlier comedies. The mob comes out on to the streets, and a ludicrous competition for control of it develops between a demagogue called Mustafa and a frantic, incompetent Mufti. Between them they caricature the whole of seventeenth-century political and religious demagoguery, with occasional precise and bitter references to specific events, such as the sacking of Catholic churches after James' flight, to keep the audience shifting in their seats. The mob demand a religion without sin. Mustafa obliges with the inspired cry, ''tis no Sin to depose the *Mufti*' (IV,ii,435), and since the Mufti can be seen as a sort of Islamic pope, the audience doubtless felt free to go along with the joke. But if they did so, they would have found themselves on the wrong side of Antonio's rejoinder: 'when Kings and Queens are to be discarded, what shou'd Knaves do any longer in the pack' (IV,ii,436–8). It cannot have felt very comfortable either to listen to Almeyda's revelation that Benducar intended first to dispose of the younger brother Zeydan, with whom he planned the insurrection, and then

> T' espouse my person, and assume the Crown
> Claym'd in my right . . .   (IV,ii,256–7)

since this was in effect what William of Orange had just done.

The contradictions and inconsistencies on the political level which these allusions point to, however, are only symptoms of deeper, more distressing confusions at the heart of the human condition, and it is these that the play is chiefly concerned with. On the night of the rising Morayma mistakes her father the Mufti for her lover Antonio, and eagerly and greedily embraces him. The blunder is a representative one. The shocking collisions of desire, as hazardous and disordered as those of public affairs, are a major theme of the play. In the first scene Dorax refers to Almeyda, whose defeat in her efforts to achieve the throne he and Moley-Moluch are celebrating, with significantly intense disgust:

> I hope she dy'd in her own Female calling,
> Choak'd up with Man, and gorg'd with Circumcision.   (I,i,132–3)

The Emperor's lust for her later is no more natural than Dorax's hatred:

> Serpent, I will engender Poyson with thee;
> Joyn Hate with Hate, and Venom to the birth.   (II,i,464–5)

This preoccupation with perversity reaches (again only apparently) its unusual climax in the Fourth Act, when Dorax's motives for turning against Sebastian are revealed. Sebastian it seems once put pressure on Dorax to surrender his mistress Violante to a rival, Enriquez, but, as Scott noted, Dorax's interest in the girl was always slight compared with his feelings for the king. It was not on Violante's account, but because of Sebastian's preference for Enriquez that the request outraged him. His rival, moreover, was effeminate:

> That Woman, but more dawbed; or if a man,
> Corrupted to a Woman: thy Man Mistress.   (IV,ii,736–7)

Sebastian openly admits that he loved Enriquez, Dorax that he would repeat the crime of striking his rival not just in the king's presence, but 'in the face of Heaven'. When the discussion of these past rivalries finally provokes Sebastian into fighting Dorax, his speech is plainly erotic:

> The sprightly Bridegroom, on his Wedding Night,
> More gladly enters not the lists of love.   (IV,ii,829–30)

In his account of Enriquez' heroic death, Sebastian makes no attempt to counter the charge that Enriquez' life was 'effeminate and soft': he argues, indeed, that this only makes his courage in battle the greater. Finally, when Dorax acknowledges Enriquez' moral superiority, Sebastian, with real tenderness, calls him for the first time by his original name, Alonzo. The relations between the three men are thus beyond question ambiguous, Dorax being as penetrating a psychological study as Pleasance in *Limberham*. (Dryden had shown similar insight in his handling of the psychologically explosive material in *Oedipus*.) This is especially remarkable in view of his detestation of homosexuality, which spoils at least one passage of his *Æneis*.[2] Nevertheless this

sympathetic study of nobility in the context of 'unnatural' feeling
intrudes with apparently unnecessary emphasis on a scene which with
all the appearance of a fifth act unites Sebastian and Almeyda in
marriage, and celebrates the return of natural order to the political
sphere with the restoration of lawful sovereignty.

But of course it is not the Fifth Act. The next scene opens with
a speech by Dorax which implies that the happy issue of the action so
far is as unstable as Eden before the Fall. This promptly proves to be the
case, with the revelation that Sebastian has unwittingly consummated a
marriage with his sister. Though this had been foreshadowed in
earlier scenes, the force of the revelation is overwhelming. This is
partly the effect of the verse—Almeyda has a wonderful speech
(V,i,270–4) in which she fatally insists on a public vindication of her
honour—but it is mainly due to the strength and significance of
Sebastian's despair, the brilliant strategem by which Dorax tempts him
away from suicide, and Sebastian's decision to live in obscurity and
sacrificial prayer. Throughout the play there have been the usual
references to the divinity of kings. Specifically, Sebastian is introduced
as a Christ-figure, as 'suff'ring Majesty' who longs to die for his
people. Now the truly 'godlike' character of kingship is revealed.
Rather than sanctioning political power, Sebastian's kingship requires
the acceptance of political impotence. To be divine like Christ is to be
of no account like Christ.

Dryden is relentless in his exposure of what this doctrine of Christian
renunciation, of passive obedience to the divine will, really means.
Man suffers not as a direct result of his own sins, but through the
action of instinct and Fate, both 'blind Guides' (II,i,628), yet both
apparently determined by the inscrutable workings of Providence.
Like Christ, Sebastian has to place himself unreservedly at the disposal
of an apparently 'unnatural' God. In the face of this call to Christian
renunciation, however, Dryden insists on an honest evaluation of
desire. Sebastian and Almeyda defiantly proclaim the sweetness of
their union, as well as its horror. The humanism of *Don Sebastian* is
thus uncompromisingly inclusive, its image of Christian surrender, of
the Christian tragedy, correspondingly complete. There is an outrage-
ousness, by human standards, at the centre of things, in history and
the human mind, which only humility can accommodate. In the face
of this, the prudential morality of poetic justice, the orderliness assumed
by decorum, and the self-aggrandisement sanctioned by the heroic
code, fall away as so much self-indulgent rubbish.

Perhaps the most distinctively 'humble' element in the play, from Dryden's point of view, is the affair between Antonio and Morayma. They embody the refreshing, reassuring ordinariness of life, man's undignified capacity for survival. The elegant gallant enthusiastically capers and postures as a bridled slave, and his sexuality is hardly discriminating. But he and Morayma suggest fertility (there is elaborate play with vegetable imagery in the subplot),[3] and they achieve a certain mutual tenderness: 'Why! thou little dun,' he says to her at one point, 'is thy debt so pressing?' (V,i,63–4). It is they who are left 'in the Middle of the Stage' at the end of the play, the representatives of ordinary humanity whose survival in a sense deprives tragedy of its self-importance. Thus *Don Sebastian* may speak of an overwhelming defeat for legitimacy and order, but it meets that defeat not only with unqualified renunciation of all claims on man and God, but also with a cheerful sense of the unimportance of great events. It meets the challenge of 1688 in other words by rising sublimely above both Revolution and Restoration and by plunging happily below them.

Dryden's next play *Amphitryon* (1690) and his last *Love Triumphant* (1694) may be taken together. They are less openly political than *Don Sebastian*, though *Love Triumphant* does deal with usurpation. It is mainly concerned, however, with reversing the pattern of Dryden's incest plays by presenting a hero and heroine who from the start believe they are brother and sister, and yet are defiantly in love. They turn out, of course, to have different parents. Dryden, apparently, was gesturing impatiently at undue pessimism about human impulses, but he does so with considerably less humanity than one finds in the subplot of *Don Sebastian*. Morally healthy as his trust of appetite may be, the play is intellectually undisciplined and dramatically confused.

Amphitryon is a little difficult to place. Scott thought it showed Dryden's 'comic powers to more advantage than anywhere, excepting the "Spanish Friar" ';[4] and though upset by its indelicacy, he praised the verse in which Jupiter's love-making is couched. There are a few political allusions in the piece, but the effect is more of Dryden teasing his audience with dangerous phrases than raising substantial issues. Jupiter, for instance, says,

> In me, my charming mistress, you behold
> A lover that disdains a lawful title,
> Such as of monarchs to successive thrones;
> The generous lover holds by force of arms,
> And claims his crown by conquest.   (II,ii, p. 45)[5]

but he is also virtually a stage incarnation of Charles II (the witty merging of Orange and Stuart was one of Dryden's favourite post-Revolution devices) and the effect seems harmless. On the other hand, it has recently been suggested that this is a play as bleak as it is funny, the mortals being cruelly abused by the gods—'sensual forces of inscrutable will and power' who 'intervene and make a mess of human life'.[6] This view of the play is entirely consistent with the vision of a helpless humanity and a ruthless providence in Dryden's final classical tragedy, *Cleomenes*.

Before looking at *Cleomenes* (1692), it is worthwhile considering briefly Dryden's general interest in pagan man. He was deeply impressed by the classical achievement, and especially by the 'vast . . . difference betwixt the productions of those souls and these of ours'.[7] He obviously preferred the humane system of education described in *The Life of Plutarch* (1683) to that meted out to his sons and himself by the stupefyingly brutal Busby, and he envied the poise of the classical mind. He praises Plutarch for opposing 'the superstitions and fopperies of Paganism', for respecting none the less the 'received custom of his country' in religious matters,[8] and for rejecting both 'extremes of the Epicurean and Stoic sects',[9] as too dogmatic. *The Character of Polybius* (1693), was published after the Revolution, and is a little more sombre, but attractive none the less. It is alive with the tensions of political duty and natural wisdom under an unlawful government. Its account of political institutions degenerating, and constitutional freedoms decaying, seems based on a firm belief in the wisdom of surrender to the tide of history. A spirit of tolerance and resignation equally informs *The Life of Lucian* (1711), but it would be wrong to assume from this that Dryden gave unqualified approval to the civilised despair of stoicism. The voice of the layman in *Religio Laici* is strongly heard in all Dryden's writings on the classical world; but so is his conviction that 'God . . . with his divine providence over-rules and guides all actions to the secret end he has ordained them'.[10] This, not stoicism, is the moral centre of his own quietism. It was not, of course, available to the pagan mind. For this very reason, however, pagan courage fascinated him, particularly the courage of naturally virtuous men who, like Cleomenes or Turnus in the *Æneid*, were 'abandoned' by history.

Cleomenes was banned for a time by Mary in her husband's absence. And though Dryden protested that it was apolitical, 'neither compliment, nor satire but a plain story',[11] there are of course allusions in it to the 'practices and principles' of Williamite and Jacobite alike. The method, however, is similar to that in the speech quoted above from *Amphitryon*. The allusions are adroitly 'inconsistent'. Cleomenes, exiled in Egypt, having lost the Spartan throne to the Macedonian Antigonus, could clearly stand for James II if the audience wanted him to. Antigonus' invasion of Sparta certainly sounds similar to William's of England:

> No noise was heard; no voice, but of the crier,
> Proclaiming peace and liberty to Sparta. (I,ii, p. 284)

But the play's effect depends on these comparisons breaking down once they have been made, so that an abstract of nobility, a sustained, uniform classical image of the sufferings and death of a great man in exile can emerge from the particularities of history, ancient or modern. When 'virtuous' brothers are discussed in the Second Act, for instance, it is important to remember who, in his time, had indeed proved 'bounteous, great, and brave' (II,ii, p. 297), precisely in the role of king's brother; but it is also important that the discussion should not have any direct application to the family relations of the Stuarts as they actually existed in 1692. Division of the characters on party lines would distract attention from altogether larger and more inclusive discriminations that Dryden wishes to make, discriminations that put the events of 1688 into a far more tragic perspective than would be possible if he indulged in mere compliment or satire.

The play has meaning only if we feel the need for poetic justice as strongly as the hero does: 'virtue in distress and vice in triumph', he says, 'Make atheists of mankind' (V,ii, p. 339). The action nevertheless relentlessly establishes a strain between nobility and moral neatness. Cleomenes and Cleanthes commit suicide when they are finally defeated. There is no question but that this is noble. There is also no question but that it is objectively wrong, not just in Christian terms, but in terms of natural morality: 'we durst not tempt the gods', Cleomenes says earlier, 'To break their images without their leave' (IV,i, p. 334). But then both he and Cleanthes, like Raymond and Alphonso in *The Spanish Friar*, first break the natural law by raising a rebellion—and they do so ostensibly in the name of the principles of 1688: 'Liberty and Magas' (Magas being the younger brother of the King of Egypt) is their very whiggish cry as Cleomenes rouses the mob against his corrupt host, while Cleanthes begs his father not to fight for an arbitrary power, 'That odious weight upon a free-born soul' (V,ii, p. 355). The Jacobites have become Williamites. This does not of course mean that the play sanctions rebellion even against a loathsome tyrant. In exile even Legitimacy (i.e. Cleomenes) can be trapped in hopeless contradictions. Thus when the rising fails, he finds that he has betrayed even the symbolic value of his kingship, which in exile is the only value it can have. Far from being 'the hunted stag, Whose life may ransome yours' (IV,i, p. 334) he cannot in the end even save himself. The pity and terror of the play arise out of the bleakly atheistical contradictions of history, in the midst of which even the noblest and most heroic of pagan kings is helpless either to assert the Right or to achieve Don Sebastian's redeeming self-abnegation.

After 1694 Dryden wrote no more plays. This is not surprising. He could no longer rely on strong and simple responses from his audience to key issues of the day. Direct comment on current affairs was denied him—he even had a prologue suppressed because of its political content—and without the robust freedom he had previously exploited so effectively, his direct addresses to the public lost their fire. The Prologue to *Don Sebastian* (1690), for instance, is rueful and concil-iatory, the Epilogue, like the Prologue and Epilogue to the *History of Bacon in Virginia* (1689), wearily indecent. The Prologue to *The Prophetess* (1690), however, combines his long-standing dislike for the whoremongers of the pit with a powerful attack on William's bloody and perfidious campaign in Ireland. He nowhere suggests the possi-bility of a Jacobite victory—his professed contempt for the Teague is too strong for that—but his picture of Irish savagery only emphasises the squalor of war. He assumes that the English will revive the custom of enslaving 'a Bogland captive', and the contrast between this and the false elegance of fashionable, excessively bewigged, London, patently revolts him. The Prologue to *Cleomenes* (1692) reworks similar ideas quite effectively, but the other prologues and epilogues are merely competent. The only exception is the Prologue to *Amphitryon* (1690) which combines a humorous complaint at the loss of his licence for satire with two of his favourite themes, the literary and sexual incom-petence of his rivals, and the loveliness of lovely women.

Dryden obviously had to discover some relatively neutral field in which to work. He found it mainly in translation, but he also turned to work of a strictly 'bespoke' character. His epitaphs provide a small sample of the professional neutrality he was able to achieve at this time. They are properly succinct and complimentary. Only one, the

Epitaph on Erasmus Lawton (n.d·), can be called moving—it is Jonsonian in its plainness, compression, and gentleness of feeling—but all are decorous and sensible. There is, however, the translation of the epitaph *Upon the Death of the Viscount Dundee* (1704) to remind us how naturally Dryden's verse turns to public affairs.

Pure professionalism had always, of course, been among his talents. Even when he temporarily stopped writing plays after 1680, he continued to produce a number of perfectly modelled and adroitly impersonal lyrics. The stream tinkles on through the excitements of the tory triumph, James' reign, and William's invasion. Some of the songs, like '*Sylvia* the fair, in the bloom of Fifteen' (1685), are bawdy, but without the sadistic grossness characteristic of similar poems by Rochester. In other poems, like the 'Amynta' and 'Amyntas' songs, the eroticism is absorbed into remote pastoral prettiness. Love-making is humorously deployed as a decorative rather than an erotic motif.

The lyrics are by and large successful to the degree that their conventionality leave the reader free to observe how obvious and easy metrical patterns can develop unexpectedly complicated tensions, which are promptly and wittily resolved. 'A Pastoral Dialogue betwixt Thyrsis and Iris' from *Amphitryon* is typical:

> Fair *Iris* and her Swain
> Were in a shady Bow'r;
> Where *Thyrsis* long in vain
> Had sought the Shepherd's hour:
> At length his Hand advancing upon her snowy Breast;
> He said, O kiss me longer,
> And longer yet and longer,
> If you will make me Blest.   (1–8)

The pause after 'said', the doubt about whether the immediately preceding pause comes before or after 'advancing', and the repetitions of 'longer' in the lines that follow combine in a gratifying flirtation with metrical disorder.

Equally professional are the small number of somewhat larger lyrical pieces which Dryden undertook during this period. The second of his three musical odes, *On the Death of Mr. Henry Purcell* (1696), for instance, is both beautifully made and notably calm in its intellectual and moral references. It is no more interested in values than the lyrics are in love-making. The only risks it takes are with the metre. Thus the third line, because it has three feet instead of four, gives a slight but pleasing harshness to the word 'strain'. The musical theme and the lush décor of Christian angels and classical gods are carefully remote. Dryden, as a virtuoso performer himself, has liberated his verse from the pressures of religious controversy, party feeling and personal exposure. His translation of the *Veni Creator Spiritus* (1693) is similarly a purely technical triumph, by which the usually clumsy octosyllabic couplet, the awkwardness of which is graphically described in *A Discourse concerning . . . Satire*,[12] is invested with 'somber and reverent dignity'.[13]

The Prefatory Epistle to *Eleonora* (1692) implies that Dryden had to work rather hard on the poem, but he was apparently pleased with the result. Although it is in heroic couplets, it is, as he says, 'of the Pindarique nature, as well in the Thought as the Expression',[14] and therefore more a panegyric than an elegy. The neutral territory marked out by the poem is correspondingly more capacious, and offers greater opportunities for a strenuous display of professional accomplishment. There is an especially rich use of scriptural allusion (notably the Book of Proverbs) by which the Countess of Abingdon is transformed into the type of a holy woman. But the two more modest pastoral elegies, *On the Death of Amyntas* (1704) and *On the Death of A Very Young Gentleman* (1704), give more pleasure. The former is a beautifully neutral lament. Its pastoral setting enables Dryden to write about the event decorously, without presuming to place the nature of his own involvement in it. His art is put simply and decently at the disposal of others.

It is not surprising, in view of Dryden's obvious relish for the role of virtuoso performer in these poems, that his later criticism should be frequently concerned with 'numbers'. Some of his most precise and telling criticism of the classical poets has to do with the musicality of their verse; Virgil's, for instance, 'is everywhere sounding the very thing in your Ears, whose sence it bears: Yet the numbers are perpetually varied'.[15] Ovid, however, has 'little Variety of Numbers and sound', while Horace is distinguished for 'the Elegance of his Words, and the numerousness of his Verse'.[16] Dryden gives detailed proof of his right to make such judgements in some acute analyses of the harmonies of ancient and modern languages, notably in the Preface to *Albion and Albanius* (1685); and if he is a little obsessive about the bad effects of Germanic monosyllables on English verse (this was a factor in making some of his later verse particularly unpleasant especially in

its repeated use of adjectives ending 'y', such as 'Oozy' and 'finny')
he does reveal a fine ear, notably for Italian. His praise of Spenser and
Milton as the nearest English poets in respect of their diction to Virgil
and Horace is acute,[17] and his intense delight in, and humility before,
the achievement of Virgil is intimately bound up with his detailed
recognition of the way in which the propriety of word to thought in
Virgil is consistently and intricately enriched by the propriety of sound
to sense.

It was impossible, however, for Dryden to remain a mere performer
of verse for long. Even among his songs there are three that call for
more than technical analysis. Two illustrate his perpetual readiness
to comment on public affairs, and the effectiveness of all three is
crucially dependent on the blank-faced inutility of most of his other
lyrics. Intimations of seriousness are particularly effective in a medium
which maintains a flawless surface of pastel-coloured innocence. *The
Lady's Song* (1704) is the first and most famous case in point. It is a
purely conventional pastoral lament, yet alive with the obvious
secret that the exiled Pan is James II and Syrinx Mary of Modena. The
last line, 'When *Pan*, and his Son, and fair *Syrinx* return', skilfully
intrudes into the lightest of metrical patterns a steely current of
uncompromising Jacobitism; 'and his Son', metrically so casual,
rhetorically so mildly stressed, tellingly exposes the new régime's
greatest weakness. Altogether different is 'Song for a Girl' from *Love
Triumphant*. Its effect depends on its having been written for a young,
beautiful, and notably innocent actress, whose singing of it must have
given an unusually poignant effect to the conventional themes of
virginity, experience, and sexual disillusionment.[18] Perhaps the subtlest
of these poems, however, *Song to a Fair, Young Lady, Going out of the
Town in the Spring* (1693) touches more dangerous matters, political
and religious, but with a graceful inconsequentiality thoroughly
representative of Dryden's later poetic tactics. Thus Chloris is an
alter Christus coming to the Temple surrounded by adoring crowds and
restoring the dead to life, but it is the poet who is 'by Love design'd
To be the Victim for Mankind' (23–4). In the same way, some cleverly
inconsistent political allusions make the third stanza pleasingly
provocative:

> Great God of Love, why hast thou made
> A Face that can all Hearts command,
> That all Religions can invade,

And change the Laws of ev'ry Land?
Where thou hadst plac'd such Pow'r before,
Thou shou'dst have made her Mercy more.   (13–18)

The professional ironist teases his audience with possibly treasonable
innuendoes in words like 'invade' and 'change the Laws'. The inconsistency increases the tension, but at least the ex-laureate can remain
undisturbed when issues of loyalty and blasphemy momentarily
intrude on a pretty, heartless charade.

The form which Dryden found most suited to his situation in his
later years, however, was the verse epistle. The panegyrics on his
literary friends at this time have an intimate character which makes the
quality of his personal life in old age intangibly vivid. Not that the
best poems in this form could ever be called private or spontaneous.
Indeed the two supposedly spontaneous pieces, *Lines on Tonson* (1704)
and *Lines to Mrs. Creed* (1800) are very unimpressive, while the
apparently informal *To Sir George Etherege* (1691) is in fact a calculated
work, almost certainly written at the request of the Earl of Middleton.
It is a chatty, admiring but unenvious celebration in octosyllabics of
Etherege's prodigious philanderings, but it tells us nothing about his
friendship with Dryden. The revealing poems, in fact, are more public
and formal. They specify the connections between Dryden's known
positions as a Jacobite and a neoclassical poet and the sort of satisfactions and affections which he enjoyed with other men of his craft
in private, and they do so with a fullness all the more striking for their
autobiographical reticence.

The verse epistle had been a familiar form to Dryden since the lines
to Hoddeson in 1650. The poems to Howard and Lee in the sixties and
seventies show how easily this branch of the art of praise came to him.
In the eighties there is the stately *To the Earl of Roscomon* (1684) which,
if it is far from being an intimate poem, does fix civilised values in the
art of poetry with some skill. It successfully combines Dryden's
delight in 'pauses, cadence and well-vowell'd Words' with another
major preoccupation of his later years, the evolution of social and
literary forms. In its long perspectives on civilisation it also anticipates
the Pope of *An Essay on Criticism* and *The Dunciad*. But Dryden's full
powers in this form are most clearly in evidence in the tighter, more
intense lines on the art of satire, *To the Memory of Mr. Oldham* (1684)
which though technically an elegaic piece rather than a verse epistle is
essentially a 'letter' to a dead friend.

Dryden had used the story of Nisus and Euryalis in *The Indian Emperour*, and had recently translated Virgil's original version of it. He had also imitated Virgil's lament on the death of Marcellus in *Absalom and Achitophel*. In *To the Memory of Mr. Oldham*, however, the allusions are more spontaneously assembled, and because they are also properly classical they place Dryden's personal involvement in Oldham's death with self-effacing propriety. This is the first poem to deal with another major theme of his later years, his relations with his literary heirs. In the friendship of young poets he found the same open, warm relations which he enjoyed with his sons. Frankness was as important to the integrity of these relationships as affection. Thus even in the presence of Oldham's death, Dryden maintains the highest literary standards, firmly answering the rhetorical question 'What could advancing Age have added more?' with a gentle statement of his dead friend's poetic limitations. It is precisely Dryden's sense of these limitations, of course, which makes the prominence he gives to a lesser poet so generous, and the Nisus–Euryalis analogy so apt. It also gives authority to the poem's generalised and comprehensively sombre vision of things in general. The pagan background makes this uncompromising pessimism plausible and appropriate.[19] The all-encompassing darkness of the final couplet involves the heirless empire of English letters, as well as the dead '*Marcellus* of our tongue', in an authentically classical as opposed to a Christian or conventionally 'Augustan' vision of death. Dryden seems to have felt in this poem the imminence of that impersonal darkness which he had already antici-pated at the end of *All for Love*, and which he was to find confirmed in the events of the next decade. At the same time, however (and this was also to be a consistent element in the work of the nineties) there is a compensating force of affirmation in the climactic triplet immediately preceding the sombre close, 'an eagerness to praise whatever can be praised' and a mellowness which 'breathes consolation'.[20]

A similar balance between personal, literary, and social relationships is to be found in the less important *To my Ingenious Friend, Mr. Henry Higden* (1687) on his octosyllabic translation of Juvenal. The most forceful phrase in the poem is the one admirably timed personal note, 'Yet you, my Friend'. Apart from two epigrams, *To Mr. J. Northleigh* (1685) and *Lines on Milton* (1688) Dryden wrote nothing more in this vein until after the Revolution. Then, however, the themes which appear in all the epistles, and in the major translations also, the evolution of literature and society and their future in the coming times, acquired even more significance for him and he returned to the form with obvious delight.

To Mr. Southern (1692) is about the failure of one of Southern's plays. It begins with a malicious political allusion:

> Sure there's a Fate in Plays; and 'tis in vain
> To write, while these malignant Planets Reign.

We are clearly meant to vary the alliteration by substituting 'Monarchs' for 'Planets'. Southern is said to have Terence's weakness in plotting and his strength in style. He is therefore recommended to model himself on Wycherley and Etherege, the masters of plotting in the present age, if he is to become a model for others in the next. In the more important and lengthier *To Sir Godfrey Kneller* (1694) Dryden turns to painting, the sister art of poetry, and again he is concerned with 'the Rudiments of Art' and of society, and their interrelated historical development. He draws into a masterly survey of classical and modern cultural history his own more private concerns as a poet and a man—his position as a 'son' and 'subordinate' of Shakespeare, the problem of his and Kneller's successors, and of the deleterious effect of the age on their work. There is an awkward moment early in the poem when the following comparisons are made:

> Thence rose and *Roman*, and the *Lombard* Line:
> One colour'd best, and one did best design.
> *Raphael*'s like *Homer*'s was the Nobler part;
> But *Titian*'s Painting, look'd like *Virgil*'s Art.
> Thy Genius gives thee both.   (61–5).

The tensions created by this audacious claim are finally resolved when Dryden admits that Kneller's achievement is in fact less than that of the Italian Masters. The admission, however, is made in equally daring terms:

> That yet thou hast not reach'd their high Degree
> Seems only wanting to this Age, not thee:
> Thy Genius bounded by the Times like mine, ⎫
> Drudges on petty Draughts, nor dare design ⎬
> A more Exalted Work, and more Divine ⎭   (145–9)

As artists both men are trapped by history. But Dryden heroically refuses to accept that as a matter of historical necessity artists will henceforth have to 'Paint to Live, not Live to Paint' (165). He therefore generously projects his younger friend into more rewarding times, with the rather sad hope that some future painting of Kneller's will somehow compensate for the heroic poem he himself has failed to produce. His lines are a just, proud, and sombre judgement on Kneller, on himself, and on the age they both worked in.

The greatest, most moving, and emotionally the most open of all these poems is *To my Dear Friend Mr. Congreve* (1694). The appearance of a young talent as great as his own on the London scene moved Dryden deeply. The love between them is evident in Dryden's repeated praise of Congreve's learning and in Congreve's affectionate *Memorial* (1717). Dryden integrates the personal warmth of this relationship with concrete and yet theoretically exact recognitions of where they both stand, one at the beginning of a literary career, the other at the end. In the first forty lives of the poem there are only five decorative adjectives ('stubborn', 'boistrous', 'Great', 'blooming', and 'Beardless'). The verse is packed with solid references to classical architecture, Roman history, renaissance painting and English literature. The assurance and precision of Dryden's judgements are paradoxically confirmed by his making Raphael Romano's pupil, and not the other way round. Because they are based on wise and passionate reading, his judgements are independent of the pedantry of fact. The almost physical grasp of seventeenth-century literary history in the first half of the poem has an authority equal to the fine survey of the same subject in the second speech in *MacFlecknoe*, but there is a greater boldness of assertion, simplicity of design, and earnestness of purpose in the later poem. Especially impressive is the naturalness with which Dryden alludes to his own loss of the laureateship in terms which bring to mind the dispute over William and Mary's accession,[21] and so the whole question of whether history enforces or ignores Right. The pride with which he is able to pass on to Congreve his own Right as England's greatest poet, whoever actually holds the laureateship, is balanced by the humility with which he is willing to allow Congreve a personal greatness wholly distinct from his own:

> Yet this I Prophesy; Thou shalt be seen,
> (Tho' with some short Parenthesis between:)
> High on the Throne of Wit; and seated there,
> Not mine (that's little) but thy Lawrel wear. (51–4)

The compression, strength and plainness of the last line make it the most Jonsonian in a poem which is deeply Jonsonian in spirit. Its carefully meditated classicism is, like Jonson's, uncompromisingly related to present historical realities. Where Dryden has the advantage over Jonson, however, is that he is aware of the instability of institutions and of human dignity in all its forms. It is this which gives such power to the touching anxiety about his own future reputation which he finally allows to displace the general issues he has in the main been concerned with in the poem. He is not dishonoured by this old man's egotism, however, because it is matched by an unqualified acceptance of Congreve's right to pass literary judgement upon his achievement. Dryden's humility in the face of the future is thus a human as well as a religious stance. It includes a generous submission to the self-creating, self-authenticating powers of young talent as well as to the Providence of God.

There are only two further verse epistles. *To my Friend* [*Peter Motteux*] (1698) contains a strong, honest reply to protests against obscenities and anti-clericalism in Dryden's plays. The political attack on the clergy which follows, however, has only an oblique relation with the defence of English irregularities against French correctness which concludes the poem. *To Mr. Granville* (1698) on the other hand is a fine poem. Ostensibly it is about the decay of English theatre in the nineties. But it is not the stage only that is in decay. James II and Louis XIV were old men, and both had had to make notable concessions to the younger 'Prince' of Orange. Superficially, therefore, Dryden might be thought to have made an odd choice of analogy when he compares himself to 'an Ancient Chief' and Granville to the young prince to whom he yields the 'Honours of the Field', since he disliked Louis almost as much as William. Within the analogy, however, is another, rather impudent, one. Granville is the schoolboy Prince of Wales, on whose growth to manhood Jacobite hopes depend:

> Young Princes Obstinate to win the Prize,
> Thô Yearly beaten, Yearly yet they rise:
> Old Monarchs though Successful, still in Doubt,
> Catch at a Peace; and wisely turn Devout.   (11–14)

In this context it is William who is numbered among the 'Old Monarchs'. Certainly he, James, and Louis grew more 'Devout' as they got older. The complaint a few lines later about degenerate

theatrical managements who 'Set up some Foreign Monster in a
Bill' (22) contains another outrageous pun, the reference being to the
establishment by Act of Parliament of a foreign 'Bill' on the throne of
England.[22] Thus, as in the Prologue to *Aureng-Zebe*, a barbarous and
crudely innovating theatre symbolises in both humorous and tragic
ways the degenerate spectacle presented by European politics. The
contrast between youth and decay, however, is not a simple one.
Dryden himself, after all, is the central figure of old age in the poem,
and there are ways in which the young Granville's 'scenes' can also be
regarded, quite properly, as old:

> Their Setting-Sun still shoots a Glimm'ring Ray,
> Like Ancient *Rome*, Majestick in decay:
> And better gleanings, their worn Soil can boast,
> Then the Crab-Vintage of the Neighb'ring Coast.
> This difference, yet the judging World will see;
> Thou Copiest Homer, and they Copy thee.   (35–40)

But though the image of a hopeful young literary prince merges
perfectly legitimately with that of the oldest of poets, there are other,
and necessary, distinctions between what is lawful, ancient and
authentic and what is usurping, innovatory and sensational, which
ought still to be maintained. The present age, however, draws even
Dryden himself into its confusion of colliding images and distorting
analogies. The old poet thus implicitly acknowledges that he is not
merely a detached observer but a participant, whether he likes it or
not, in the corruptions and ambiguities of his time. He insists also,
however, that in spite of the sensationalism and dishonour of the
modern 'scene', Right remains, incontestably and eternally Right.
The business of accepting with deep seriousness and warm humour this
absolute dichotomy between historical change and his own most
cherished values was, in the end, Dryden's major task as a poet out of
tune with the Revolution of 1688.

1. *Four Tragedies*, p. 281.
2. X, pp. 449–52.
3. See *Four Tragedies*, p. 283.
4. Scott–Saintsbury I, p. 300.
5. Quoted from Scott–Saintsbury VIII.

6. Earl Miner, 'On Reading Dryden' in *Writers and their Background: John Dryden*, Ed. Earl Miner (1972), p. 18.

7. 'Dedication of Plutarch's *Lives*', Scott–Saintsbury XVII, p. 6.

8. *The Life of Plutarch*, ibid., p. 33.

9. ibid., p. 31.

10. ibid., pp. 56–7.

11. *Cleomenes*, Preface, Scott–Saintsbury VIII, p. 222.

12. See Kinsley II, p. 663.

13. Paul Ramsey, *The Art of John Dryden* (1969), p. 130.

14. Kinsley II, p. 583.

15. Preface to the *Sylvae*, Kinsley I, p. 392.

16. ibid., p. 399.

17. See *The Dedication of the Æneis*, Kinsley III, p. 1051.

18. See Earl Miner, *Dryden's Poetry* (1967), p. 241.

19. See Howard Erskine-Hill, 'John Dryden: The Poet and Critic', *Dryden to Johnson*, Ed. R. Lonsdale (1971), p. 48.

20. Mark Van Doren, *John Dryden: A Study of His Poetry* (1960), p. 66.

21. See Alan Roper, *Dryden's Poetic Kingdoms* (1965), pp. 170–1.

22. ibid., p. 138.

9

REACTIONS TO HISTORY:

TRANSLATIONS AND CRITICISM 1681–1698

The case against Dryden was put forcefully by Wordsworth. Dryden, he wrote to Scott, 'had neither a tender heart nor a lofty sense of moral dignity: where his language is poetically impassioned it is mostly upon unpleasing subjects'.[1] In particular Wordsworth established the tradition of using the translations and adaptations as the prime evidence against Dryden, whose appropriations of small parts of Theocritus, Sophocles and Horace, and large sections of Homer, Lucretius, Persius, Juvenal, Ovid, Boccaccio, Chaucer, Shakespeare and Milton, certainly suggest a poetic appetite more capacious than subtle. It is inappropriate, however, to make direct comparisons between Dryden and his originals. He was very conscious of having different historical and literary perspectives from theirs, and he felt it essential to his work as a translator to be seen to exploit them.

Of course Dryden had deficiencies of sensibility. He may always have respected the importance of strategy in art, of the fable, its design and disposition, but he was never completely consistent in his approach to matters of detail. Neoclassical decorum tended to coarsen his sense of manners, and false analogies with painting sometimes made his theory of diction dangerously superficial. Against this one can set his intense concentration in the eighties and nineties on problems of sound in verse, and his much reiterated definition of wit as 'Propriety of thoughts and words', the product, he claimed, of his Virgilian studies. *A Parallel of Poetry and Painting* (1695), for instance, only comes to life on the question of colouring and diction, and the account of Horace's language in the Preface to the *Sylvae* (1685) is manifestly the product of an acute ear for the proprieties of Latin.

In practice, too, Dryden was generally a master of verbal tactics: the strength of the transitions in the famous description of the feast at the end of the First Book of the *Æneis* (1697) 'lies in the diction',[2] and it is easy to overstate the deleterious effect of neoclassical vocabulary on his Virgil. The heroic couplet, after all, does not move with the measured dignity of a Latin hexametre. Its greater pace and more obvious resonances justify, even require, a less discriminating choice of figurative expressions than Virgil's. Objection has been taken, for instance, to Dryden's 'fearsome' use of the word 'war' to describe any violent action, such as the shooting of the deer in the First Book.[3] But the incident, from the sighting of the deer to the feast, is over so quickly that the far from unusual periphrasis does not register as a poeticism.

The fact remains, however, that both wit and diction are astonishingly undervalued in the Preface to the *Fables* (1700), and in practice it is certainly true that Dryden often is 'florid and fulsome'[4] notably in his use of words like 'insatiate', 'tumultuous', 'admires', and 'devours' to describe sexual feeling. The descriptions of Dido's passion for Æneas in the stock vocabulary of stagey love are made especially unpleasant by the gross prominence given to the diction by the rhyme:

> The Heroe's Valour, Acts, and Birth inspire
> Her Soul with Love, and fann the secret Fire.
> His Words, his Looks imprinted in her Heart,
> Improve the Passion, and increase the Smart.   (IV,3–6)

The effects of such a vocabulary not only on the Virgil, but also on the translations of Theocritus, proved disastrous. It is not just the subtleties of love, however, that Dryden fails to register. All purely personal emotions are outside his range. Neither Æneas gazing at the images of the fall of Troy in Africa, nor the numberless souls on the bank of the Styx compel him to a careful or truly passionate choice of words. His translation of *The Last parting of Hector and Andromache* (1693) from the Sixth Book of the *Iliad*, is equally crass. Even his favourite episodes of Nisus and Euryalus from the *Æneid* reveal him as unfit to render simple human sorrow.

Dryden's severest critics, however, concede the power of his translations of Lucretius, Juvenal, and (more problematically) Persius. The Lucretius was his only successful piece of sustained translation before 1688. His powers of argumentation, eloquence, and intoxicated but menacing eroticism are magnificently displayed. The platonised abstractions and unyielding periphrases of restoration love poetry function perfectly in the relentless, impersonal determinations of Lucretius' cosmos. *The Fourth Book. Concerning the Nature of Love* is especially satisfying. There is a sense of intellectual release in Dryden's implacable exposition of the inexorability of process. He loves combining the self-indulgent decoration of baroque with the mental freedom of a plain dealer. The lines in which the tranditional torments of Hades are reinterpreted in terms of the pains and penalties of human vice and folly in this life, especially the Sisyphus passage (III,200–17), also provide an excellent opportunity for drawing the England of Charles II into the translation. There is, incidentally, a remarkable anticipation of *The Hind and the Panther* in the psychologically penetrating figure in the concluding couplet;

> Yet nothing to be seen in all the store
> But still the Wolf within thee barks for more.   (III,216–17)

The skill with which Dryden integrates his topical allusions with the authoritative generalisations of Lucretius is not an accidental grace.

With the Revolution Dryden lost his freedom as a satirist. He mourned it good humouredly in the Prologue to *Amphitryon*:

> How can he show his Manhood, if you bind him
> To box, like Boys, with one hand ty'd behind him?   (9–10)

He could make indirect allusions to the contemporary scene, but a full frontal attack on Orange England was forbidden him. Unable to challenge his principal enemy, he relieved his feelings, like Lucretius' frustrated lover, by attacking all the others:

> . . . When one molests thy mind
> Discharge thy loyns on all the leaky kind;
> For that's a wiser way than to restrain
> Within thy swelling nerves that hoard of pain.   (IV,19–20)

The Satires (1693) of Juvenal and Persius were the result.

The *Discourse concerning the Original and Progress of Satire* which prefaces this volume is intricately relevant to the poems themselves (at least to those translated by Dryden). It has admittedly little interest as a work of speculative scholarship, but as a statement and illustration of critical principles and procedures it is one of Dryden's greatest achievements. It is a difficult work to get along with, however, and needs placing in the context of Dryden's later critical works generally if it is to be fully understood. The problem is one of manner. Dryden's later criticism often seems doctrinaire, disorganised, and vindictive. The urbanity and control seem to have gone. This is particularly noticeable if the Preface to the *Sylvae* (1685) is compared with *A Parallel of Poetry and Painting* and the Dedication of *Examen Poeticum* (1693). The Preface, written in Dryden's prosperity, when he was at the height of his powers, has been justly praised for 'the unfailing precision and illumination of [its] similitudes, the sophistication of [its] analysis of the single poet, and [its] conspicuous comparisons and contrasts.'[5] It humanises its solid and sensitive learning with an air of proprietary ease. The *Parallel*, in contrast, is stiff. Dryden lacks an intricate intimacy with the art of painting, and so cannot test, modify, or refine the tensions created by theory and practice when comparing the two arts. The word 'parallel' indicates precisely the generalised, systematic orthodoxy of its neoclassicism. The Dedication of *Examen Poeticum* is uneasy too, but in a different way. It reads like a bullying, egotistical display of prejudice. Politicians are 'Timeservers and Blockheads',[6] over-correct critics a 'sort of Insects'.[7] Linked to some insensitive remarks about Hector and Andromache, and in the light of the allegedly fulsome dedications elsewhere to aristocratic critics and politicians, it apparently confirms the whig view of Dryden in old age, as a rambling, arrogant, self-pitying flatterer.

Its true nature, however, is subtly different from this. As a prose writer Dryden may never have assumed a completely fictional personality, but he calculated the effects of his manner very carefully none the less. He might address men stupider than himself, like the Duke of York in the Dedication of *The Conquest of Granada* (1672), but he expected to be overheard by his intellectual peers. Hence the comparison of the Duke to Achilles, and the discreet list of Achilles' faults in the subsequent essay. Very different sides to his personality are revealed, for instance, by the ferocity of his contempt for Rochester, in the Preface to *All for Love* (1678), and the intricate blend of anger and *pietas* in his letter to Busby on an injustice done by that savage mentor to his eldest son.[8] In both cases, however, major parts of

Dryden's real feelings are concealed. The Dedication of *Examen Poeticum* in its turn carefully calculates the effects of its ill-temper. It is packed with fierce references to the Revolution which are publishable only because the disorganised savagery of an angry old man seems helpless and therefore licensed.

It is as a very much more elaborate exercise in deliberate garrulity that the *Discourse* must be read. Thus the rambling discussion of epic poetry with which it begins enables Dryden both to state almost casually a position on the problem of evil, which, as we shall see, is fundamental to his satiric vision, and to prepare the ground for the as yet unrevealed purpose of the essay, which is to confer heroic status on the art of satire. This raises other important matters which are crucially relevant to the Juvenal translations, the joint evolution of literature and society (an obsessive theme of the later epistles also), the maintenance of native traditions, and by implication their treasonable repudiation. The latter, of course, bears directly on the Revolution, which is alluded to indirectly but specifically in the lavish praise of Dorset, now Lord Chamberlain, to whom *The Satires* are dedicated. The garrulous, bitter old flatterer wittily addresses the usurper's censor, not just as the legal 'King of Poets . . . absolute by your Office', but as the possessor of a literary authority 'which is inborn and inherent in your Person'.[9] Like the Preface to *An Evening's Love*, but more extensively, since it includes political theory, Roman and English history, and moral philosophy as well as criticism, the *Discourse* establishes a series of firm positions of principle, apparently disconnected, but in fact significantly if informally related. Thus the account of Horace's education in the manners of a gentleman is subtly modified by its taking place in the court of Augustus, whose glorious revolution, we are told elsewhere, 'tory' republicans like Persius found offensive. The analyses of Persius, Horace, and Juvenal, and the distinctions between Varronian, Horatian, and Juvenalian satire yield in addition a complex of related insights into history and ethics. The *Discourse* thereby becomes a major statement about the relationship of literature and society, even if many of the important things it says are not so much stated as implicit both in the wit with which Dryden exploits his licence to ramble and rage, and in the elaborate connections between the essay and the poems it accompanies. Taken together, however, they demonstrate that what Dryden possessed was a noble and compassionate sense precisely of the tragic *in*dignity which is woven into the human condition.

The chief end of the Juvenal translations, then, is not mere fidelity to the original text. *The First Satire*, for instance, being the only one in which Juvenal keeps 'to no one subject, but strikes indifferently at all Men in his way,'[10] gives Dryden the chance to inject himself into the verse by keeping up the effect of structural informality which gives the *Discourse* so idiosyncratic a character. The casualness, however, is only a matter of appearance. In paragraphs which are in fact organised with even more power and purpose than usual, Dryden establishes a casual, angry familiarity with the world of Rome, and as the pointedly generalised translation of the closing lines suggests, blends it with that of London. Not surprisingly he shares a number of attitudes with Juvenal, as the later satires further illustrate, notably a distaste for commerce and social mobility, but he is not content to express these and other attitudes in purely Roman terms. In *The Tenth Satire*, for instance, he writes:

> But we who give our Native Rights away,
> And our Inslav'd Posterity betray,
> Are now reduc'd to beg an Alms, and go
> On Holidays to see a Puppet show.   (X,128–31)

The first couplet, for which there is no warrant in Juvenal, is general enough to apply to Augustus' imperial usurpation, but obviously refers more emphatically to the Settlement of 1689. The second, translating Juvenal's *panem et circenses*, brilliantly conflates the Roman and English worlds. In addition it has a cruel appropriateness to Dryden's own reduced circumstances and his new dependence on a theatre he despised. By a mass of such allusions, sometimes as slight as the description of Juvenal's Greek immigrants as 'Refugies' (a hit at the Huguenots), he makes sure that Juvenal's Rome is perpetually shadowed by his own London. The effect is not, as it could have been, a mere generalisation or abstraction of vice and folly. The two worlds remain specific; the reader's awareness of the difference gives the translation its historical depth; and the *Discourse* in the background, with its emphasis on historical development, gives the awakened historical sense a theoretical significance.

The two couplets from *The Tenth Satire* quoted above also point up a vitally important difference between Dryden and Juvenal's satirical method. In the original it is the mob who have surrendered their rights under the constitution of the republic; Juvenal himself is not involved. In the translation, as in the later *To Mr. Granville*, Dryden allows himself to be degraded with his countrymen. It is this which makes the egotism of his version not merely tolerable but impressive. It could easily have been otherwise, for Dryden thrusts himself forward rather shamelessly in *The Satires*. He manages to make Juvenal's complaints about censorship sound as if they applied uniquely to his own case, and he simply takes over Umbricius in *The Third Satire*, changing Juvenal's Roman knight, denied the public employment appropriate to his caste, into an out-of-office laureate:

> Since Noble Arts in *Rome* have no support,
> And ragged Virtue not a Friend at Court,
> No Profit rises from th'ungrateful Stage,
> My Poverty encreasing with my Age;
> 'Tis time to give my just Disdain a vent,
> And, Cursing, leave so base a Government. (III,39–44)

The reason why this self-centredness is not offensive but morally dignified becomes clearer later. Umbricius is still speaking:

> For want of these Town Virtues, thus, alone,
> I go conducted on my way by none:
> Like a dead Member from the Body rent;
> Maim'd and unuseful to the Government. (III,85–8)

Dryden identifies himself not with the injured man, but the amputated limb. If the body-politic is corrupt, so, willy-nilly, is he. Unlike Juvenal he is not a mere spectator-moralist. His bitterness is infected by the corruption against which it declaims. There is thus less hope of escape in Dryden than there is in Juvenal. Instead of standing on the Archimedean platform of indignation, Dryden is stuck inside the inextricable tangle of human good and evil, not abstractly but historically conceived.

Nothing illustrates this more clearly than his handling of heroic conventions and values in the *Discourse* and *The Satires*. Since satire is now his chief *métier*, it is obvious that a great deal of self-esteem is involved in the assertion in the *Discourse* that the greatest satire 'is undoubtedly a Species' of heroic poetry.[11] Yet it is precisely the heroic and all it stands for that he puts under the strongest satiric pressure. The account of Hannibal's career in *The Tenth Satire* reveals how deeply disillusioned he was with the conventions of the mode, at least as they were practised in his own time. It begins with an energetic, propulsive strength that is authentically epic. It ends with a deadly attack on the literary dignity of modern heroic writing:

> Now what's his End, O Charming Glory, say
> What rare fifth Act, to Crown this huffing Play? (X,256–7)

The heroic mode shares Hannibal's degradation, yet its satirist still argues strenuously for his own work to be accorded heroic status.

Nor is this the only ambiguity in the heroic ideal. The slow historical convergence of heroic and satirical poetry by which Dryden sets such store in the *Discourse* turns out to be a highly revealing part of the whole history of man's development from a primitive to an Augustan order of things, a process Dryden regards with serious misgivings. The following lines from *The Third Satire*, about both the virtue and the crudity of country life, are suggestive in this connection:

> On Theatres of Turf, in homely State,
> Old Plays they act, old Feasts they Celebrate:
> The same rude Song returns upon the Crowd;
> And, by Tradition, is for Wit allow'd. (III,285–8)

This obviously echoes the discussion in the *Discourse* on the primitive rural world in which satire originated. The fact that satire is thus native to Italy, part of the 'Tradition' of Latin civilisation, should presumably be a legitimate source of Roman pride (at least in Dryden's system of values—there is nothing about Tradition in Juvenal's description of the rural theatre). Unfortunately the evolution of this one literary form with a uniquely Roman pedigree from a crude medley of peasant insult into a firmly designed, stoically dignified species of heroic poetry is not something of which Rome can unreservedly boast, since it requires not only the emergence of civilised standards of literary correctness for satire to refine itself against, but degenerate ways of life to provide it with a subject. The heroic dignity which time confers on satire necessarily involves also the corruption of heroic virtue.

This important irony is especially evident in *The Sixth Satire*, where a powerful description of the rude virtue of primitive Italy introduces a sophisticated satire on the degeneracy of civilised Rome. This notorious attack on the unchastity of Roman women is especially penetrating in its exposure of how deep-seated corruptions in the human spirit inevitably infect even the noblest human experience. The lust of women, Dryden says in the *Discourse*, is 'the most heroick of their Vices'.[12] The remark is, admittedly, lightly enough made, and hardly threatens the moral standing of heroic values and conventions. It is equally true that a great proportion of Dryden's version of *The Sixth Satire* manages to be outrageously obscene, urbanely amusing, and heroically eloquent without in any way compromising the poet's or the reader's commitment to high seriousness in art or life. Thus the women in *The Sixth Satire* are heroic performers even in the slightly bowdlerised version it seems Dryden gave to the public[13]—

> One sees a Dancing-Master Capring high,
> And Raves, and Pisses, with pure Extasie:
> The Country Lady, in the Box appears,
> Softly She Warbles over, all she hears;
> And sucks in Passion, both at Eyes, and Ears.
>
> (VI,91–2;97–9)

Verse sprung on such solid nouns and vigorous verbs creates literary satisfactions akin to epic *admiratio* but without compromising our pleasure in Homer. The same cannot be said, however, of the famous description of the noblewoman's heroic fencer-lover, the eroticism of which is rank enough to infect everything subsequent to it in the poem:

> A Promontory Wen, with griesly grace,
> Stood high, upon the Handle of his Face:
> His blear Eyes ran in gutters to his Chin;
> His Beard was Stubble, and his Cheeks were thin.
> But 'twas his Fencing did her Fancy move;
> 'Tis Arms and Blood and Cruelty they love.   (VI,153–8)

In considerably toughening the original (the urban gutter image and the final couplet are his) Dryden does not burlesque the heroic. He does make it very clear, however, that just as the satirist shares the corruption of the society he is attacking, so the epic vigour of such language uninhibitedly exploits the same impulses in the reader which it finds disgusting in the woman. It reminds us also of the unabashed and essential brutality of epic literature (the Twenty-second Book of the *Odyssey*, for example, or the Ninth of the *Æneid*). In the tangle of pleasure and pain, heroism and degeneracy in which human life has to be lived, even 'the greatest Work which the Soul of Man is capable to perform',[14] would seem to be dangerously close, psychologically and morally, to the most hideous of Roman excitements.

For all the complexity of these entanglements, however, certain clear positions emerge. Dryden demonstrates the convergence of the satiric and heroic modes because he believes that heroic wonder is, in spite of everything, a supremely valuable experience. Tangled the human situation may be, but Dryden as always is clear on points of principle. His various pictures of primitive and sophisticated man, in the *Discourse* and *The Satires*, admittedly point to a sort of ironic equation in the human condition by which the proportions of good and evil remain constant, even though the elements change: barbarous vigour is roughly in balance with polite enfeeblement; it follows that there is no hope of extrication from the moral confusions and ambiguities of history for poet, or reader, or poem. But the luminous validity of moral truth, and the clarity and exactness of its many distinctions, remain. The fact that history proceeds with a total disregard for human values does not invalidate them. Courage, politeness, and purity are forever themselves.

These convictions have an important bearing on a second major preoccupation of *The Satires*; the vanity of human calculations, the great theme of *The Tenth Satire*. Dryden's alterations to the conclusion of this 'Divine' poem are very significant. He introduces quite casually and apparently gratuitously the exclusively Christian controversy about the relation of power to love in the divine nature. Of the gods he declares, 'In Goodness as in Greatness they excell', and then promptly qualifies his implicit orthodoxy with the ambiguous exclamation: 'Ah that we lov'd our selves but half so well!' (X,539–40). His divinities are then seen rewarding an innocent man with a wife who is an 'audacious Strumpet' and a son who is 'ungracious'. Finally, we are told to pray only for 'Health of Body and Content of mind' and to 'Forgive the Gods the rest' (548–9). Dryden's long-standing preoccupation with fortitude in the face of a Providence which, from a human point of view, operates without visible regard for justice, is thus a major factor in co-ordinating the moral vision of *The Satires*.

Fortitude and Providence have a crucial if informal place also in the

Discourse. In his analysis of the Christian epic, for instance, Dryden points out that Christian fortitude 'consists in Patience, and Suffering for the Love of God . . . Humility and Resignation are our prime Vertues'.[15] (He then goes on to argue that this does not apply to Christian princes, but the point has been made, and its relevance to the unqualified pessimism of *The Tenth Satire* does not need stating.) He next turns to a consideration of the 'machinery' of a Christian epic, arguing that angels could properly oppose each other as fiercely as the pagan gods do, since 'as Finite beings [they are] not . . . capable of discovering the final Purposes of God, who can work Good out of Evil, as he pleases'.[16] On the evidence of *The Tenth Satire*, the bitter implications of this omnipotent secretiveness penetrate Dryden's satirical vision as profoundly as they do the tragic insights of *Don Sebastian*, and both are firmly based in his basic aesthetic and moral decision not to separate good from evil simplistically or comfortingly in man, in history, in literature, or in God.

The resulting recognition of what I have called the tragic indignity woven into all human experience is nowhere more in evidence than in the famous account of Priam's death in *The Tenth Satire*, and this is linked to the other major preoccupation of Dryden's later years, a controlling factor both in the translations and the *Discourse*, the fate of the Stuarts. It deserves quotation in full:

> How Fortunate an End had *Priam* made,
> Among his Ancestors a mighty shade,
> While *Troy* yet stood: When *Hector* with the Race
> Of Royal Bastards might his Funeral Grace:
> Amidst the Tears of *Trojan* Dames inurn'd,
> And by his Loyal Daughters, truly mourn'd.
> Had Heaven so Blest him, he had Dy'd before
> The fatal Fleet to *Sparta Paris* bore.
> But mark what Age produc'd; he liv'd to see
> His Town in Flames, his falling Monarchy:
> In fine, the feeble Syre, reduc'd by Fate,
> To change his Scepter for a Sword, too late,
> His last Effort before *Jove*'s Altar tries;
> A Souldier half, and half a Sacrifice:
> Falls like an Oxe, that waits the coming blow;
> Old and unprofitable to the Plough.   (X,402–19)

Priam is almost a royal victim-priest immolated for his people in this passage. In the end, however, he is a beast unfit for sacrifice, a James II.

The language is cruelly appropriate to the latter's futile behaviour in 1688 and afterwards, while the phrase 'Loyal Daughters' has a bitter applicability also. The earlier, hypothetical lines, however, apply equally to Charles II, who did indeed die in time to be duly mourned by his bastards. Dryden thus deliberately links the Stuarts as a family with an irreversible dynastic disaster. He even follows Juvenal in the subsequent lines of Hecuba's old age, thereby violating the lovely image of Mary of Modena which he had so memorably celebrated in the 'Prologue to the Dutchess'. There are few harsher examples of his willingness to confront all the implications of a surrender to the relentless dispositions of time. Yet *The Tenth Satire* generally and this passage in particular also confirm, if with tragic impressiveness, his hard-earned faith in the heroic dignity of the art of satire.

There were of course other translators at work on *The Satires* as well as Dryden. Coherent as the vision of man in history may be, therefore, in the *Discourse* and the four major satires of Juvenal which Dryden himself translated, the volume as a whole is not the single co-ordinated work the *Fables* were to be. Dryden probably translated *The Sixteenth Satire*, for instance, simply to attack William of Orange's interest in maintaining a standing army. His relation to the Persius translations is similarly doubtful. Johnson thought that they were 'written merely for wages',[17] but this ignores Dryden's manifestly sincere respect for Persius' loyalty to the Roman republic through 'the dangerous times of the Tyrant *Nero*'.[18] His Persius 'has not forgotten that *Rome* was once a Commonwealth',[19] and Dryden enjoys the innocent irony of being able to dress tory principles in flagrantly republican colours. There is also a degree of thematic continuity between the Juvenal and Persius translations. *The Fifth Satire*, for instance, contains some robust writing on fustian heroics ('Words unchaw'd, and fit to choak the Muse') and inevitably on 'fond notions of false liberty'. In *The Fourth Satire* there is well-controlled tension between polite neoclassical circumlocution and the plain speech called for by subjects like depilation, impotence, and military brutality; and in *The First Satire* an admirable attack on excessive and un-English correctness in verse:

> The verse in fashion, is, when Numbers flow
> Soft without Sence, and without Spirit slow;
> So smooth and equal, that no sight can find
> The Rivet, where the polish'd piece is join'd.   (I,123–6)

No one who feels the propriety and force of 'The Rivet' could agree with Johnson that this was written 'without any eager endeavour after excellence'.[20]

The main reason for the inclusion of Persius, however, is his theoretical importance. It was Persius, we are told in the *Discourse*, who 'discover'd to us this important Secret, . . . that [satire] ought only to treat of one Subject . . . As in a Play in the English fashion, which we call a *Tragecomedy* . . . tho' there be an Under-plot, or Second Walk of Comical Characters and Adventures, yet they are subservient to the Chief Fable.'[21] Persius is important also for his moral perspectives. Without falling into any of the absurdities and impieties of pagan pride, he is a Stoic: 'The most noble, most generous, most beneficial to Humane Kind, amongst all the Sects, who have given us the Rules of Ethiques, thereby to form a severe Virtue in the Soul.'[22] It is a small but representative sign of Dryden's moral suppleness that the man who in his view brought satire to technical perfection, and who also maintained the noblest ethical principles open to mankind without the aid of sanctifying grace, should be 'the least in Dignity'[23] of the great Roman satirists. For Dryden, every kind of success, in a man or a civilisation, is counterbalanced, but never cancelled out, by a different kind of failure.

Of the various Prefaces to *The Works of Virgil* (1697), only the Dedication of the *Æneis* has any importance, and even so it reads rather tamely. The 'loose Epistolary way . . . after the Example of Horace',[24] in which it is written, however, is as calculated as the *Discourse*. It begins in epic fashion with a large assertion: 'A Heroick Poem, truly such is undoubtedly the greatest Work which the Soul of Man is capable to perform.' Only later is the poem's patron addressed and praised. Its full, thoroughly neoclassical account of epic theory and of the *Æneid* is unfortunately nearer in spirit to the *Parallel betwixt Poetry and Painting* than the more flexible *Discourse*, mainly because there are too few great epics for the subtle discriminations between different kinds and degrees of success which make the latter so dense with meaning. Its aggressive, persistent and witty Jacobitism, however, is highly relevant to the translations which accompany it.

The *Pastorals* begin with a poker-faced note on Augustus' confiscations once he had 'setled hinself in the Roman Empire',[25] relevant of course to the poem, but relevant also to Dryden's own situation as ex-laureate. Melibœus in *The First Pastoral* asks a particularly pointed question:

> Are we condemn'd by Fates unjust Decree,
> No more our Houses and our Homes to see?
> Or shall we mount again the Rural Throne,
> And rule the Country Kingdoms, once our own!   (I,93–6)

Plain good men everywhere could meditate with either pleasure or pain on the fact that Meliboeus never regained his estate, but Virgil did. The contrast between town and country in *The Second Pastoral* raises again the ironic calculus of good and evil in primitive and civilised societies, and in *The Seventh Pastoral* the dispute between Corydon and Thyrsis revives critical issues treated in Persius' *First Satyr*. *The Fourth Pastoral*, full of alexandrines and fourteeners, keeps somewhat lushly alive the theme of triumphant restoration, but by and large, after a provocative start, these are properly neutral poems. Inevitably there is an unpleasant clash between idyllic values and manners on the one hand, and Dryden's diction on the other, notably in *The Fifth Pastoral*. *The Third*, however, is as 'lyrical' as the best of Dryden's songs.

The Georgics are very different. The opening of *The First Georgic*, which Dryden greatly admired, gives him space enough for a brilliant exhibition of the resources of the couplet. One feels at once why he thinks this 'the best poem of the best poet'.[26] The themes of *The First Georgic*; ploughing, the weather, sea, stars, the evolution of crafts and ultimately Rome itself—bring nature and civilisation into massive fluctuating relationships in which patterns of recurrence and change are equally evident, and repeatedly relevant to events in Dryden's own world. In drawing attention to these coincidences he incidentally pays tribute, at times humorously, to Virgil's capacity to speak to the human condition. Thus the 'Jacobite' bull in *The Third Georgic* is both comic and courageous:

> Often he turns his Eyes, and, with a groan,
> Surveys the pleasing Kingdoms, once his own.
> And therefore to repair his strength he tries:
> Hardning his Limbs with painful Exercise,
> And rough upon the flinty Rock he lies.   (III,333–7)

Giving his animals human emotions amused Dryden; giving an animal shape to human entanglements and feelings—the bull is hardly a person—proved as rewarding. Dryden delighted in combining a

subtle mockery of public affairs with his usual unyielding loyalty to
political principle. This is nowhere more in evidence than in the account
of civil strife among the bees in *The Fourth Georgic*:

> Yet all those dreadful deeds, this deadly fray, ⎫
> A cast of scatter'd Dust will soon alay,   ⎬
> And undecided leave the Fortune of the day.   ⎭
> When both the Chiefs are sund'red from the Fight,
> Then to the lawful King restore his Right. (IV,130–5)

The sudden shift from belittling contempt to four, hard, Jacobite
words in the last line is particularly satisfying.

Neoclassical periphrasis works surprisingly well in *The Georgics*.
There are, admittedly, passages where it is happily eschewed—the
country-woman very properly

> . . . boils in Kettles Must of Wine, and skims
> With Leaves, the Dregs that overflow the Brims. (I,393–4)

but when her husband waters his fields and

> Sends in his feeding Flocks betimes t'invade
> The rising bulk of the luxuriant Blade . . . (I,165–6)

the elaboration of the rhetoric enacts the richness of the harvest. One
of the great strengths of the poem, indeed, is its feeling for dense,
vegetable fertility. *The Second Georgic* is especially rich in this respect,
and in the clarity and emphasis of its generalised vocabulary:

> Happy the Man, who, studying Nature's Laws,
> Thro' known Effects can trace the secret Cause.
> His Mind possessing, in a quiet state,
> Fearless of Fortune, and resign'd to Fate. . . .
> Nor hopes the People's Praise, nor fears their Frown, ⎫
> Nor, when contending Kindred tear the Crown,   ⎬
> Will set up one, or pull another down.   ⎭
> (II,698–701;706–8)

The alternative to party quarrels is rediscovering in the countryside
the primitive virtue of the golden age 'E're *Saturn*'s Rebel Son usurp'd
the Skies' (II,785). Always, however, the implication that virtue makes

for strength, strength for empire, and empire for both civility and corruption implies an ironic perspective. But Dryden is now on his home ground, following 'Virgil through the *Georgics* with delight and the same gentlemanly knowledge of sky, field and fold';[27] and his response to the irony is warmer and more humane than it had been in the Satires, just as his diction is cleaner and more appropriate than it had been in the *Pastorals*.

His attitude to his version of the *Æneid* is significant. In the 'Postscript to the Reader' he displays a decent pride in his technical success, but he had already urged the reader, in the Dedication, to 'Lay by *Virgil* ... when you take up my Version' precisely because he could not 'Copy his Harmonious Numbers ... [nor] imitate his Noble Flights; where his Thoughts and Words are equally sublime'.[28] In effect he acknowledges the case against himself, but also justly asserts that his coarsening of Virgil can be largely attributed to the inadequacies of literary English at the end of the seventeenth century. It is important, therefore, to take his advice to lay Virgil by when reading his *Æneis*, except in so far as comparison between the two texts highlights his calculated modifications of the original, all of which were concerned to use the coming of Æneas to the kingdom of Latinus, of Augustus to the Roman republic, and of William of Orange to the kingdom of England as representative instances of the historical process.

The first six books admittedly come much closer to being a direct translation of Virgil than this suggests. They are also less successful than the last six. Their virtues, 'clarity and rapidity, . . . dextrous changes of pace and image and sound, ... use of a decor of ... dazzling brilliance',[29] are inexorably accompanied by a complementary incapacity to render Virgil's 'pathos, graciousness without formality, power of suggestion, effortless dignity, above all the sustained heroic note'.[30] The eloquent decisive opening illustrates all these virtues with none of the faults. The verse moves from action to rest with strength and grace. Dryden does, admittedly, make the occasional political reference at this stage, even to the extent of having Venus punningly protest to Jove that her Trojans are 'Entitled to your Heav'n, and Rites Divine' (I,341), but the theme is a minor one. The odyssey of Virgil's hero holds our attention. When he begins the story of the fall of Troy he may lack tragic dignity, but his narrative effectively conveys a sense of massive destruction, violence and loss. The couplets are not sensitive enough for individual moments of suffering, but a collective sorrow, monumental and terrible, does dignify the images of destruction. The effect is epic, brutal and historical. The quieter movement of the *Third Book* also requires pace. The meeting with Helenus and Andromache is at least not bathetic, and the brief conclusion, with Anchises' death, is decorously done. The *Fourth Book* contains some of Dryden's most publicised failures, though here again the speed of his narrative suggests the relentless pressure on the lovers. The account of their passion and its conclusion is theatrically if unfeelingly organised. The *Fifth Book* works well, notably the famous descriptions of the snake and of Ascanius' troop. Dryden generally succeeds in the vigorous deployment of solidly physical material. Only the last couplet fails to catch the enormous sorrow of Æneas' lament for Palinurus. The *Sixth Book*'s account of Æneas in the underworld is exactly what one would expect. Dryden's verse fails to record the sadness of pagan death, but it grasps with great intellectual power the scale of Virgil's historical vision. And it is in the account of the variety of wickedness in Hell that Dryden decisively intrudes his own historical and political preoccupations into the Virgilian text (VI,824–8). The remaining six books are organised around the themes of usurpation, the rule of foreign princes, and the repeal of ancient laws which are here given striking emphasis.

The invocation near the beginning of the *Seventh Book* is significant:

> Relate how *Latium* was, her ancient Kings:
> Declare the past, and present State of things,
> When first the *Trojan* Fleet *Ausonia* sought;
> And how the Rivals lov'd, and how they fought.
> These are my Theme, and how the War began,
> And how concluded by the Godlike Man.
> For I shall sing of Battels, Blood, and Rage,
> Which Princes, and their People did engage.   (VII,54–61)

Virgil's first statement of the 'greater matters' (*maior rerum*) which he was about to relate makes no reference to 'how the Rivals lov'd, and how they fought', nor does it single out Æneas' role from that of the other princes drawn to death by their courage. Dryden's version thus adds stereotyped and mechanical motivation to the action, but it also gives Æneas the ideologically important title 'Godlike', and involves the people as well as the princes in the wars. As is usual with Dryden, psychological simplification is balanced by an elaboration of theoretical allusiveness.

As in all his best political writings Dryden does not represent
historical characters allegorically in his poem, but allows situations to
echo and shadow each other in an elaborate and often provocative
intellectual design. Thus in both Æneas' son, Ascanius, and in Pallas,
the son of his ally Evander, there is something of the exiled Prince of
Wales. In the *Tenth Book*, Pallas rallies his forces with these words:

> By my great Sire, by his establish'd Name,
> And early promise of my Future Fame;
> By my Youth emulous of equal Right,
> To share his Honours, shun ignoble Flight. . . .
> 'Tis thro' that forward Path that we must come:
> There lies our Way, and that our Passage home.
>
> (X,516–19;522–3)

There is nothing about an 'establish'd Name' nor of Pallas' 'Right' in
Virgil; and Dryden has reshaped the final couplet. In the original the
fatherland simply recalls the men to the thick of battle; Dryden makes
this a call to the exiles to fight their way home. The shift in emphasis is
especially important because Pallas is of course killed. The young
Ascanius enters his divine inheritance, but the House of Evander is
left heirless. Though an epic action necessarily ends in the hero's
triumph, Dryden always qualified the simplistic optimism of neoclassical poetic justice with repeated images of Right violated and
destroyed.

The story of the exiled tyrant Menzentius, whom Dryden calls an
atheist, and his virtuous son, Lausus, further complicates the body of
allusion to the Stuarts and the more general theme of the relative
standing of 'Right' and Fate in human affairs. When Lausus dies
saving his father, Menzentius declares:

> To see my Son, and such a Son, resign
> His Life a Ransom for preserving mine? . . .
> My Guilt thy growing Virtues did defame;
> My Blackness blotted thy unblemish'd Name.
> Chas'd from a Throne, abandon'd, and exil'd
> For foul Misdeeds, were Punishments too mild:
> I ow'd my People these.   (X,1208–9;1214–18)

Dryden blackens Menzentius' confession apparently gratuitously in
order to highlight the purity and innocence of his son. Though first

written before 1688, the passage reads like a defiant concession of the Williamite case against James in order to intensify the moral dilemma posed by the impeccable claims of the Prince of Wales. But as in *The Assignation*, we have in addition the striking paradox of a son acting as 'Ransom' for a father's guilt, a distinctively Christian turn of phrase unwarranted by the Latin. The effect is to confirm the nightmare of godlessness implicit in a historical disjunction between Fate and Right, and simultaneously to defy it with a shining image of truly 'Godlike' sonship.

The conflict between Fate and Right is never finally resolved in the poem. Dryden himself believed that Virgil had bound even Jove by the decrees of Fate,[31] a view perfectly consistent with the pagan perspectives of the poem. He also tends to stress rather more than Virgil does Jove's own usurpation of Saturn's throne, and naturally exploits Saturn's subsequent reign in the golden age of primitive Latium. The coming of Æneas into his divine inheritance thus takes place against a background in which the relation of Fate to Right is confused even at an Olympian level, just as in the subsequent history of Rome, first as an elective monarchy, then as a republic, the whole question of legitimacy involves a Jacobite poet in a mass of familiar paradox, in which kings can be lawfully exiled and 'The *Roman* Youth' can justly 'assert their Native Rights' (VIII,860) against them. (Virgil's sons of Æneas fight simply *pro libertate*—it is Dryden who makes the issue a constitutional one.) Even at the supreme moment of the poem, when Juno submits to the will of Jove and ceases to protect Turnus, and Virgil introduces his final and most emphatic assertion of the divine right of Æneas, the Julian line, and the *imperium* of Augustus, Dryden hints at the doubtful standing of the two Olympians. For Virgil's '*es germana Iovis Saturnique altera proles*' (XII *Æn.* 830), Dryden writes, 'Can *Saturn*'s Issue, and Heav'n's other Heir' (XII,1205), thus fleetingly blending the images of Jove and Juno with those of William and Mary. Such fusions are deliberately momentary and illusory since the essence of the problem is the insecurity created by the ambiguous flux of history. In Dryden's *Æneis* heroic virtue has precisely the task of asserting Right simply and strongly amid all these obscurities and doubts as they emerge from the secular, anti-human processes of time.

Three figures dominate the second half of the poem; Latinus, Æneas, and Turnus. They are related to each other as Sancho, Torrismond and Bertram are in *The Spanish Friar*. Latinus, typically the

figure of an old king, courageous but uncertain and confused by
weakness and age, perfectly reflects the situation of James II, without
in any way being a portrait of him. In Virgil he is a quasi-mythical
figure, meditating unhappily on his daughter's marriage and the oracle
of Faunus. In Dryden the traditional dilemmas of legend precipitate
precise political and constitutional questions—'Succession, Empire,
and his Daughter's Fate' (VII,346)—and to keep Latium and England
in continual association Dryden repeatedly emphasises that Æneas'
future relationship with Latinus parallels that between William and
James. He succeeds in giving his Latinus a considerable measure of the
original's dignified suffering, even when he is emphasising the relationship between his situation and that of the Stuarts. When according
to Virgil the king enters his palace and abandons the reins of state,
Dryden writes:

> He said no more, but in his Walls confin'd,
> Shut out the Woes which he too well divin'd:
> Nor with the rising Storm wou'd vainly strive,
> But left the Helm, and let the Vessel drive.   (VII,829–32)

This is just what Charles II did during the Exclusion crisis, and in very
different fashion, and to very different effect, what the helpless James
did at the approach of William's army. There are thus allusions both to
Stuart craft and Stuart weakness in the lines, which the altered and
enlarged metaphor of a ship driven before the wind admirably
dignifies and generalises. (The contrast with Achitophel, the 'daring
Pilot in extremity', is noteworthy.) What these lines definitively illustrate is Dryden's capacity to incorporate contemporary tensions into
his *Æneis* and at the same time to subordinate them to the grave
generality of the heroic convention.

Æneas is thus, in important ways, the Prince in Orange in Dryden's
version of the poem—but with the crucial difference that he is also the
embodiment of 'Piety', which according to the Dedication 'compre-
hends the whole Duty of Man towards the Gods, towards his Country,
and towards his Relations'.[32] Dryden tellingly reminds his readers in
the Dedication that Æneas came of a cadet line of the Trojan royal
house, that in first marrying Priam's daughter he had still no claim on
the Trojan throne 'while any of the Male Issue were remaining', and
that in later marrying Lavinia, 'tho' he Married the Heiress of the
Crown yet [he] claim'd no Title to it during the Life of his Father-in-

Law'.[33] This is why he so insistently points up the godlike virtue of his hero. Æneas has a truly royal personality and presence, and a capacity to integrate his legitimate aspirations to empire with an unreserved commitment to a fully human sense of duty. Yet for all the substantiated grandeur of Æneas' piety, small touches of doubt remain. The facetiousness with which the feelings of Dido and Lavinia are discussed in the Dedication is itself ambiguous. In relation to the former Dryden concedes that 'humanely speaking . . . there was a fault somewhere',[34] and blames Jove, while his remarks about Lavinia's 'folly' in preferring the young Turnus are at least open to ironic interpretation. Moreover Dido's complaint against Æneas bears indirectly but disturbingly on the great theme of Right of which in all other respects he is the heroic embodiment:

> The Gods, and Jove himself behold in vain
> Triumphant Treason, yet no Thunder flyes:
> Nor *Juno* views my Wrongs with equal Eyes;
> Faithless is Earth, and Faithless are the Skies! (IV,532–5)

Far more complex and interesting is the case of Turnus, in whom the spirit of Homeric rather than Virgilian virtue most obviously flourishes, and who thus in a sense represents legitimacy at least of a kind in an epic context. He is also Lavinia's original betrothed, whose claim Æneas 'usurps'. Moreover he fights on behalf of native rights against the incursions of a foreign prince. As Juno declares to Venus, in lines considerably at variance with Virgil's,

> You think it hard, the *Latians* shou'd destroy
> With Swords your *Trojans*, and with Fire your *Troy*:
> Hard and unjust indeed, for Men to draw
> Their Native Air, nor take a foreign Law. (X,112–15)

Of course in other respects Turnus is impious and unjust. He is guilty, apparently, of desiring 'Universal Sway', a thoroughly 'Bourbon' vice, and at the same time of 'Orange' perfidy, in so far as he is responsible for

> A broken League, a Bride unjustly sought,
> A Crown usurp'd, which with their Blood is bought! (XI,333–4)

Nevertheless he makes an overwhelming impression of barbarian greatness and primitive Right. Numanus' speech of defiance to the 'civilised' Trojans who have come to replace the ancient heroic order is hard and alive—the structure of the couplets being noticeably irregular but toughly disciplined for all that—justifying to some extent Dryden's later feeling that his talents were more Homeric than Virgilian in character:

> We plow, and till in Arms; our Oxen feel
> Instead of Goads, the Spur, and pointed Steel:
> Th' inverted Lance makes Furrows in the Plain;
> Ev'n time that changes all, yet changes us in vain:
> The Body, not the Mind: Nor can controul
> Th' immortal Vigour, or abate the Soul. (IX,833–8)

But of course it is the relentless decision of time, for all Turnus' magnificent butchery in invading the Trojan camp and then fighting his way out of it, that change must be. In a slight but crucial shift of emphasis, however, Dryden makes sure that the trapped and already defeated Turnus of the *Twelfth Book* achieves incontestably full and unqualified human status before he dies. When called upon by Saces to redeem his people, Virgil's Turnus looks back towards the city full of rage and with blazing eyes. In Dryden, however,

> By slow degrees his Reason drove away
> The Mists of Passion, and resum'd her Sway. (XIII,973–4)

Moreover, when he and Æneas fight, it is not to discover whom battle will destroy, who will sink into death, but rather 'With Swords to try their Titles to the State' (XII,1033). The issue is thus in Dryden's terms (and possibly in ours) fully human for the very reason that it is pressingly and practically historical. The destruction of his Turnus is not something that takes place in a remote, mythological past, which might as easily be an archetypal dream-present. It happens in a real world where kingdoms and dynasties rise and fall, and where liberties and proprieties, rooted in a heroic if impoverished and barbarous past, are sophisticated, betrayed, and destroyed forever. What is striking and courageous about Dryden's *Æneis*, and what makes it consistent with the terrible enigma at the end of *Absalom and Achitophel*, is that the establishment of a Right as fated and just as that of the 'Godlike' Æneas must nevertheless smash and extinguish for

ever the spontaneous, barbarian, but noble and virtuous, humanity of
Turnus.

1. *The Letters of William and Dorothy Wordsworth. The Early Years' 1787–1805*, Ed. Ernest de Selincourt and Chester L. Shaver (1967), p. 641.
2. L. Proudfoot, *Dryden's Æneid and its Seventeenth Century Predecessors* (1960), p. 195.
3. ibid., p. 225.
4. See Kinsley IV, pp. 1448–9.
5. Charles E. Ward, *The Life of John Dryden* (1961), p. 206.
6. Kinsley II, p. 790.
7. ibid. II, p. 793.
8. See *The Letters of John Dryden*, pp. 18–20.
9. Kinsley II, p. 606.
10. *Argument of The First Satyr*, Kinsley II, p. 670.
11. Kinsley II, p. 665.
12. Argument of *The Sixth Satyr*, Kinsley II, p. 695.
13. See W. B. Carnochan, 'Dryden's Juvenal', *TLS*, 21 January 1972, pp. 73–4.
14. *The Dedication of the Æneis*, Kinsley III, p. 1003.
15. Kinsley II, p. 611.
16. ibid. II, p. 614.
17. *Lives*, p. 447.
18. Argument of the Prologue to the *First Satyr*, Kinsley II, p. 741.
19. Argument of the *First Satyr*, ibid. II, p. 742.
20. *Lives*, p. 447.
21. Kinsley II, p. 661.
22. ibid. II, p. 643.
23. ibid. II, p. 661.
24. ibid. III, p. 1009.
25. Argument of *The First Pastoral*, Kinsley II, p. 873.
26. *The Dedication of the Georgics*, Kinsley II, p. 913.
27. Earl Miner, *Dryden's Poetry* (1967), p. 174.
28. Kinsley III, pp. 1058–9.
29. Proudfoot, op. cit., p. 184.
30. ibid., p. 192.
31. See *The Dedication of the Æneis*, Kinsley III, pp. 1024–5.
32. Kinsley III, p. 1020.
33. ibid. III, p. 1017.
34. ibid. III, p. 1027.

10

NATURE, LOVE AND WAR:
THE FABLES AND THE SECULAR MASQUE

'Ovid's genius', John Oldmixon wrote in 1728, 'has more of Equality' with Dryden's than Virgil's.[1] In the Dedication to *Examen Poeticum*, Dryden himself declared, 'my Translations of *Ovid* . . . appear to me the best of all my Endeavours in this kind'.[2] To turn from the grandeur of his translation of Lucretius' atomical flux to the superficially not dissimilar *First Book of Ovid's Metamorphoses* (1693) is certainly a relaxing experience. Dryden was right when he claimed to have exhausted the resources of the English poetic style in his translations of Virgil. In them, and in his Lucretius and Juvenal translations, he had driven his rhetoric, his diction, and the heroic couplet magnificently but hard. His Ovidian translations are much calmer. The *Metamorphoses* suggested a more casual but subtler stance, just as in the critical essays satire provided richer opportunities for exercising his critical intelligence than the supreme experience of the epic. Ovidian flux is less solemn, less responsible, but by no means less rich in potential meaning than Lucretian science or Virgilian history, providing opportunities for mellow acceptance rather than tragic submission, for wisdom rather than sublimity.

No claim to wisdom, however, could be made for the other Ovidian translations in the *Examen Poeticum*. The sexual transformation of Iphis and the grotesque pastoral wooing of Polyphemus are tolerably treated, but the experience is a minor one. What is missing is any sense of the intellectual power or ethical discrimination which characterise the earlier Horatian translations in the *Sylvae* (1685). Admittedly two of these four poems are minor pieces also. *The Third Ode from the First Book* is in octosyllabics, effective, but not quite as expertly handled as in the *Veni Creatus Spiritus*. *The Ninth Ode from the First Book* is light, pointed, graceful, and clever without being slick. *The Twenty-Ninth Ode from the Third Book*, however, was Dryden's first exercise in pindarics, and is one of the finest irregular odes in English. Nor is its excellence only a matter of technique, but of wit, the propriety of the thoughts to the words and the intrinsic value of those thoughts. It combines an appetite for life with a willingness to accept loss, a recognition of the uncontrollability of things, and an unpretentious acknowledgement of the need for self-control, which remarkably anticipate the graver, ampler meditations on these themes in the nineties. It illustrates, too, the continuity of Dryden's poetic development. The storm image looks back to *Tyrannick Love*, the theme of poverty forward to the *Fables*. This poem and the lines from the Second Epode clearly demonstrate the base of Dryden's classicism to be, as Jonson's was, in the traditions of rural life. Jonson's version of the Second Epode is better than Dryden's, but not strikingly so: Dryden's diction in particular is notably clear and pure compared with the corrupt eroticism and false pastoralism of his Theocritus poems.

Taken together, the Horatian and Ovidian translations, and the epistolary poems to his friends in the Horatian manner, formed a base for Dryden's richest work, the *Fables Ancient and Modern* (1700). At this modest level, urbane and familiar, yet public and formal as well, he achieved, without ambitious pains, one of the great purposes of neoclassicism, a unification of classical, mediaeval and modern experience. The dedication of the whole volume to the Duke of Ormonde, a complicated blend of loyalty and idealisation, exemplifies the method of the entire work.[3] Though the present Duke had cautiously supported William's invasion, if not his assumption of the crown, the service of his family in the Stuart cause was famous. His grandfather ('Barzillai') was the best lord lieutenant Ireland had had in the seventeenth century. His grandson had returned to Ireland in 1697 in an attempt to placate his bitter, defeated, and persecuted countrymen. Later he became an avowed Jacobite. Through the Butlers, therefore, Dryden was in touch almost tangibly, but judiciously, with the kingship of the Stuarts, if only by association. Judicious association, however, is the method of the work that follows.

The volume is elaborately organised in a series of casual allusions to deeply meditated correspondences. The strategy is far more complex than that in the earlier translations in which analogies between Virgil's or Juvenal's worlds and Dryden's were deftly suggested. In the *Fables* Dryden takes three civilisations, the classical, the mediaeval and his own—and records echoes of each in the others. This all takes place in a fourth world, the fictitious artificial world of neoclassical fable, in which the various tales in the miscellany shadow each other, modifying, qualifying, even negating the values each on its own might appear to confirm. The effect is of Ovidian insecurity removed from a purely mythological medium and reconstituted in a generalised human psychology on the one hand, and three historically differentiated civilisations on the other. The sense of flux is thereby intensified and made historically concrete, but within it repetitions and correspondences begin to emerge which define certain abiding facts about the human condition and suggest the lasting relevance of certain values in a way altogether wiser, more persuasive and more inclusive than would normally be possible in the language of reasoned neoclassicism.

This process begins in the first paragraph of the Dedication, in which Dryden alludes to himself both as another Nestor and as a hereditary client of the Butler family. Since the themes of inherited titles, rights, and virtues figure prominently in the subsequent poems, it is no accident that he should then group examples of all three in Roman, English, and even 'Peruvian' history round the figure of the Duke, in whom title, right, and virtue are perfectly embodied. It is part of the volume's meaning and value that the Duke combines 'heroical' courage with gentleness and learning. He is not 'one of those Athletick Brutes whom undeservedly we call Heroes', 'a Man-killing Ideot' like Ajax.[4] Dryden's hatred of violence is a prominent feature of the *Fables* but it is combined with a real respect for intelligent courage, and a grim acceptance of the inevitability of war.

The Preface begins with an account of the origins of the volume as a whole. It was apparently the product of that process of metamorphosis which the *Fables* themselves illustrate. They had their origins, Dryden tells us, in an experimental translation of Homer, which led him to translate the very different summary of the Trojan war in *The Twelfth Book of the Metamorphoses*. This in turn brought to his attention the great generalised vision of flux in *The Fifteenth Book*. Ovid now took over from Homer. Dryden translated five more stories, sensed a connection between what he had done and Chaucer, and so tried his hand at the 'Homeric' *Knight's Tale*, as well as the 'Ovidian' *Nun's Priests' Tale* and *The Wife of Bath's Tale*. Chaucer led to

Boccaccio, and Dryden finally decided to include some poems of his own, an epistle, *To my Honour'd Kinsman, John Driden*, an ode, *Alexander's Feast*, which he had already published, and *The Monument of a Fair Maiden Lady, Who dy'd at Bath*. He insists, however, that though the procedure was a casual one the whole volume makes up a single work. 'I have built a House', he claims, 'where I intended a Lodge'.[5]

The Preface itself is alleged to have been written in similar fashion. It meanders into unity. The Nestor of English letters uses the device of free association, to ensure that certain important themes crop up again and again in different contexts and at strategically significant moments. Thus on three separate occasions he wanders off the subject in hand to defend himself against the charges of obscenity, anticlericalism, and political infidelity which had recently been levelled at him by two clergymen, Collier and Millbourne, and a doctor, Blackmore. These apparently egotistical ramblings, however, lay the foundations for a series of important allusions in the poems that follow to chastity and lust, and to clerical corruption and clerical virtue. And just as Ovid is to emerge as the centrally unifying factor in the *Fables*, so Chaucer emerges as the centralising figure in the vision of the Preface. In the most brilliant and original of all Dryden's studies of an individual poet, he is first compared with Ovid, then with Boccaccio. With the exception of the comments on Chaucerian metrics, the assessment is astonishingly exact, original, and complete. But Chaucer is not praised for the sake of his poems only. Through him Dryden creates a detailed picture of a densely peopled literary world full of evolving languages, lines of poetic descent, and borrowed tales intricately consistent with the great theme of change which binds the *Fables* together. In addition Chaucer is placed in a significant historical as well as a representative literary context. Dryden records his belief, for instance, that Chaucer was involved in the deposition of Richard II and that he flirted with heresy. The idea that 'the Father of *English* Poetry' had been a bad tory and a bad Catholic does not disturb him, however, since the great vision of continuity as well as change which Chaucer the poet did so much to specify makes possible an intelligent accommodation of all such contradictions.

We have our Fore-fathers and Great Grand-dames all before us as they were in Chaucer's Days [Dryden says of the *Canterbury Tales*]; their general Characters are still remaining in Mankind, and even in *England*, though they are call'd by other Names than those of *Moncks*, and *Fryars*, and *Chanons*, and Lady *Abbesses*, and *Nuns*: For Mankind is ever the same, and nothing is lost out of Nature, though everything is alter'd.[6]

The *Fables* may be divided, if only for convenience, into four sections. The first consists of Chaucer's *Palamon and Arcite*, a miniature mediaeval epic set in Theseus' Athens, with a regally feminine dedication to the Duchess of Ormonde preceding it and an informally masculine Horatian epistle to John Driden following it. Having thus established poetic roots in the classical, mediaeval and modern worlds, Dryden then introduces, in the second phase, four minor Ovidian stories and one by Boccaccio, in which themes and allusions established in the first three poems are ironically amplified. The third section begins with *The First Book of Homer's Ilias* and includes stories by Boccaccio and Chaucer, one of Ovid's minor tales, *Ceyx and Alcyone*, and a notable contribution by Dryden himself, *Alexander's Feast*—but its principle of organisation is that laid out in the Preface: it develops by association from Homer's Troy to the climactic 'Of the Pythagorean Philosophy' from *The Fifteenth Book of the Metamorphoses*, which Dryden regarded as Ovid's finest achievement. The final section is a sort of coda, with two studies of Christian virtue qualifying the impressions left by the paganism of Ovid and the lewdness of *The Wife of Bath's Tale*, but these in their turn are qualified by a last poem, *Cymon and Iphigenia* from Boccaccio, a curious, tough little tale which brings the collection to an end on an abruptly realistic note.

The dedicatory verses *To Her Grace the Dutchess of Ormonde* are flattering, elaborate and decorative, after the manner of the prologue to the Duchess of York, and with none of the clever purposelessness of the lines to Lady Castlemain. The Duchess' descent from the Plantagenets enables Dryden to associate her with the mediaeval monarchy and with Emily, the heroine of *Palamon and Arcite*. By implication this makes Palamon a type of Ormonde himself, Theseus of William of Orange, and Thebes (which he lays waste) of Ireland. The Duchess' visit there in 1697 preparatory to her husband's return had been a great popular success. Dryden's description of it cleverly draws on his own hyperbolic account of Charles II's return in 1660, written nearly forty years before, and so secretly anticipates the restoration, in his turn, of James II:

> The Land, if not restrain'd, had met Your Way,
> Projected out a Neck, and jutted to the Sea.
> *Hibernia*, prostrate at Your Feet, ador'd,
> In You, the Pledge of her expected Lord.   (51–4)

The Duchess' 'Lord' is of course her husband; but the lines can be read as referring also to her lawful king. She symbolises also restorations of a sublimer kind. She is the dove returning to the ark after the Flood, and Christ Himself, at the Second Coming. The fact that she fell dangerously ill on her return from Ireland enables Dryden to introduce the themes of health and sickness, and of the true and false physician which were first introduced with the references to Blackmore in the Preface. None of these allusions seems forced, however; or rather, just as in the Preface Dryden craftily exploits his old man's licence to wander from the point, so here he indulges his licence as a poet to flatter a beautiful noblewoman with extravagant analogy. He is particularly successful in suggesting that the idea of the Duchess spontaneously evokes astonishing and beautiful images. But the surface of mindless, rococo prettiness that results only serves to give a peculiarly ironic force and flavour to the body of intelligent allusion it conceals.

Successful as Dryden is in rendering a mature and public femininity like that of the Duchess, he unquestionably coarsens Chaucer's Emily in *Palamon and Arcite*. To translate 'Hir body wesshe with water of a welle' as 'They wash the Virgin in a living Stream' (III,198) betrays moral as well as verbal insensitivity. Nevertheless Dryden's Emily is appropriate to his purposes. He needs, not Chaucer's helpless and tender girl, but a representative Woman, a generalised 'Virgin', who can be the centre of a representative love-dispute without drawing attention to herself as an individual. Love in Dryden is rarely a matter of the private feelings of real men and women, but approximates to the modern 'libido' or 'Eros', by which all human hungers of body and heart are brought under a single head and considered as a single factor in the general human situation.

Dryden's ability to generalise Chaucer like this, for ethical and poetic purposes of his own, is admirably illustrated in his description of the temples at the end of Book II. Though we may find Chaucer's sharp and detailed pictures intrinsically more enjoyable, the allusions to events in Dryden's own day do stiffen his abstractions with telling particularity:

> There saw I how the secret Fellon wrought, ⎫
> And Treason lab'ring in the Traytor's Thought; ⎬
> And Midwife Time the ripen'd Plot to Murder brought. ⎭
>
> (II,560–2)

(Note the thudding movement of the alexandrine with its two heavy caesuras.) Dryden offers us in the three temples the three basic ingredients of the human condition, love, war, and (a less easily defined but recurring element in this and the other fables) nature, or, to be more precise, the world of trees, seasons, and hunting symbolised by a forest which acts as a sort of fertile, innocent setting for human violence and desire. It is in a wood that Palamon and Arcite fight, and in a wood that Arcite is burned. Amid all the chaste vitality of nature, man-in-love is the source of anger and the victim of Fate:

> Love is not in our Choice, but in our Fate . . . [Arcite declares]
> Each Day we break the Bond of Humane Laws
> For Love . . .   (I,328;331–2)

'Love' thereby calls in question the freedom of the will, the relevance of Right (it is very useful from the Jacobite point of view that Palamon has the 'Eldership of Right' in the dispute over Emily) and the usefulness of prayer. What is at issue, in fact, as so often in Dryden, is the inhumanity of history, or, to put it another way, the wickedness of God.

Dryden is particularly adroit at exploiting in this connection the inevitable ambiguities arising out of Christian allusions to the pagan gods. Thus he not only gives us lesser divinities who frankly rejoice at Arcite's unjust victory;

> Laugh'd all the Pow'rs who favour Tyranny;
> And all the Standing Army of the Sky . . .   (III,671–2)

but he himself takes obvious pleasure in the fact that presiding over them is Chaucer's terrible and, from Dryden's point of view, notably 'godless' god, Saturn, who openly admits, for instance that 'Bought Senates, and deserting Troops are mine' (III,411). Saturn's image on earth is Theseus, as patronising towards Palamon and Arcite and his own subjects generally as Saturn is towards the other gods, yet because he is human finally as blind as everyone else to the long results of time.

Like Saturn, too, Dryden's Theseus is a magnificently ambiguous character. He is clearly linked with William of Orange in the first phase of the poem; yet by the end he makes a point of consulting the wishes of his parliament, something William was believed to be reluctant to do after Ryswick; and even if he does ravage Thebes as ruthlessly as William had ravaged Ireland, his war against Creon is in a just cause. His final speech, moreover, is possibly Dryden's richest statement of his deep conviction that the essence of wisdom is

> To thank the gracious Gods for what they give,
> Possess our Souls, and while we live, to live.   (III,1113–14)

This basic wisdom is the poem's ultimate control, sharpening its comedy and deepening its seriousness. It is this which makes love seem a folly:

> Who now but *Palamon* exults with Joy?
> And ravish'd *Arcite* seems to touch the Sky . . .   (II,426–7)

and the pretensions of kings—as Egeus notes—ridiculous:

> Like Pilgrims, to th' appointed Place we tend;
> The World's an Inn, and Death the Journeys End.
> Ev'n Kings but play; and when their Part is done,
> Some other, worse or better, mount the Throne.   (III,887–90)

Egeus' cynicism, however, is only a partial kind of wisdom. The poem ends on a note of humanely moderated resignation. Taken as a whole, therefore, *Palamon and Arcite* may be a robust, extravagant, authentically heroic performance, but it is infiltrated by an irony which consistently compromises the impressiveness of heroic effort. The resulting moral stance, however, is not one of despairing quietism but is manifestly connected to the great central assertion of Theseus' speech, that, hidden behind the chaos of jarring atoms and human change, there is the perfection and stability of divine love.

Having thus firmly established a highly abstract but densely imagined complex of ethical, historical, and literary references, it was time for Dryden, in his next poem, to return to the concrete conditions of the historical present, to his own world, that of the English squirearchy. *To my Honour'd Kinsman*, despite its title, is a far less intimate poem than the lines to Congreve. It is a respectful yet fantastically good-humoured address to the head of the Dryden family. Formally the most important and ideologically the most serious of its analogies are blessed with mildly comic implications. Sir John was a bachelor, a naturally hale, rather serious but hard-hunting country squire. His life therefore is like Adam's without Eve, a condition of natural virtue and well-being beside the Tree of Life, in contrast to the acrimonious state of matrimony, or a life of ill-health under the control of physicians, or the recriminations of Adam and Eve beside the tree of knowledge.[7] The poem is based on Horace's Second Epode, and is therefore seriously appreciative of rural values, but its distinctly un-Horatian praise of Sir John's celibacy, and the slightly bizarre implications of a middle-aged hunting squire replacing Emily's divine huntress as the type of sylvan chastity, suggest that Dryden was discreetly appreciative of his kinsman's eccentricities.

The poem also departs from Horace in praising Sir John's involvement in public affairs. It becomes as a result a serious statement of political principle[8] and an urgent if allusive contribution to the rather ill-tempered debate between William of Orange and the Commons on the question of a standing army. As a good county member, Sir John had urged a reduction in the armed forces after Ryswick while remaining a firm anti-Jacobite. He had in fact played an archetypally moderate and independent part in the dispute. The tory commitment to isolationism from European wars and to social values and practices grounded in country life and manners, the squirearchal dream of parliamentary monarchy which figures idealistically in *The Hind and the Panther*, is thus realistically specified in the life and person of Sir John. It does not matter that he is a Williamite. He is the hunting squire both James and William long to be:

> Thus Princes ease their Cares: But happier he,
> Who seeks not Pleasure thro' Necessity,
> Than such as once on slipp'ry Thrones were plac'd;
> And chasing, sigh to think themselves are chas'd.   (67–70)

The tenses in the last couplet are precisely chosen. James used to occupy a slippery throne; William (note the passive voice) was placed on one; both were still hunting at the time of writing, William barely escaping an assassination attempt after one such expedition, James doubtless sighing at Saint-Germaine. But these lines' most crucial and

the most daring figure is the pun in 'chas'd'—with its clear implication
that celibacy has few pleasures.[9] The monarchical and parliamentary
ideal, which the poem illustrates in throughly modern terms, is thus
indirectly, facetiously, but effectively placed. The couplet immediately
following these is interestingly eccentric:

> So liv'd our Sires, e'er Doctors learn'd to kill,
> And multiply with theirs, the Weekly Bill . . . (71–2)

The association of Sir John with an ideal past now irretrievably
vanished develops by some deliberately forced wordplay into a
consciously self-indulgent attack on doctors, and the inevitable blast
against Blackmore. The poet thus links an admission that Sir John, as a
man of the world, is something of an anachronism with his own
personal quirkishness. They are both old-fashioned men. Yet this is
also their strength, poetically in the use of analogies which may be
far-fetched but are also weighty, and politically in preserving that
humane, historically-sanctioned social ideal which Sir John virtually
incarnates.

The five tales forming the second major grouping in the *Fables*
provide important instances of tonal metamorphosis. *Meleager and
Atalanta* is a striking mixture of horror and farce, set in a vigorous
primitive world, but retold with a sophistication that could appear
slick but for the toughness with which Dryden emphasises the main
fact of the story, that Diana destroys forever the royal house of
Oeneus. The young Nestor leaping out of the way of the Calydonian
boar may be funny enough, but the mourning of the sisters of Meleager,
killed by his mother for murdering her brothers, is appalling. The
apparent tastelessness of neoclassical diction intensifies the effect:

> They beat their Breasts with many a bruizing Blow,
> Till they turn'd livid, and corrupt the Snow. (381–2)

A similar grossness is evident in the next story, *Sigismonda and
Guiscardo*, from Boccaccio, notably when Tancred sends his daughter
her husband's heart in a goblet:

> Then, to the Heart ador'd, devoutly glew'd
> Her Lips, and raising it, her Speech renew'd. (641–2)

Yet this story too, against a background of impossible violence between father and daughter (instead of the mother and son in *Meleager and Atalanta*) has passages of flamboyant humour, notably when the lovers leap on each other in the presence first of the priest who marries them, and later of the father who discovers their secret. The salacity of the comedy and the bad taste of the horror in both stories finally combine, however, to challenge the smart tolerance they apparently assume. The forest where the boar is hunted, and the thicket surrounding Sigismonda's secret chamber through which Guiscardo has to force his way to reach her, suggest a kind of nightmare landscape against which lust and anger enact ludicrous and tragic confusions.

The vacuousness of neoclassical romance settings in these stories is also offset by the shadowy presences of 'history' and 'theology' in both. Very occasionally the references are precise. Guards, we are told (and William of Orange was doubtless if unfairly in Dryden's mind), of the kind who slew Guiscardo in the night, are

> Dang'rous to Freedom, and desir'd alone
> By Kings, who seek an Arbitrary Throne.   (600–1)

More generally we are reminded of positions on politics and divinity which Dryden has taken elsewhere and which his stories apparently contradict. Thus the union of Sigismonda and Guiscardo raises the whole problem of rank, and so of societies as well as monarchies founded on the hereditary principle, in ways hardly compatible with the poems to the Duchess of Ormonde and Sir John Driden. The comic terror of these stories is no mere fantasy, but a matter of precise concern for Dryden and his age. The madness, however approached, with cries of alarm or cold-hearted slickness, is a fact of history as well as of mind. Thus Sigismonda tells her father that her plebeian marriage is 'The Fault of Fortune',

> Or call it Heav'ns Imperial Pow'r alone,
> Which moves on Springs of Justice, though unknown;
> Yet this we see, though order'd for the best,
> The Bad exalted, and the Good oppress'd;
> Permitted Laurels grace the Lawless Brow,
> Th' Unworthy rais'd, the Worthy cast below.   (492–8)

Rank and virtue are equally insecure amidst the anarchy of lust and the Providence of God.

The two consecutive stories from Book X of the *Metamorphoses*, *Pygmalion* and *Cinyras and Myrrha* bring this nightmare of instability to a climax distinctly reminiscent of the verbal chaos of *Aureng-Zebe*. The incestuous passion of Myrrha for her father reverses the father-daughter antagonism of *Sigismonda and Guiscardo* and amplifies the theme of natural law which is raised by Sigismonda's defence of her marriage in the earlier story: 'State-Laws', she argues, 'may alter: Nature's are the same' (418). But nature includes not only law but impulse, and the effect of the latter is to abolish distinctions of kin as well as of class. The result is a grotesque parody of Guiscardo's rendezvous with Sigismonda as Myrrha gropes her way into her father's bed. Yet the story is prefaced by the comedy of Pygmalion's assault on his statue, which is funny in itself and puts celibacy like Sir John Driden's in an odd light.

Between *Sigismonda and Guiscardo* and *Cinyras and Myrrha*, however, is Ovid's very Chaucerian *Baucis and Philemon*, in which the virtues of simplicity, both poetic and human, are beautifully rendered. The urbanity of this pastoral piece (reminiscent of parts of the *Georgics*) is typified in the following passage which weaves into the Ovidian text a range of comic allusion which points it intellectually and enriches it emotionally. It concerns an old couple trying to kill their only goose to feed two guests, who are really Jove and Hermes in disguise. Not the least enjoyable element in the passage is the anticipation, in the final line, of Alexander's behaviour in *Alexander's Feast*:

> Her, with malicious Zeal, the Couple view'd;
> She ran for Life, and limping they pursu'd:
> Full well the Fowl perceiv'd their bad intent,
> And wou'd not make her Masters Compliment;
> But persecuted, to the Pow'rs she flies,
> And close between the Legs of *Jove* she lies:
> He with a gracious Ear the Suppliant heard,
> And sav'd her Life; then what he was declar'd,
> And own'd the God. (133–41)

The story, we are assured in the headnote, was originally told by Helex to counter the atheism of Perithous, but the deft salacity with which Jove is rendered ridiculous here, and the naivety of the whole tale tend to strengthen the case for sophisticated unbelief. This effect is silently countered, however, by the inevitable echoes of scripture both

in the basic tale (an analogue of the story of Lot), and in the metic-
ulously rendered virtue of Baucis and Philemon themselves, whose
poverty, humility and simplicity give the lie to atheistic cleverness and
considerably modify the moral and ontological insecurities which the
other tales so lavishly illustrate.

The original epic impulse, deriving from *Palamon and Arcite* but
lost perhaps in the stories that follow, is renewed in *The First Book of
Homer's Ilias*, which introduces the third and structurally the most
important phase of the whole work. It is an odd achievement, less
impressively organised than the *Æneis*, and morally less ambitious. In
its way, however, it is a very intelligent rendering, at least in so far as it
takes up and intensifies two important areas of tension in the volume
as a whole—the grandeur and folly of primitive violence, and the
doubtful moral standing of the gods. There is some fine comic writing
towards the end on the quarrels of Jove and Juno over the fate of
Achilles, which Vulcan manages to soothe with some notably ungodlike
arguments:

> What end in Heav'n will be of civil War,
> If Gods of Pleasure will for Mortals jar?   (772–3)

These are not the gods of religion but the lordlings of Charles II's
court. As an 'atheist's god', Vulcan is not terrible like Chaucer's
Saturn but flippant like Mercury in *Amphitryon*. Enjoyable as this
flippancy may be, it is also radically anti-Homeric, so that even if we
accept Dryden's civilised objections to the athletic brutalities of epic
heroes, his version of Homer still seems perilously close to being a
violation of the original. But perhaps this is a calculated effect. While
establishing a fresh set of legendary references for exploitation in
subsequent poems, Dryden economically traps the reader in the
uncomfortable middle ground between primitive heroism and modern
scepticism.

Such a process of deflation is certainly evident in the decision to
follow Homer with Chaucer's *The Cock and the Fox*, in translating
which Dryden also managed to mock his own portentous preoccupation with incest. Yet his version never quite commits itself to the
deflation it plays with so pleasingly. Dame Partlet's submission to
Chanticleer's mountings may cheerfully parody the Anglican doctrine
of passive obedience, but it is hard to be certain how seriously we
should take Chanticleer's own Tale of the Two Friends, with its

firm assertion that Heaven's 'darling Attribute . . . is boundless Grace, and Mercy to Mankind' (281–2), or his meditations on free will, which Dryden has expanded from the original. It is certainly significant that the lies of literature should be so prominent a theme of the poem:

> Ye Princes rais'd by Poets to the Gods,
> And *Alexander'd* up in lying Odes.   (659–60)

The literary enterprise as such is virtually called in question. As in a dream, however, this particular fable lies like truth:

> Dreams are but Interludes, which Fancy makes,
> When Monarch-Reason sleeps, this Mimick wakes:
> Compounds a Medley of disjointed Things,
> A Mob of Coblers, and a Court of Kings.   (325–8)

This ironic turning of the *Fables* on its own themes and ideas does not, however, end in mere Pyrrhonistic cleverness. The negation is itself negated:

> The Cock and Fox, the Fool and Knave imply;
> The Truth is moral, though the Tale a Lie,
> Who spoke in Parables, I dare not say.   (814–16)

Indeed just as the heroic scale of the *Iliad* is put into perspective by *The Cock and the Fox*, so the latter's flippancy is in turn rebuked by its moral.

Theodore and Honoria continues the process but far more shockingly. It is virtually original, though formally adapted from Boccaccio. The thick wood on Theodore's country estate, where the ghost of Guido Calvacanti urges his hell-hounds after the ghost of his mistress till they tear her phantom body apart, points to Dryden's keen sense of how violence and frustrated eroticism collide in compulsive repetitions of evil which challenge both the peace of Sir John Driden's celibacy and his own jocular ease in the previous tale. That it is a reply to the latter is clear from the emphasis on Friday as the fatal day—Chanticleer too attaches importance to Fridays—and from the seriousness with which it treats of dreams and visions. The hideous transformations which it depicts not only of love but of justice turning into the grossest cruelty are as psychologically penetrating as the insights in *Don Sebastian* and *The Sixth Satire of Juvenal*. Dryden's mellow confidence in man and secured faith in God have to prove themselves not only against the inhuman processes of history, but the terrible fusions of the human heart as well.

A healing of these terrors of mind is, however, suggested by the next fable, *Ceyx and Alcyone*, a gentle, sometimes humorous story which brings its lovers (changed finally into kingfishers) into a rich calm idyll of 'conjugal Affection'. Dreams, prayers, prophecies, and implicit in them the whole question of determinism on the one hand and the benevolence of Fate on the other, are prominent enough themes to make the poem's function within the larger design of the *Fables* obvious enough. Nor is the story, however it may end, untouched by the violence which haunts the entire volume. In this instance, however, it is of an external rather than psychological character. Ceyx's shipwreck is a perfect instance of the powerlessness of kings in the face of Fate—one is reminded of Latinus letting the ship of state drive before the wind—which links it with a more overt yet still discreet political bias in the next fable, the allegedly Chaucerian *The Flower and the Leaf*. Here, once more in a wooded setting, though this time one of Marvellian sweetness, a dispute about armed chastity and amorous ease ends in a frankly dreamlike dance of reconciliation and concord. The allegory, if such it is, is handled with gracefully attenuated allusiveness which unobtrusively softens and modernises a substantial body of theme and symbol drawn from the previous tales. The entire volume is thus brought back to its beginnings in the idealised femininity of the Duchess of Ormonde, and the poet's own urbane and thoroughly contemporary sense of the relationship between courtly fictions and the real world.

Its delicacy, however, is promptly met with the brash masculinity of *Alexander's Feast*. The heroic note is once more loudly and ambiguously sounded in a 'lying ode' so flamboyantly expert that it makes a theme of its own technical brilliance: 'We listen', as Scott noted of the Anne Killigrew Ode, 'for the completion of Dryden's stanza, as for the explication of a difficult passage in music; and wild and lost as the sound appears, the ear is proportionally gratified by the unexpected ease with which harmony is extracted from discord and confusion'.[10] This effect is a matter of meaning as well as of ear. There is a fundamental disjunction between the response which the spectacle and the rhetoric appear to invite, and that manifest coldness of the poet

towards his hero which enables him to forget Alexander and concen-
trate like Timotheus on effects. Folly, when Alexander drunkenly
'Assumes the God', impotence when with the gorgeous Thias beside
him he can only sigh and look and sigh again, and wickedness, when
they burn down Persepolis, clash discordantly with achieved effects of
wonder, pity, and terror in the poem. The resolution of these tonal
tensions, however, is not as well handled as resolutions of a more
technical kind. The satire against William of Orange's triumph in his
wars against France, for instance, is especially obvious in the context
of the *Fables*, but the sort of balance between irony and triumphalism
which it points to is difficult to integrate with the vision of St Cecilia
in Stanza VII and the Grand Chorus which follows it. The motives
and perspectives of the enigmatic Timotheus/Dryden figure, who has
played so cleverly with the victory-intoxicated king, have failed to
reveal themselves. But perhaps, like the curious effect of *The First
Book of Homer's Ilias*, this undoubted weakness in the poem, considered
in isolation, has a function in the collection as a whole, since it keeps
in abeyance too decisive a resolution of the tensions between irony and
splendour at this stage of the volume's development.

The unresolved tensions between heroic magnificence and comic
hubris, which *Alexander's Feast* sustains so ostentatiously, are at any
rate further exemplified in *The Twelfth Book of Ovid. His Metamorphoses*, which follows it. Achilles' powerful defiance of Cygnus, his
enraged impotence at his enemy's divinely secured invulnerability,
and, when he does kill him, his disappointment at the disappearance
of the body, repeatedly suggest the closeness of genuinely Homeric
effort to farce. Moreover it is possible to see in Nestor (who tells the
bloody tale of the Battle of the Centaurs) an illuminating extension of
the Timotheus/Dryden figure of *Alexander's Feast*. His tale indulges
in a pornography of violence which, like the obscenity of *The Sixth
Satire of Juvenal*, dextrously blends effects of grossly heroic brutality
with an air of civilised imperturbability:

> Him *Peleus* finish'd, with a second Wound, ⎫
> Which through the Navel pierc'd: He reel'd around; ⎬
> And drag'd his dangling Bowels on the Ground. ⎭
> Trod what he drag'd; and what he trod he crush'd:
> And to his Mother-Earth, with empty Belly rush'd.   (519–23)

The detached narrator of heroic brutalities, however, has enough simplicity of heart to discover a dignity and beauty in the centaur lovers, Cyllarus and Hylonome, which all the farcical ugliness of primitive violence cannot extinguish. And the death of Cæneus, though very like that of Cygnus, is not funny at all, but in a titanic way terrible, just as his metamorphosis into an eagle is almost glorious.

In *The Speeches of Ajax and Ulysses*, however, we are at last given a decisive, but by no means simplistic, placing of the 'Athletick Brutes' called heroes. The debate (about who should inherit the armour of the dead Achilles) resolves itself into a competition between 'Right' and 'Success'. It is thus discreetly relevant to the problem of the English succession, though Dryden never makes it clear if in fact there is any Right in the case at all. Moreover it is the despised Ajax who grounds his claim to the armour in inherited 'Right Divine' as well as in his pre-eminence as a warrior. Ulysses, on the other hand, adroitly deploys the arts of the rhetorician to involve the entire Greek army in the guilt of his own unprincipled political guile. It is thus possible that Ajax represents James II (whose youthful stupidity and senile cowardice Dryden was by no means blind to), and Ulysses William of Orange. What is certain is that the apparent victory of eloquence over force (which it would be altogether too easy to applaud) is in fact the victory of cold-hearted pragmatism over militaristic bombast. In view of the fact that it was Paris, 'The base Adult'rer' who killed Achilles in the first place, it would seem that Dryden's sense of the bleakness of the human condition is stronger here than it was even at the end of *Troilus and Cressida*, which does at least emphasise the restoration of Agamemnon's legitimate authority.

It is no doubt to counteract some of this pessimism that the next fable is from Chaucer. There is no mystery about why Dryden decided to include *The Wife of Bath, Her Tale* in the collection. Like *The Cock and the Fox*, it contains a tale within a tale, and offers opportunities for reworking some major themes; anti-clericalism, distaste for literary obscenity, the ludicrous aspects of kingship, the relationship of virtue to rank, chance, free will, and marriage. Its function in relation to the two extracts preceding it, however, is to perform the typically English trick of miniaturising important themes without trivialising them, and so to put the titanic gestures of classical literature firmly in their place.

This is a necessary task, since the greatness of the ancient world, as the *Fables* represent it, would seem to lie not in its heroic traditions but in the scope of its philosophical speculations, and in its great myth of a golden age, the chaste, bloodless, fertile peace of man's first encounter with nature. Both are celebrated in *Of the Pythagorean Philosophy*, which concludes the third phase of the collection, and presents the major meditation on the fundamental problems of human life towards which the whole work has been moving. Yet even here Dryden's perspectives as a learned man of his own age expose the superstitious fantasies as well as the brilliant insights in Pythagoras' vision, suggesting the element of *hubris* as well as of splendid daring in pagan speculation. Philosophy and myth, however, have more to reveal than their own limitations. Philosophy teaches the necessity of submitting to the sovereignty of history:

> . . . For former Things
> Are set aside, like abdicated Kings:
> And every moment alters what is done,
> And innovates some Act till then unknown.   (274–7)

(Note the passive 'abdicated' and the unobtrusive pun in 'Act'.) Myth, in the fable of the phoenix, on the other hand, offers images of miraculous restoration. The sublime Jacobitism of the closing passages of the *Pythagorean Philosophy* is especially courageous and moving, coming as it does so soon after the unqualified disillusionment of the Ajax–Ulysses debate. Any possibility of its being read as an essay in naive triumphalism, however, is countered by the brilliant adaptation of Chaucer's *Character of a Good Parson* which follows. This careful and loving study of a non-juring priest convincingly blends Dryden's deepest convictions about religion and politics with humane and distinctly Catholic ideals of spirituality and asceticism. The modesty of its faith in both God and man perfectly counters the tendency towards over-reliance on a glorious, but defiantly extra-historical, symbolism at the end of the Pythagorean extract.

   The Monument of a Fair Maiden Lady is less ambitious and less impressive. It does, however, affirm the validity of chastity, and so connects with Dryden's very personal introduction to the last and in some respects the greatest of the fables, *Cymon and Iphigenia*. This final statement by the poet in his own person is typically indirect in its method. A jibe at the non-celibate Anglican clergy casually opens a plea for a discriminating and supple response to literary eroticism, and an affirmation of the importance of sexuality in both poetry and life. But the final, deftly expanded celebration of the civilising effects of love (joined to a last graceful allusion to the Duchess of Ormonde) contains a hidden irony. Exactly what sort of 'lib'ral Acts' and reconciliations the civilising powers of Eros actually achieve the ensuing poem reveals in a brilliantly organised allegory of social evolution, a subtle, exact, and honest image of *all* that 'civilisation' entails, which by no means enforces the claims made for love in the opening section.

The fable begins in Cyprus, birthplace of Venus, with an ineducable boy being sent by his father to live obscurely on a country estate, where he encounters the barely nubile, half-naked Iphigenia lying carelessly asleep in the pure, archetypal setting of a grove. In lines reaching back to *Religio Laici* and possibly even the Lucretian chaos of mind described in *To . . . S*^r *Robert Howard*, the stirrings of love are seen to drive the light of reason for the first time through Cymon's brain. The representative transformation of country clown into courtly lover, however, is unavailing since Iphigenia is already betrothed to Pasimond, a nobleman from Rhodes. Cymon, who as a gaping sot was careful not to wake his beloved, as a dashing gallant decides to take her by force; and what was a simple allegory of emotional development suddenly becomes a politically sophisticated parable. Physically victorious, Cymon openly admits to the defeated Rhodians, 'Love taught me Force, and Force shall Love maintain' (303), echoing the words of Arcite in *Palamon and Arcite* and pointedly contradicting the optimism of the introduction.

Significantly, 'Right' is far from clear in the dispute between him and Pasimond anyway. Iphigenia's preference is for Cymon, but Dryden pointedly compares them to Paris and Helen. 'Right' certainly has less effect than Fate. In a storm as symbolic of man's political powerlessness as that in *Ceyx and Alcyone*, Cymon loses control of his vessel, and Iphigenia feels the pangs of conscience, blaming her lover for daring to 'Invade, and violate another's Right' (360). Whatever the objective force of these womanish complaints, Cymon and Iphigenia, as representatives of the civilising power of love, do not emerge from the storm with much moral dignity. Shipwrecked on Rhodes, they are rather oddly overcome by a troop of militia such as tories normally preferred to a regular standing army, but which are here treated as clownish brutes. Cymon is then imprisoned, and Iphigenia, who, like Dame Partlet, has to endure the undignified lot of the 'passive . . . Church of Womankind' (424), is prepared for marriage to Pasimond.

There is neither ambiguity nor humour, however, in what follows. In order to prevent Pasimond's brother from marrying the girl he also loves, Lysymachus, a young magistrate made a slave to his lusts as a direct result of the Hobbist freedom deriving from political power, enters into a conspiracy with Cymon: 'let Losers talk in vain of Right' (523), he declares; all that matters is that they should make good their escape with the women. The treachery at the wedding feast of Pasimond and his brother which he arranges is thus an exact repetition of the centaurs' treason at the wedding of Perithous and Hippodame in *The Twelfth Book of Ovid*. Only this time, in the persons of Cymon and Lysymachus and their men—they are referred to repeatedly as 'Ravishers'—the 'centaurs' are victorious and the brothers brutally slain. Then in a miraculously deft complication of the issues, Dryden suddenly transforms the very Williamite Lysymachus into an image of James II, whose flight in 1688, from any point of view, was a gross dereliction of duty. Dryden's Jacobitism is no more sentimental than his delight in women:

> What should the People do, when left alone?
> The Governor, and Government are gone . . .
> *Rhodes* is the Sovereign of the Sea no more;
> Their Ships unrigg'd, and spent their Naval Store;
> They neither could defend, nor can pursue,
> But grind their Teeth, and cast a helpless view . . .
> Mean while the Ravishers their Crimes enjoy.
>
> (615–16;619–22;625)

If the image of the Duchess of Ormonde landing in Ireland with which the *Fables* opened evoked brilliant memories of *Astræa Redux*, this hopeless image of naval impotence and shabby pragmatic success contrasts bitterly with the mercantilist ebullience and monarchical idealism of the early sixties. There is no loss of moral idealism, however, no misanthropic dismissal of human reason and human love, which are enshrined with ineffaceable beauty and humour in the description of Cymon's first encounter with Iphigenia at the beginning of the tale. But the idealism, the simple loyalty to principle which Dryden has consistently asserted through all the urbanely shifting instabilities of the *Fables*, is finally qualified by this wise, sad, and uncensorious recognition that the sweetness and nobility of natural humanity will always be soiled by the inevitably unprincipled compromises of human life, that the sophistications of history will always conceal with cruel completeness the virtues of men and the superhuman purposes of God.

The *Fables* are the work of an old man. Dryden died less than two months after their publication. A brief survey of so vast and deeply considered an achievement inevitably distorts and hardens the subtleties of its subject, especially when there has been no general recognition that the volume does indeed form a single work. In addition the deliberately rambling, associative nature of their construction makes explication a singularly self-defeating activity. But the major difficulty in the way of a full appreciation of this extraordinary work is the idiom in which it was written, the systematically generalised psychology, the mechanically available diction, the whole neoclassical tradition in short, which Dryden seems to manipulate with such undiscriminating strength. It is just this attachment to dying but traditional conventions, however, that makes the idiom of Dryden's later writing so much of a piece with the vision of God, man and society which obsessed him during the last fifteen years of his life. He was a great reconciler of opposites; of worldliness with faith, of contempt with loyalty, of scepticism with reason, of irony with idealisation. But perhaps his greatest effort went into reconciling a deep knowledge of, and an unfaltering attachment to, established traditions of all kinds, philosophical, literary and historical, with a patient, good-humoured, humble, and generous openness to a future that denied them.

It is a view of the world which is perfectly encapsulated in his last work, *The Secular Masque*, which he wrote with a Prologue, an Epilogue, and a Song for a benefit performance of *The Pilgrim* staged on his behalf in April 1700. It celebrates the passing of the seventeenth century in lyrics as intellectually weighty as any of his couplets and yet as light and alive as the most sparkling of his songs. It is a distillation of the *Fables*, in which the passing century is presented as opening with the country freshness of a hunt under the patronage of Emily's Diana; it is then transformed by Arcite's Mars into a field for 'Arms and Honour'; and is finally softened into the pleasurable but fleeting world of Palamon's Venus. The allegory is bare, its figures simple and conventional, the effect casual and pretty; yet the vision of the times is also amazingly complete, wise, moderate, and sad. The sense of futility in all human endeavour is perfectly caught in the long spondaic opening of the final chorus:

> All, all, of a piece throughout;
> Thy Chase had a Beast in View;
> Thy Wars brought nothing about;
> Thy Lovers were all untrue.   (92–5)

Yet the chorus manages to end with a perfect restatement of that openness to the future which gave such moral dignity to Dryden's old age, and which was first so beautifully suggested by the lines to Congreve in 1694:

> 'Tis well an Old Age is out,
> And time to begin a New.   (96–7)

The Masque concludes with a 'Dance of Huntsmen, Nymphs, Warriours and Lovers'. The century ends with humanity holding the stage, like Antonio and Morayma at the end of *Don Sebastian*. It is a thoroughly characteristic and appropriate conclusion to Dryden's life and to his work.

1. Quoted in California I, p. 324.

2. Kinsley II, p. 795.

3. The 'unifying conception' which underlies the *Fables* is definitively and extensively documented in Earl Miner, *Dryden's Poetry* (1967), pp. 289–317.

4. Kinsley IV, p. 1442.

5. ibid. IV, p. 1444.

6. ibid. IV, p. 1455.

7. See Alan Roper, *Dryden's Poetic Kingdoms* (1965), pp. 128–9.

8. See *The Letters of John Dryden*, p. 120.

9. William after his wife's death, and James in guilty old age were both 'chaste' at this time.

10. Scott–Saintsbury I, p. 410.

FURTHER READING

The Works of John Dryden, Ed. Walter Scott and George Saintsbury (Edinburgh 1882)

The Works of John Dryden Ed. H. T. Swedenberg, Jr, and Vinton A. Dearing (Berkeley and Los Angeles 1956); six vols. have so far been published

The Poems of John Dryden, Ed. James Kinsley (Oxford 1958)

Essays of John Dryden, Ed. W. P. Ker (Oxford 1900)

Of Dramatick Poesie and other Critical Essays, Ed. George Watson (London 1962)

Selected Criticism, Ed. James Kinsley and George Parfitt (Oxford 1970)

Four Comedies, Ed. L. A. Beaurline and Fredson Bowers (Chicago and London 1967)

Four Tragedies, Ed. L. A. Beaurline and Fredson Bowers (Chicago and London 1967)

The Letters of John Dryden, Ed. Charles E. Ward (Chapel Hill 1942)

John M. Aden, 'Dryden and the Imagination. The First Phase', *PMLA* LXXIV (1959)

Ann T. Barbeau, *The Intellectual Design of John Dryden's Heroic Plays* (New Haven and London 1970)

Louis I. Bredvold, *The Intellectual Milieu of John Dryden* (Ann Arbor 1934)

Sanford Budick, *Dryden and The Abyss of Light. A Study of 'Religio Laici' and 'The Hind and the Panther'* (New Haven and London 1970)

Howerd Erskine-Hill, 'John Dryden: the Poet and Critic', *Dryden to Johnson*, Ed. R. Lonsdale (London 1971)

William Frost, *Dryden and the Art of Translation* (New Haven 1955)

Thomas H. Fujimara, 'Dryden's *Religio Laici:* an Anglican Poem', *PMLA* LXXVI (1961)

Phillip Harth, *Contexts of Dryden's Thought* (Chicago and London 1968)

Arthur W. Hoffman, *John Dryden's Imagery* (Gainesville 1962)

Robert D. Hume, *Dryden's Criticism* (Ithaca and London 1970)

Ian Jack, *Augustan Satire* (Oxford 1952)

Samuel Johnson, *Lives of the English Poets*, Ed. George Birbeck Hill (Oxford 1905)

Bruce King, *Dryden's Major Plays* (Edinburgh and London 1966)

Bruce King (Ed.), *Dryden's Mind and Art* (Edinburgh 1969)

James Kinsley and Helen Kinsley (Eds.), *Dryden. The Critical Heritage* (London 1971)

Arthur C. Kirsch, *Dryden's Heroic Drama* (Princeton 1965)

F. R. Leavis, '*Antony and Cleopatra* and *All for Love*', *Scrutiny* V (1936)

C. S. Lewis, 'Shelley, Dryden, and Mr. Eliot', *Rehabilitations and Other Essays*, (London 1939)

Earl Miner, *Dryden's Poetry* (Bloomington and London 1967)

Earl Miner (Ed.), *Writers and their Background: John Dryden* (London 1972)

Frank Harper Moore, *The Nobler Pleasure. Dryden's Comedy in Theory and Practice* (Chapel Hill 1933)

James M. Osborne, *John Dryden: Some Biographical Facts and Problems* (revised ed., Gainesville 1965)

Martin Price, *To the Palace of Wisdom. Studies in Order and Energy from Dryden to Blake* (New York 1964)

Moody E. Prior, *The Language of Tragedy* (New York 1967)

Paul Ramsey, *The Art of John Dryden* (Lexington 1969)

Alan Roper, *Dryden's Poetic Kingdoms* (London 1965)

George Saintsbury, *Dryden* (London 1881)

Bernard N. Schilling, *Dryden and the Conservative Myth. A Reading of 'Absalom and Achitophel'* (New Haven and London 1961)

Bernard N. Schilling (Ed.), *Dryden. A Collection of Critical Essays* (Englewood Cliffs 1963)

H. T. Swedenberg, Jr (Ed.), *Essential Articles for the study of John Dryden* (London 1966)

Mark Van Doren, *John Dryden; A Study of His Poetry* (Bloomington 1960)

A. W. Verral, *Lectures on Dryden* (Cambridge 1914)

Charles E. Ward, *The Life of John Dryden* (Chapel Hill and London 1961)

INDEX